GLENCOE FRENCH 1A

# Bon voyage!

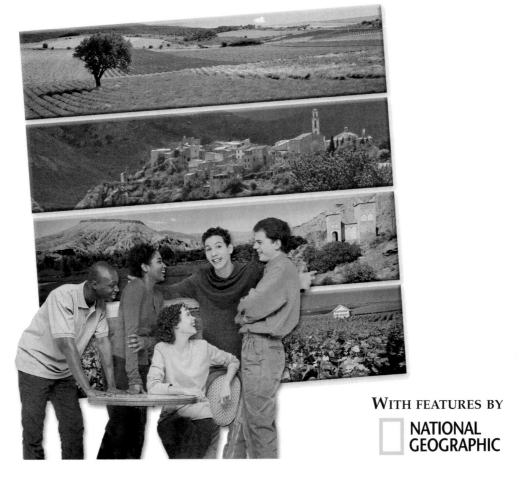

WITH FEATURES BY

NATIONAL
GEOGRAPHIC

## Conrad J. Schmitt • Katia Brillié Lutz

 **Glencoe**

New York, New York    Columbus, Ohio    Chicago, Illinois    Peoria, Illinois    Woodland Hills, California

# About the Authors

## Conrad J. Schmitt

Conrad J. Schmitt received his B.A. degree magna cum laude from Montclair State University. He received his M.A. from Middlebury College. He did additional graduate work at New York University.

Mr. Schmitt has taught Spanish and French at all levels—from elementary school to university graduate courses. He served as Coordinator of Foreign Languages for the Hackensack, New Jersey, public schools. He also taught Methods of Teaching a Foreign Language at the Graduate School of Education, Rutgers University. Mr. Schmitt was Editor-in-Chief of Foreign Languages and ESL/EFL materials for the School Division of McGraw-Hill and McGraw-Hill International Book Company.

Mr. Schmitt has authored or co-authored more than one hundred books, all published by Glencoe/McGraw-Hill or by McGraw-Hill. He has addressed teacher groups and given workshops in all states of the United States and has lectured and presented seminars throughout the Far East, Latin America, and Canada. In addition, Mr. Schmitt has traveled extensively throughout France, French-speaking Canada, North Africa, French-speaking West Africa, the French Antilles, and Haiti.

## Katia Brillié Lutz

Katia Brillié Lutz has her **Baccalauréat** in Mathematics and Science from the Lycée Molière in Paris and her **Licence ès Lettres** in languages from the Sorbonne. She was a Fulbright scholar at Mount Holyoke College.

Ms. Lutz has taught French language at Yale University and French language and literature at Southern Connecticut State College. She also taught French at the United Nations in New York City.

Ms. Lutz was Executive Editor of French at Macmillan Publishing Company. She also served as Senior Editor at Harcourt Brace Jovanovich and Holt Rinehart and Winston. She was a news translator and announcer for the BBC Overseas Language Services in London.

Ms. Lutz is the author of many language textbooks at all levels of instruction.

---

**Glencoe**

The *McGraw-Hill* Companies

The feature in this textbook entitled **Reflets** was designed and created by the National Geographic Society's School Publishing Division. Copyright 2005. National Geographic Society. All rights reserved.

The name "National Geographic" and the yellow border are registered trademarks of the National Geographic Society.

Send all inquiries to:
Glencoe/McGraw-Hill
8787 Orion Place
Columbus, OH 43240-4027

ISBN: 0-07-865622-2 *(Student Edition)*
ISBN: 0-07-865623-0 *(Teacher Wraparound Edition)*

Printed in the United States of America.

3 4 5 6 7 8 9 10  079/055  10 09 08 07 06 05

# Teacher Reviewers

We wish to express our appreciation to the numerous individuals throughout the United States and the French-speaking world who have advised us in the development of these teaching materials. Special thanks are extended to the people whose names appear below.

**Anne-Marie Baumis**
Bayside, NY

**Claude Benaiteau**
Austin, TX

**Sr. M. Elayne Bockey, SND**
St. Wendelin High School
Fostoria, OH

**Linda Burnette**
Rockville Junior/Senior
High School
Rockville, IN

**Linda Butt**
Loyola Blakefield
Towson, MD

**Betty Clough**
Austin, TX

**Yolande Helm**
Ohio University
Athens, OH

**Jan Hofts**
Northwest High School
Indianapolis, IN

**Kathleen A. Houchens**
The Ohio State University
Columbus, OH

**Dominique Keith**
Lake Forest, CA

**Raelene Noll**
Delmar, NY

**Nancy Price**
Fort Atkinson High School
Fort Atkinson, WI

**Sally Price**
Marysville-Pilchuck
High School
Marysville, WA

**Bonita Sanders**
Eisenhower High School
New Berlin, WI

**Deana Schiffer**
Hewlett High School
Hewlett, NY

**Julia Sheppard**
Delaware City Schools
Delaware, OH

**James Toolan**
Tuxedo High School
Tuxedo, NY

**Mary Webster**
Romeo High School
Romeo, MI

**Marian Welch**
Austin ISD
Austin, TX

**Richard Wixom**
Miller Middle School
Lake Katrine, NY

**Brian Zailian**
Tamalpais High School
Mill Valley, CA

# For the Parent or Guardian

We are excited that your child has decided to study French. Foreign language study provides many benefits for students in addition to the ability to communicate in another language. Students who study another language improve their first language skills. They become more aware of the world around them and they learn to appreciate diversity.

You can help your child be successful in his or her study of French even if you are not familiar with that language. Encourage your child to talk to you about the places where French is spoken. Engage in conversations about current events in those places. The section of their Glencoe French book called **Le monde francophone** on pages xxi–xxxv may serve as a reference for you and your child. In addition, you will find information about the geography of the French-speaking world and links to foreign newspapers at **french.glencoe.com**.

The methodology employed in the Glencoe French books is logical and leads students step by step through their study of the language. Consistent instruction and practice are essential for learning a foreign language. You can help by encouraging your child to review vocabulary each day. As he or she progresses through the text, you will to want to use the study tips on pages H51–H61 to help your child learn French. If you have Internet access, encourage your child to practice using the activities, games, and practice quizzes at **french.glencoe.com**.

# Table des matières

## La francophonie

## Why Learn French?

## L'alphabet français

## Leçons préliminaires

### Objectifs
**In these preliminary lessons you will learn to:**
- ✔ *greet people*
- ✔ *say good-bye to people*
- ✔ *ask people how they are*
- ✔ *ask and tell names*
- ✔ *express simple courtesies*
- ✔ *find out and tell the days of the week*
- ✔ *find out and tell the months of the year*
- ✔ *count from 1 to 30*
- ✔ *find out and tell the time*

# CHAPITRE 1 Une amie et un ami

## Objectifs

**In this chapter you will learn to:**

✔ *ask or tell what someone is like*

✔ *ask or tell where someone is from*

✔ *ask or tell who someone is*

✔ *describe yourself or someone else*

✔ *talk about students from France and Martinique*

# CHAPITRE ② Les cours et les profs

## Objectifs

**In this chapter you will learn to:**

✔ *describe people and things*

✔ *talk about more than one person or thing*

✔ *tell what subjects you take in school and express some opinions about them*

✔ *speak to people formally and informally*

✔ *talk about French-speaking people in the United States*

# CHAPITRE  Pendant et après les cours

## Objectifs

**In this chapter you will learn to:**

✔ *talk about what you do in school*

✔ *talk about what you and your friends do after school*

✔ *identify and shop for school supplies*

✔ *talk about what you don't do*

✔ *tell what you and others like and don't like to do*

✔ *discuss schools in France*

# Table des matières

## CHAPITRE  4   La famille et la maison

### Objectifs

**In this chapter you will learn to:**

✔ *talk about your family*

✔ *describe your home and neighborhood*

✔ *tell your age and find out someone else's age*

✔ *tell what belongs to you and others*

✔ *describe more people and things*

✔ *talk about families and homes in French-speaking countries*

# CHAPITRE ⑤ Au café et au restaurant

## Objectifs

**In this chapter you will learn to:**

✔ *order food or a beverage at a café or restaurant*

✔ *tell where you and others go*

✔ *tell what you and others are going to do*

✔ *give locations*

✔ *tell what belongs to you and others*

✔ *describe more activities*

✔ *compare eating habits in the United States and in the French-speaking world*

# CHAPITRE ⑥ La nourriture et les courses

## Objectifs

**In this chapter you will learn to:**

✔ *identify more foods*

✔ *shop for food*

✔ *tell what you or others are doing*

✔ *ask for the quantity you want*

✔ *talk about what you or others don't have*

✔ *tell what you or others are able to do or want to do*

✔ *talk about French food-shopping customs*

# CHAPITRE 7 Les vêtements

## Objectifs

**In this chapter you will learn to:**

✔ *identify and describe articles of clothing*

✔ *state color and size preferences*

✔ *shop for clothing*

✔ *describe people's activities*

✔ *compare people and things*

✔ *express opinions and make observations*

✔ *discuss clothes and clothes shopping in the French-speaking world*

# Literary Companion

## Video Companion

# Handbook

# Guide to Symbols

Throughout **Bon voyage!** you will see these symbols, or icons. They will tell you how to best use the particular part of the chapter or activity they accompany. Following is a key to help you understand these symbols.

 **Audio Link**  This icon indicates material in the chapter that is recorded on compact disk.

 **Recycling**  This icon indicates sections that review previously introduced material.

 **Paired Activity**  This icon indicates sections that you can practice orally with a partner.

 **Group Activity**  This icon indicates sections that you can practice together in groups.

 **Encore Plus**  This icon indicates additional practice activities that review knowledge from current chapters.

 **Allez-y!**  This icon indicates the end of new material in each section and the beginning of the recombination section at the end of the chapter.

 **Literary Companion**  This icon appears in the review lessons to let you know that you are prepared to read the literature selection indicated if you wish.

 **Interactive CD-ROM**  This icon indicates that the material is also on an Interactive CD-ROM.

# Le monde francophone

The French geographer Onésime Reclus first coined the word *francophonie* in 1880 to designate geographical entities where French was spoken. Today, *la francophonie* refers to the collective body of over one hundred million people all over the world who speak French, exclusively or in part, in their daily lives. The term *francophonie* refers to the diverse official organizations, governments, and countries that promote the use of French in economic, political, diplomatic, and cultural exchanges. Politically, French remains the second most important language in the world. In some Francophone nations, French is the official language (France), or the co-official language (Cameroon); in others, it is spoken by a minority who share a common cultural heritage (Andorra). The French language is present in Europe, Africa, the Americas, and Oceania.

# Le monde

**LE MONDE FRANCOPHONE**

**Le monde**

The areas in color indicate the vast Francophone world.

OCÉAN GLACIAL ARCTIQUE

Mer de Beaufort

Baie de Baffin

Mer de Bering

Golfe de l'Alaska

Baie d'Hudson

CANADA

Mer du Labrador

AMÉRIQUE DU NORD

ÉTATS-UNIS

OCÉAN ATLANTIQUE

MEXIQUE

Golfe du Mexique

OCÉAN PACIFIQUE

Mer des Caraïbes

VENEZUELA

GUYANA
SURINAME
GUYANE FRANÇAISE

COLOMBIE

ÉQUATEUR

PÉROU

AMÉRIQUE DU SUD

BRÉSIL

SAMOA

TONGA

BOLIVIE

PARAGUAY

URUGUAY

CHILI   ARGENTINE

## La Mer des Antilles

Golfe du Mexique

BAHAMAS

ÎLES TURKS ET CAICOS (G.B)

OCÉAN ATLANTIQUE

CUBA

MEXIQUE

ÎLES VIERGES (É.-U. et G.B.)

ANTIGUA-ET-BARBUDA

HAÏTI

RÉPUBLIQUE DOMINICAINE

BELIZE

JAMAÏQUE

PORTO RICO (É.-U.)

ST KITTS-ET-NEVIS

GUADELOUPE (FR.)

GUATEMALA

HONDURAS

Mer des Caraïbes (Antilles)

DOMINIQUE

MARTINIQUE (FR.)

SAINTE-LUCIE

SALVADOR

SAINT-VINCENT-ET-GRENADINES

BARBADE

NICARAGUA

ARUBA

ANTILLES NÉERLANDAISES

GRENADE

TRINITÉ-ET-TOBAGO

COSTA RICA

PANAMÁ

VENEZUELA

OCÉAN PACIFIQUE

COLOMBIE

GUYANA

GUYANE FRANÇAISE

SURINAME

OCÉAN GLACIAL ARCTIQUE

Mer du
Groenland
Mer de
Norvège
Mer de
Barents
Mer de Kara
Mer des Laptev

ISLANDE

ASIE

Mer du
Nord
RUSSIE
Mer
d'Okhotsk

EUROPE
KAZAKHSTAN
MONGOLIE

GÉORGIE
ARMÉNIE
OUZBÉKISTAN
KIRGHIZISTAN
CORÉE
DU NORD
Mer
du
Japon
JAPON

TURQUIE
TURKMÉNISTAN
TADJIKISTAN
CHINE
CORÉE
DU SUD

LIBAN
SYRIE
AZERBAÏDJAN
AFGHANISTAN
Mer de
Chine
orientale

MAROC
TUNISIE
ISRAËL
IRAK
JORDANIE
IRAN
TAÏWAN

Mer Méditerranée

SAHARA
OCCIDENTAL
ALGÉRIE
LIBYE
ÉGYPTE
KOWEÏT
BAHREÏN
PAKISTAN
NÉPAL
BHOUTAN

QATAR
ÉMIRATS
ARABES
UNIS
INDE
BANGLADESH
MYANMAR
LAOS
Mer
de Chine
méridionale

MARSHALL

MAURITANIE
ARABIE
SAOUDITE
OMAN
Golfe
du Bengale
THAÏLANDE
VIÊT NAM
PHILIPPINES

ÉT. SÉNÉGAL
MALI
NIGER
TCHAD
SOUDAN
ÉRYTHRÉE
YÉMEN
DJIBOUTI

ÉTATS FÉDÉRÉS
DE MICRONÉSIE

GAMBIE
BURKINA
FASO
NIGERIA
ÉTHIOPIE
SRI
LANKA
CAMBODGE
BRUNEI
PALAU
KIRIBATI

GUINÉE-
BISSAU
GUINÉE
BÉNIN
AFRIQUE
RÉPUBLIQUE
CENTRAFRICAINE
MALAISIE

RA LEONE
GHANA
TOGO
CAMEROUN
OUGANDA
SOMALIE
MALDIVES
NAURU

LIBERIA
CÔTE D'IVOIRE
SÃO TOMÉ ET PRÍNCIPE
KENYA
INDONÉSIE
PAPOUASIE-
NOUVELLE-
GUINÉE
ÎLES
SALOMON

GUINÉE ÉQUATORIALE
GABON
RWANDA
BURUNDI
ÎLES
SEYCHELLES
OCÉAN
INDIEN
TUVALU

CONGO
RÉP. DÉM.
DU CONGO
TANZANIE
WALLIS-ET-
FUTUNA

ANGOLA
MALAWI
ZAMBIE
COMORES
VANUATU
FIDJI

MOZAMBIQUE
MADAGASCAR
ÎLE MAURICE
Mer de
Corail

NAMIBIE
ZIMBABWE
RÉUNION
NOUVELLE-
CALÉDONIE

OCÉAN
ATLANTIQUE
BOTSWANA
AUSTRALIE

AFRIQUE
DU SUD
SWAZILAND
LESOTHO
Mer de
Tasman

NOUVELLE-
ZÉLANDE

ANTARCTIQUE

## L'Europe

NORVÈGE
FINLANDE

SUÈDE

ESTONIE

IRLANDE
GRANDE-
BRETAGNE
DANEMARK
LETTONIE

LITUANIE
RUSSIE

PAYS-BAS
RUSSIE
BIÉLORUSSIE

OCÉAN
ATLANTIQUE
BELGIQUE
ALLEMAGNE
POLOGNE

LUXEMBOURG
RÉPUBLIQUE
TCHÈQUE
UKRAINE

FRANCE
• PARIS
SLOVAQUIE

SUISSE
AUTRICHE
HONGRIE
MOLDAVIE

SLOVÉNIE
CROATIE
ROUMANIE

PORTUGAL
MONACO
BOSNIE-
HERZÉGOVINE
SERBIE
GÉORGIE

ESPAGNE
ITALIE
YOUGOSLAVIE
BULGARIE
Mer Noire

MONTÉNÉGRO
MACÉDOINE

ALBANIE

GIBRALTAR
(Brit.)
Mer Méditerranée
GRÈCE
TURQUIE

AFRIQUE
MALTE
SYRIE

CHYPRE
LIBAN

# La francophonie

## L'Afrique

### La République Centrafricaine

**CAPITAL**
Bangui

**POPULATION**
3,684,000

**FUN FACT**
The Central African Republic has two very expensive exports—gold and diamonds.

### Le Burkina Faso

**CAPITAL**
Ouagadougou

**POPULATION**
13,228,000

**FUN FACT**
Burkina Faso is known for its friendly people. Villagers are fond of allowing foreigners to live in their homes and take part in village life.

### L'Algérie

**CAPITAL**
Algiers

**POPULATION**
32,818,000

**FUN FACT**
Algeria is called "the geographic giant" of the Maghreb. It is four times the size of France. Most of the country lies in the Sahara desert.

### Le Burundi

**CAPITAL**
Bujumbura

**POPULATION**
6,096,000

**FUN FACT**
Burundi was first under German control. It then became Ruanda-Urundi under Belgian control. It became independent in 1962.

### Le Cameroun

**CAPITAL**
Yaoundé

**POPULATION**
15,746,000

**FUN FACT**
Cameroon is known for its fantastic landscapes: Saharan desert, equatorial rain forest, tree-laden savannah, grassy plains, volcanic mountains with crater lakes, the swampy basin of Lake Chad, and one of the highest mountains in Africa.

### Le Bénin

**CAPITAL**
Porto-Novo

**POPULATION**
7,041,000

**FUN FACT**
Benin has one of the most popular tourist attractions in all of West Africa—the fishing village of Ganvié built on stilts in the middle of a lagoon not far from the capital, Porto Novo.

### Les Comores

**CAPITAL**
Moroni

**POPULATION**
633,000

**FUN FACT**
The beautiful Comores Islands in the Indian Ocean are known for their lovely, isolated beaches. These islands are among the few areas in the world where natural beauty reigns.

### La République du Congo

**CAPITAL**
Brazzaville

**POPULATION**
2,954,000

**FUN FACT**
Seventy percent of the population lives in the capital city or near the railroad between it and Pointe-Noire about 250 miles to the west.

## La République Démocratique du Congo

**CAPITAL**
Kinshasa

**POPULATION**
56,625,000

**FUN FACT**
The population of the Democratic Republic of the Congo is made up of six major ethnic groups which are divided into over 250 subgroups.

## La Côte d'Ivoire

**CAPITAL**
Yamoussoukro

**POPULATION**
16,962,000

**FUN FACT**
The Ivory Coast's principal city, Abidjan, is West Africa's most cosmopolitan city and is often referred to as the "Paris of West Africa."

## Djibouti

**CAPITAL**
Djibouti

**POPULATION**
457,000

**FUN FACT**
Djibouti is the name of both the republic and its capital. Its position at the entrance to the Red Sea makes it one of the most important seaports in Africa.

## Le Gabon

**CAPITAL**
Libreville

**POPULATION**
1,322,000

**FUN FACT**
More than three-quarters of the territory of Gabon is covered by forests. Its capital, Libreville (appropriately named), was founded by Catholic missionaries to house liberated slaves.

## La Guinée

**CAPITAL**
Conakry

**POPULATION**
9,030,000

**FUN FACT**
Guinea is a country known for its strong tradition of live music. Almost any evening, you can find a wonderful musical celebration in the streets of Conakry, its capital.

## La Guinée Équatoriale

**CAPITAL**
Malabo

**POPULATION**
510,000

**FUN FACT**
Equatorial Guinea is the only country in Africa where both Spanish and French are spoken even though French is considered the official language.

## Madagascar

**CAPITAL**
Antananarivo

**POPULATION**
16,980,000

**FUN FACT**
Madagascar is a beautiful and, in some areas, rocky volcanic island in the Indian Ocean.

## Le Mali

**CAPITAL**
Bamako

**POPULATION**
11,626,000

**FUN FACT**
Mali is the home of Timbuktu, which was and still is the terminus of a camel caravan route across the Sahara, linking Arabia with West Africa since ancient times.

## Le Maroc

**CAPITAL**
Rabat

**POPULATION**
31,689,000

**FUN FACT**
Morocco is a country of many beautiful, fascinating cities, such as Casablanca, Tangiers, Fez, and Marrakech.

## L'île Maurice

Port Louis

**CAPITAL**
Port Louis

**POPULATION**
1,210,000

**FUN FACT**
Mauritius is a volcanic island in the Indian Ocean known for its natural beauty.

## La Mauritanie

Nouakchott

**CAPITAL**
Nouakchott

**POPULATION**
2,913,000

**FUN FACT**
Mauritania is a bridge between the Maghreb in the North and sub-Saharan Africa in the South.

## Le Niger

Niamey

**CAPITAL**
Niamey

**POPULATION**
11,059,000

**FUN FACT**
Niger is a starkly dramatic country with its desert terrain. The capital, Niamey, on the fringe of the Sahara, is a city of modern buildings and wide boulevards—where many times you will see camels walking.

## La Réunion

Saint-Denis

**PRÉFECTURE**
Saint-Denis

**POPULATION**
755,000

**FUN FACT**
Réunion, a French overseas department, is a beautiful island in the Indian Ocean with many beaches. It has a very hot, tropical climate.

## Le Rwanda

Kigali

**CAPITAL**
Kigali

**POPULATION**
7,810,000

**FUN FACT**
Ruanda, located in Central Africa, is a country of many lakes. It has one of the densest populations in all of Africa.

## Le Sénégal

Dakar

**CAPITAL**
Dakar

**POPULATION**
10,580,000

**FUN FACT**
Senegal is a country that has a fabulous mix of Afro-French characteristics. More visitors go to Senegal than to any other Western African country.

## Les Seychelles

Victoria

**CAPITAL**
Victoria

**POPULATION**
86,000

**FUN FACT**
The Republic of the Seychelles is made up of more than one hundred islands and is a vacationer's paradise. The Seychelles attract people from all over the world.

## Le Tchad

N'Djamena

**CAPITAL**
N'Djamena

**POPULATION**
9,253,000

**FUN FACT**
Chad has a lake in the southwest of the country that doubles in size during the rainy season.

## Le Togo

**CAPITAL**
Lomé

**POPULATION**
5,429,000

**FUN FACT**
Togo is a pencil-thin strip of land whose capital, Lomé, has some of the most beautiful beaches just a block or two from the heart of town.

## La Tunisie

Tunis

**CAPITAL**
Tunis

**POPULATION**
9,925,000

**FUN FACT**
Tunisia contains Roman archaeological sites second only to Rome itself.

# L'Amérique du Nord et du Sud

## La Guadeloupe

Basse-Terre

**PRÉFECTURE**
Basse-Terre

**POPULATION**
440,000

**FUN FACT**
Guadeloupe, a French overseas department in the Caribbean, is made up of two major islands in addition to some smaller ones. It is known for its jungle highlands and beautiful seaside resorts.

## La Guyane française

Cayenne

**PRÉFECTURE**
Cayenne

**POPULATION**
187,000

**FUN FACT**
French Guyana on the east coast of South America is an overseas French department. It is famous for its Devil's Island, which once served as a French penal colony.

## Haïti

Port-au-Prince

**CAPITAL**
Port-au-Prince

**POPULATION**
7,528,000

**FUN FACT**
Haiti shares the island of Hispaniola with the Dominican Republic. Its friendly people are known for their musical and artistic talents. Haitian primitive art is sought after in art galleries around the world.

## La province de Québec

**CAPITAL**
Québec

**POPULATION**
7,040,000

**FUN FACT**
Quebec is the oldest and largest of Canada's provinces. About 90 percent of Quebec's inhabitants are French-speaking.

## La Martinique

**PRÉFECTURE**
Fort-de-France

**POPULATION**
426,000

**FUN FACT**
Martinique, like Guadeloupe, is a French overseas department in the Caribbean Sea. It is a highly developed island famous for its beautiful, exotic flowers—orchids, hibiscus, and flamingo flowers.

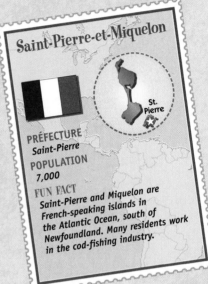

## Saint-Pierre-et-Miquelon

**PRÉFECTURE**
Saint-Pierre

**POPULATION**
7,000

**FUN FACT**
Saint-Pierre and Miquelon are French-speaking islands in the Atlantic Ocean, south of Newfoundland. Many residents work in the cod-fishing industry.

# L'Europe

## La principauté d'Andorre

**CAPITAL**
Andorre-la-Vieille

**POPULATION**
69,000

**FUN FACT**
Andorra is a co-principality governed by France's president and a Spanish bishop.

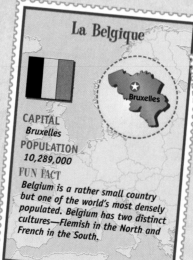

## La Belgique

**CAPITAL**
Bruxelles

**POPULATION**
10,289,000

**FUN FACT**
Belgium is a rather small country but one of the world's most densely populated. Belgium has two distinct cultures—Flemish in the North and French in the South.

## La France

**CAPITAL**
Paris

**POPULATION**
60,181,000

**FUN FACT**
France is a country known for its savoir vivre, delicious cuisine, and beautiful scenery, which changes dramatically from province to province.

## Le grand-duché de Luxembourg

**CAPITAL**
Luxembourg
**POPULATION**
454,000
**FUN FACT**
Luxembourg is smaller than the state of Rhode Island. The native Luxembourgers all speak three languages fluently: Luxembourgish, German, and French.

## La principauté de Monaco

**CAPITAL**
Monaco
**POPULATION**
32,000
**FUN FACT**
Monaco is one of the world's smallest sovereign states. It is located on a horseshoe-shaped strip of land bathed by the Mediterranean on one side and shielded by alpine peaks on the other.

## La Suisse

**CAPITAL**
Berne
**POPULATION**
7,319,000
**FUN FACT**
The beautiful country of Switzerland is dominated by the Alps. Its population density is among the lowest in Europe. Thus, it has fabulous wide-open spaces.

# L'Océanie

## Vanuatu

**CAPITAL**
Port-Vila
**POPULATION**
199,000
**FUN FACT**
The republic of Vanuatu is an archipelago in the South Pacific, made up of forty islands of volcanic origin. Some of the volcanoes are still active.

## La Nouvelle-Calédonie

**CAPITAL**
Nouméa
**POPULATION**
211,000
**FUN FACT**
New Caledonia is a French overseas territory in the South Pacific. It is made up of one large island and numerous small, beautiful coral islands.

## La Polynésie française

**CAPITAL**
Papeete
**POPULATION**
262,000
**FUN FACT**
French Polynesia is a French overseas territory made up of approximately 130 islands. The islands are known for their volcanic mountains, tropical climate, and beautiful bays and coves.

## Wallis-et-Futuna

**CAPITAL**
Mata-Utu
**POPULATION**
16,000
**FUN FACT**
Wallis-et-Futuna is a French overseas territory in the South Pacific. The mountainous islands of the archipelago are surrounded by coral reefs.

# La France

ANGLETERRE

Mer du Nord

PAYS-BAS

BELGIQUE

ALLEMAGNE

Manche

Calais

Nord-Pas-
de-Calais

Lille

LUXEMBOURG

Le Havre

Haute-
Normandie

Amiens

Caen

Picardie

Rouen

Brest

Basse-
Normandie

Seine

Châlons-
en-Champagne

Marne

Metz

Bretagne

Paris

Île-de-
France

Meuse

Lorraine

Rennes

Champagne-
Ardenne

Strasbourg

Rhine

Le Mans

Orléans

Pays de la Loire

Alsace

Nantes

Loire

Centre

Bourgogne

Besançon

Poitiers

Dijon

Franche-
Comté

OCÉAN
ATLANTIQUE

Poitou-
Charentes

Moulins

SUISSE

Limoges

Clermont-
Ferrand

Saône

Limousin

Auvergne

Lyon

Bordeaux

Rhône-Alpes

Garonne

Grenoble

Aquitaine

Rhône

ITALIE

Biarritz

Midi-Pyrénées

Toulouse

Montpellier

Provence-Alpes-
Côte d'Azur

Monaco

Nice

Languedoc-
Roussillon

MONACO

Marseille

ESPAGNE

Corse

Mer Méditerranée

Saint Denis

Périphérique

Boulevard Périphérique

Bd Mortier Bd Davout

Bd Sérurier

Av Jean Lolive

Rue de Paris

Cité des Sciences et de l'industrie

Bd MacDonald

19e arr.

Parc des Buttes-Chaumont

Rue de Belleville

Bd de Belleville

Rue de Ménilmontant

20e arr.

Av Ph Auguste

Rue Gambetta

Rue Belgrand

Av Jean Jaurès

Rue de Flandre

Bd de la Villette

10e arr.

Av de la République

Bd du Temple

11e arr.

Bd Voltaire

PL DE LA RÉPUBLIQUE

PL DE LA NATION

PL DE LA Cours de Vincennes

Bd de Picpus

Av Daumesnil

Parc Zoologique

Bois de Vincennes

Bd Soult

12e arr.

Bd de Reuilly

Bd de Bercy

Av de Bercy

Quai de Bercy

Palais Omnisports

Pont de Bercy

Rue de la Chapelle

Bd de la Chapelle

Gare de l'Est

Canal St. Martin

Rue du Faubourg du Temple

3e arr.

Rue de Turbigo

Bd de Sébastopol

Rue St Antoine

Bd du Temple

Bd Beaumarchais

PL des Vosges

PL DE LA BASTILLE

Opéra Bastille

Rue du Faubourg St Antoine

4e arr.

Bd Diderot

Opéra de Lyon

Quai de la Rapée

Gare de Lyon

Ministère des Finances

Rue de Bercy

Quai d'Austerlitz

Gare d'Austerlitz

Quai de la Gare

Bibliothèque Nationale de France

Bd Vincent Auriol

Av des Gobelins

13e arr.

PL D'ITALIE

Av de Choisy

Av d'Italie

Bd Masséna

Rue de la Chapelle

Gare du Nord

Rue Marx Dormoy

Bd de la Chapelle

Bd de Strasbourg

Bd de Magenta

Rue La Fayette

Bd Barbès

Bd Omano

Bd Barbès

Sacré-Cœur

MONTMARTRE

18e arr.

Rue de Rochechouart

9e arr.

Bd de Clichy

Rue de Clichy

Opéra Garnier

2e arr.

Av de l'Opéra

Rue de Rivoli

1er arr.

Louvre

Jardin des Tuileries

Centre Pompidou

Hôtel de Ville

ÎLE DE LA CITÉ

Notre Dame

ÎLE ST LOUIS

Sorbonne

Panthéon

QUARTIER LATIN

5e arr.

Bd St Michel

Jardin du Luxembourg

Jardin des Plantes

Institut du Monde Arabe

Bd de l'Hôpital

Av des Gobelins

Bd Arago

Bd de Port Royal

Rue Claude Bernard

Av Denfert

Bd St Jacques

Av du Général Leclerc

PL DENFERT ROCHEREAU

14e arr.

Bd A Blanqui

Bd Auguste Blanqui

Rue d'Alésia

Bd Jourdan

Cité Universitaire

Bd Kellermann

Bd Brune

Périphérique

Ney

Bd

Périphérique

Bd Omano

Boulevard

Av de St Ouen

Av de Clichy

Bd Bessières

Rue de la Chapelle

17e arr.

Bd Berthier

Bd J Jaurès

Rue Victor Hugo

Av de Clichy

Bd des Batignolles

PL DE CLICHY

Bd de Clichy

Gare Saint Lazare

Bd des Batignolles

Bd Malesherbes

Bd Haussmann

La Madeleine

PL DE LA CONCORDE

8e arr.

Av des Champs Élysées

Av de Friedland

Arc de Triomphe

PL CHARLES DE GAULLE

Av Marceau

Av d'Iéna

Av Kléber

Av Foch

Palais de Chaillot

16e arr.

Av Victor Hugo

Av G Mandel

Av P Doumer

Av H Martin

Av Mozart

Bd Suchet

Bd Lannes

Av de Villiers

Av de Wagram

Av de la Grande Armée

Bd G St Cyr

Palais des Congrès

ÎLE DE PUTEAUX

LA DÉFENSE

Bd du Cdt Charcot

Av de Madrid

Allée de Longchamp

Bd Bineau

ÎLE DE LA GRANDE JATTE

Seine

Bd de Verdun

Rue Victor Hugo

Av du Général de Gaulle

Bois de Boulogne

Rue de Vaugirard

Rue de la Convention

15e arr.

Rue Lecourbe

Av Émile Zola

Quai André Citroën

Quai de Grenelle

7e arr.

Bd des Invalides

des Invalides

École Militaire

Av de Tourville

Av de la Motte-Picquet

Av Bosquet

Quai d'Orsay

Musée d'Orsay

St Germain des-Prés

Rue de Rennes

6e arr.

Bd St Germain

Bd du Montparnasse

Raspail

Tour Montparnasse

Gare Montparnasse

Av du Maine

Rue de Vaugirard

Rue de la Convention

Parc du Champ de Mars

Tour Eiffel

Quai Branly

Av de Suffren

Bd de Grenelle

Bd Garibaldi

Rue Balard

Bd Victor

Bd Lefebvre

Rue de Vouillé

Av de Choisy

Rue Balard

Quai Louis Blériot

Rue de Versailles

Rue St-Exupéry

Bd Exelmans

Bd Murat

ÎLE SAINTE GERMAINE

Quai du Point-du-Jour

Quai de Stalingrad

Av Victor Cresson

Seine

Périphérique

Boulevard

Av P Brossolette

# Le Canada

OCÉAN GLACIAL ARCTIQUE

ALASKA (ÉTATS-UNIS)

YUKON

Whitehorse

COLOMBIE-BRITANNIQUE

Victoria

TERRITOIRES DU NORD-OUEST

Yellowknife

ALBERTA

Edmonton

SASKATCHEWAN

Regina

MANITOBA

Winnipeg

NUNAVUT

Iqaluit

Baie D'Hudson

GROENLAND (DANEMARK)

ÉTATS-UNIS

ONTARIO

Toronto

Ottawa

Québec

Montréal

Fredericton

QUÉBEC

NOUVEAU-BRUNSWICK

ÎLE-DU-PRINCE-ÉDOUARD

Charlottetown

Halifax

NOUVELLE-ÉCOSSE

TERRE-NEUVE

St-John's

ST-PIERRE-ET-MIQUELON (FR.)

Mer du Labrador

OCÉAN ATLANTIQUE

OCÉAN ATLANTIQUE

EUROPE

# L'Afrique

ASIE

Mer Méditerranée

Alger
Tunis
Rabat
TUNISIE
MAROC
Tripoli
Le Caire

ALGÉRIE
LIBYE
ÉGYPTE

SAHARA
OCCIDENTAL
(MAROC)

MAURITANIE
Nouakchott

MALI
NIGER
TCHAD

Khartoum
ÉRYTHRÉE
Asmara

SOUDAN

Dakar
SÉNÉGAL
Banjul
GAMBIE
GUINÉE-BISSAU
Bissau
GUINÉE
Conakry
SIERRA
LEONE
Freetown
Monrovia
LIBERIA

Bamako
BURKINA
FASO
Niamey
Ouagadougou
BÉNIN
TOGO
GHANA
Yamoussoukro
CÔTE
D'IVOIRE
Lomé
Abidjan
Accra

NIGERIA
Abuja
N'Djamena

DJIBOUTI
Djibouti

Addis
Ababa
ÉTHIOPIE

Porto-
Novo
Malabo
CAMEROUN
Yaoundé

RÉPUBLIQUE
CENTRAFRICAINE
Bangui

OUGANDA
Kampala
KENYA
Nairobi
SOMALIE
Mogadishu

GUINÉE ÉQUATORIALE
SÃO TOMÉ
ET PRÍNCIPE
São Tomé
Libreville
CONGO
GABON
Brazzaville
CABINDA
(ANGOLA)
Luanda

RÉPUBLIQUE
DÉMOCRATIQUE
DU CONGO
Kinshasa
RWANDA
Kigali
BURUNDI
Bujumbura
TANZANIE
Dodoma

OCÉAN
ATLANTIQUE

ANGOLA

ZAMBIE
Lusaka

MALAWI
Lilongwe

Moroni
COMORES

Harare
ZIMBABWE
MOZAMBIQUE

MADAGASCAR
Antananarivo

NAMIBIE
Windhoek
BOTSWANA
Gaborone
Pretoria
Maputo
Mbabane
SWAZILAND
Bloemfontein
LESOTHO
Maseru
AFRIQUE
DU SUD
Le Cap

# Why Learn French?

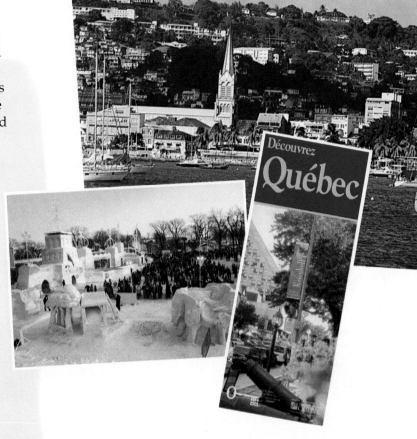

## The Francophone World

**Culture** Knowing French will open doors to you around the world. As you study the language, you will also come to understand and appreciate the way of life, customs, values, and cultures of people from many different countries. Look at the map on page xxii to see the areas of the world in which French is spoken, either as a first or second language. You might be surprised to see that people speak French in places as close to home as Haiti, Martinique, Quebec, and Louisiana.

Learning French can be fun and will bring you a sense of accomplishment. You'll be really pleased when you are able to carry on a conversation with a French-speaking person in French. You will also be able to read French literature, keep up with current events in French magazines and newspapers, and understand French films without relying on subtitles. The French language will be a source of enrichment for the rest of your life.

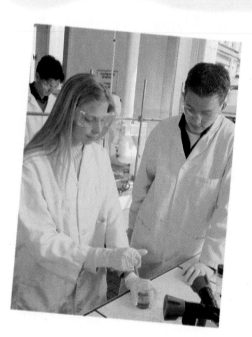

## Career Opportunities

**Business** Your knowledge of French will also be an asset to you in a variety of careers. Many French companies are multinational and have branches around the world, including the United States. Some of the fields in which French companies excel are: clothing and fashion, cosmetics, tourism, agriculture, the automotive and aerospace industries, and technology.

**Research** France is also a world leader in high-energy physics research and medical genetics. Did you know that French and English are the two major languages of the Internet? French can help you in almost any career path you choose.

## Language Link

Another benefit to learning French is that it will improve your English. Once you know another language, you can make comparisons between the two and gain a greater understanding of how languages function. As a result, your use of English will be more effective. You'll also come across many French words that are used in English. Just a few examples are: **rouge, chaise longue, chic, crêpe, à la mode, omelette, chargé d'affaires, déjà vu, détente,** and **laisser faire.** French will also be helpful if you decide to learn yet another language. Once you learn a second language, the learning process for acquiring other languages becomes much easier.

French is a beautiful, rich language that is spoken on many continents. Many people use French on a daily basis as their second language. Whatever your motivation is for choosing to study it, French will expand your horizons and increase your job opportunities. **Vive la langue française! Et bon voyage!**

# L'alphabet français

**a** *a*mis

**b** *b*ébé

**c** *c*irque

**d** *d*eux

**e** *le*çon

**f** *f*enêtre

**g** *g*iraffe

**h** *h*uit

**i** *i*gloo

**j** *j*eu

**k** *k*ilo

**l** *l*ivre

**m** *m*aison

**n** *n*ez

**o** *o*live

**p** *p*ain

**q** *q*uatre

**r** *r*eine

**s** *s*oupe

**t** *t*able

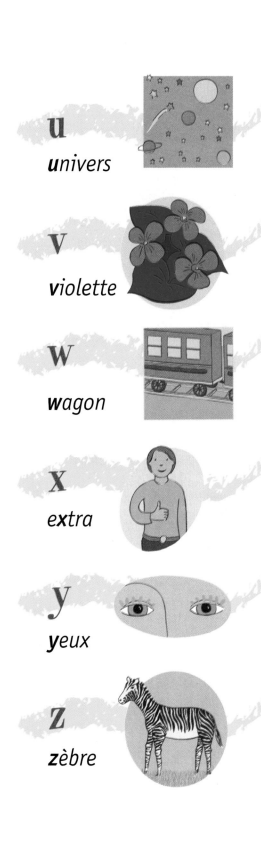

**u** *u*nivers

**v** *v*iolette

**w** *w*agon

**x** ex*t*ra

**y** *y*eux

**z** *z*èbre

# Leçons préliminaires

# Bienvenue

## Objectifs

**In these preliminary lessons you will learn to:**

✓ *greet people*

✓ *say good-bye to people*

✓ *ask people how they are*

✓ *ask and tell names*

✓ *express simple courtesies*

✓ *find out and tell the days of the week*

✓ *find out and tell the months of the year*

✓ *count from 1 to 30*

✓ *find out and tell the time*

1. Karim Ashour, Tunis, Tunisie
2. Yvonne Senghor, Abidjan, Côte d'Ivoire
3. Jacques Ferrand, Montréal, Canada
4. Thérèse Nguyen, Lyon, France
5. Yves Clémenceau, Fort-de-France, Martinique
6. Ahmed Rashid, Paris, France
7. Vincent Daudet, Rouen, France
8. Élodie Lutz, Strasbourg, France
9. Marie Robert, Marseille, France

# Greeting people 🎧

When someone wants to know how you are doing and asks **Ça va?**, there are several different answers you can give.

**Ça va.**
**Bien, merci.**
**Ça va très bien.**
**Pas mal, merci.**

## 1 Salut!

Get up from your desk. Walk around the classroom. Say hello to each classmate you meet.

## 2 Ça va?

Work with a classmate. Greet one another and find out how things are going.

# More greetings 🎧

1. **Salut!** is an informal greeting that you can use with people your own age. When you greet an older person, you may use the following expressions.

Bonjour, monsieur.

Bonjour, madame.

Bonjour, mademoiselle.

2. Note that the titles **monsieur, madame,** and **mademoiselle** are almost always used without the last name of the person.

## 3 Bonjour!

Draw some figures on the board. Some will represent friends your own age and others will represent older people. Greet each of the figures on the board properly.

## 4 Salutations

Look at these photographs of young people in France and Martinique. As they greet one another they do some things that are different from what we do when we greet each other. What do you notice in the photographs?

# Préliminaire B

## Saying good-bye 🎧

Au revoir, madame.

Au revoir, Christine.

Ciao, Thomas. À tout à l'heure.

Ciao, Charlotte.

**1.** A very common expression to use when saying good-bye to someone is **Au revoir.**

**2.** If you plan to see the person again soon, you can say **À bientôt!** If you plan to see the person very soon, you can say **À tout à l'heure.** If you plan to see the person the next day, you can say **À demain.**

**3.** An informal expression you often hear is **Ciao.** It comes from Italian and is used in many parts of Europe.

### 1 Ciao!

Go over to a classmate and say good-bye to him or her.

### 2 À bientôt!

Work with a classmate. Say **Ciao** to each other and let one another know when you will be getting together again.

### 3 Au revoir!

Say good-bye to your French teacher. Use **monsieur, madame,** or **mademoiselle,** as appropriate. Then say good-bye to a friend. Use a different expression with each person.

# Conversation

**4** **Salut!**

Work with a classmate.
Have a conversation
in French. Say as
much as you can to
each other.

**5** **Bonjour!**

Work with a classmate. One of you will pretend to be an older person.
Have a conversation. Say as much as you can to each other.

# Préliminaire C *Les noms*

## Finding out a person's name 🎧

> Tu t'appelles comment?

> Moi, je m'appelle Nicolas. Et toi?

> Je m'appelle Marie.

> Salut, Nicolas.

> Salut, Marie.

When you want to find out the name of a person who is about the same age as you, you can ask **Tu t'appelles comment?** However, you would not use this expression with an older person. You will learn the more formal forms at a later time.

**1** **Tu t'appelles comment?**

Get up from your desk. Walk around the room. Find out several of your classmates' names. Let them know your name, too.

# Conversation

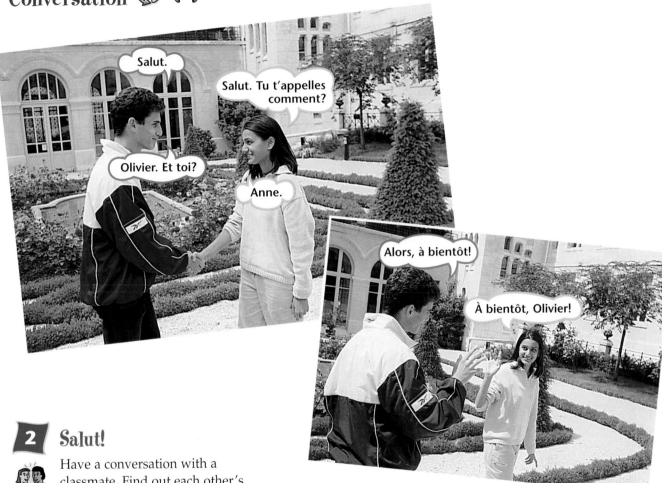

Salut.

Salut. Tu t'appelles comment?

Olivier. Et toi?

Anne.

Alors, à bientôt!

À bientôt, Olivier!

## 2 Salut!

Have a conversation with a classmate. Find out each other's name, how things are going, and say good-bye to each other.

## 3 Je m'appelle...

Look at this photograph of young French people introducing each other. Are they doing something that you probably would not do? What is it?

## Ordering food politely 🎧

Expressions of politeness are always appreciated. The following are the French expressions for "please," "thank you," and "you're welcome."

| Formal | Informal |
|---|---|
| S'il vous plaît. | S'il te plaît. |
| Merci (madame). | Merci. |
| Je vous en prie. | Je t'en prie. |

## 1 La politesse

With a classmate, practice reading the preceding conversation aloud.
Be as animated and as polite as you can.

## 2 Une limonade, s'il vous plaît.

You are at a café in Canada. Order the following things. Your partner will be
the server. Be polite when you order.

1. un sandwich

2. un coca

3. une limonade

4. un café

5. une pizza

6. une saucisse de Francfort,
un hot-dog

7. une crêpe

# Préliminaire E

## La date

## Telling the days of the week 🎧

To find out and give the day of the week, you say:

**C'est quel jour aujourd'hui?**
**(Aujourd'hui), c'est lundi.**
**Demain, c'est mardi.**

| LUNDI | MARDI | MERCREDI | JEUDI | VENDREDI | SAMEDI | DIMANCHE |
|-------|-------|----------|-------|----------|--------|----------|
| 1 | 2 | 3 | 4 | 5 | 6 | 7 |
| 8 | 9 | 10 | 11 | 12 | 13 | 14 |

**1**  **C'est quel jour?**

 Answer the following questions in French.

1. C'est quel jour aujourd'hui?
2. Et demain? C'est quel jour?

## Telling the months 🎧

| | | |
|---------|---------|-----------|
| janvier | mai | septembre |
| février | juin | octobre |
| mars | juillet | novembre |
| avril | août | décembre |

### Les nombres de 1 à 30

| | | | | |
|--------|-----------|--------------|----------------|--------------|
| 1 un | 7 sept | 13 treize | 19 dix-neuf | 25 vingt-cinq |
| 2 deux | 8 huit | 14 quatorze | 20 vingt | 26 vingt-six |
| 3 trois | 9 neuf | 15 quinze | 21 vingt et un | 27 vingt-sept |
| 4 quatre | 10 dix | 16 seize | 22 vingt-deux | 28 vingt-huit |
| 5 cinq | 11 onze | 17 dix-sept | 23 vingt-trois | 29 vingt-neuf |
| 6 six | 12 douze | 18 dix-huit | 24 vingt-quatre | 30 trente |

# Finding out and giving the date

**Quelle est la date aujourd'hui?**

**(C'est) le trente et un août.**

| AOÛT | | | | | | |
|---|---|---|---|---|---|---|
| LUNDI | MARDI | MERCREDI | JEUDI | VENDREDI | SAMEDI | DIMANCHE |
| 1 | 2 | 3 | 4 | 5 | 6 | 7 |
| 8 | 9 | 10 | 11 | 12 | 13 | 14 |
| 15 | 16 | 17 | 18 | 19 | 20 | 21 |
| 22 | 23 | 24 | 25 | 26 | 27 | 28 |
| 29 | 30 | ③① | | | | |

**Premier** is used for the first day of the month. For other days you use **deux, trois, quatre,** etc.

> **le premier août**
> **le deux septembre**

## 2  La date, s'il vous plaît.

Answer the following questions in French.

1. Quelle est la date aujourd'hui?
2. Et demain?

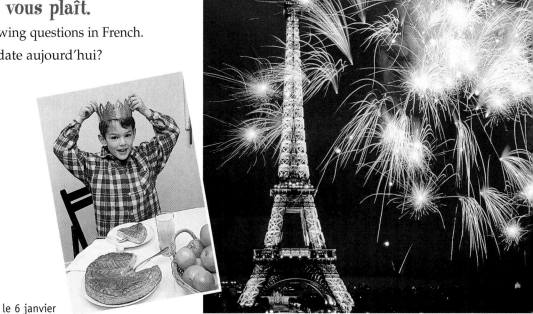

le 6 janvier

le 14 juillet à Paris

## 3  En quel mois?

Each of you will stand up in class and give the date of your birthday in French. Listen carefully and keep a record of how many of you were born in the same month. Then tell in French in which month the greatest number of students were born. In which month were the fewest born?

# Préliminaire F — L'heure

## Telling time 🎧

**1.** To find out the time, you ask:

> **Il est quelle heure?**

**2.** To give the time on the hour, you say:

**1 h**
**Il est une heure.**

**2 h**
**Il est deux heures.**

**10 h**
**Il est dix heures.**

**12 h**
**Il est midi.**

**12 h**
**Il est minuit.**

**3.** To give the time after the hour, you say:

**1 h 05**
**Il est une heure cinq.**

**3 h 10**
**Il est trois heures dix.**

**4 h 25**
**Il est quatre heures
vingt-cinq.**

**4.** To give the time before the hour, you say:

**4 h 50**
**Il est cinq heures
moins dix.**

**5 h 40**
**Il est six heures moins
vingt.**

**9 h 35**
**Il est dix heures moins
vingt-cinq.**

**5.** To express time on the quarter hour and half hour, you say:

**2 h 15**
**Il est deux heures et quart.**

**6 h 45**
**Il est sept heures moins
le quart.**

**6 h 30**
**Il est six heures et demie.**

**6.** If you need to specify whether it is A.M. or P.M., you can use the following expressions.

**Il est six heures du matin.**

**Il est quatre heures
de l'après-midi.**

**Il est onze heures du soir.**

**1** Il est quelle heure?

Look at each clock and give the time.

1.

2.

3.

4.

5.

6.

## Conversation

> Salut, Julie. Il est quelle heure, s'il te plaît?

> Il est trois heures vingt.

> Trois heures vingt! Déjà? Zut! Au revoir!

> Au revoir, Vincent. À bientôt!

### 2 Ciao!

Work with a classmate. Greet each other. Find out the time and react as if you have to get going.

### 3 Il est quelle heure, s'il te plaît?

Get up from your desk and walk around the room. Go up to a classmate. Greet the person quickly and ask the time. Show your classmate a piece of paper with a time on it. He or she will give you the time.

## Greeting people

| | | |
|---|---|---|
| Salut! | Ça va? | Bien. |
| Bonjour! | Pas mal. | Très bien. |

## Giving titles

| | | |
|---|---|---|
| Monsieur | Madame | Mademoiselle |

## Saying good-bye

| | |
|---|---|
| Au revoir. | À bientôt. |
| Ciao! | À demain. |
| À tout à l'heure. | |

## Finding out a person's name

Tu t'appelles comment?
Je m'appelle…

## Being courteous

| | |
|---|---|
| S'il te plaît. | Je t'en prie. |
| S'il vous plaît. | Je vous en prie. |
| Merci. | |

**How well do you know your vocabulary?**

- Choose an expression from the list to begin a conversation.
- Have a classmate respond.
- Take turns.

## Telling the days of the week

| | | | |
|---|---|---|---|
| lundi | jeudi | samedi | C'est quel jour? |
| mardi | vendredi | dimanche | aujourd'hui |
| mercredi | | | demain |

## Telling the months of the year

| | | | |
|---|---|---|---|
| Quelle est la date? | avril | août | novembre |
| janvier | mai | septembre | décembre |
| février | juin | octobre | |
| mars | juillet | | |

## Telling time

| | |
|---|---|
| Il est quelle heure? | Il est midi. |
| Il est _____ heure(s). | Il est minuit. |
| du matin | |
| de l'après-midi | |
| du soir | |

# Une amie et un ami

## Objectifs

In this chapter you will learn to:

- ask or tell what someone is like
- ask or tell where someone is from
- ask or tell who someone is
- describe yourself or someone else
- talk about students from France and Martinique

Victor Gabriel Gilbert *Enfants jouant au cerceau*

# Vocabulaire

Comment est la fille? 🎧

brune

petite

amusante

grande

C'est qui?
C'est Julie Lacroix.
Julie est française.

Elle est d'où, Julie?
Julie est de Paris.

# Comment est le garçon?

brun

petit

amusant

grand

C'est qui?
C'est Olivier Charpentier.
Olivier est français aussi.

Il est d'où, Olivier?
Il est de Nice.

## Note

Many words in French and English look alike even though they are pronounced differently. These words are called "cognates." You can use the following cognates to describe people.

| | |
|---|---|
| américain | intelligent |
| blond | intéressant |
| patient | |

Here are some words used to express degree.

**Il est amusant.**
**Il est assez amusant.**
**Il est très amusant.**
**Il est vraiment amusant.**

# Quel est le mot?

## 1 Historiette   Une fille française

Inventez une histoire. *(Make up a story.)*

1. Sophie est française ou américaine?
2. Elle est de Paris ou de New York?
3. Elle est brune ou blonde?
4. Elle est amusante?
5. Elle est grande ou petite?

Sophie Legrand

## 2 Historiette   Un garçon français

Inventez une histoire. *(Make up a story.)*

1. Christophe est américain ou français?
2. Il est de Lyon ou de Houston?
3. Il est brun ou blond?
4. Il est amusant?
5. Il est très intelligent?
6. Il est assez patient?

Christophe Gaudin

Bill

Henri

## 3 Un Français ou un Américain?

Répondez d'après les photos.
*(Answer according to the photos.)*

1. Qui est américain?
2. Qui est français?
3. Qui est de Paris?
4. Qui est de Los Angeles?
5. Qui est blond?
6. Qui est brun?

**4** **Il est... ? Elle est... ?** Look at the following people and say two things about each of them. Then, find out who they are. They are all famous.

 **5** **C'est qui?** Think of a student in the class. A classmate will ask you questions about the person and try to guess who it is. Take turns.

 *For more practice using words from **Mots 1**, do Activity 1 on page H2 at the end of this book.*

ENCORE
PLUS

UNE AMIE ET UN AMI

# Vocabulaire

## Une sœur et un frère 🎧

le frère

la sœur

Voilà Nathalie et Luc Simonet.
Nathalie est la sœur de Luc.
Luc est le frère de Nathalie.

une amie

un ami

Voilà Philippe.
Philippe n'est pas le frère de Nathalie.
Philippe est un ami de Nathalie.

## Une école et un collège 🎧

une école
américaine

WESTERVILLE NORTH

OPEN HOUSE
SEPT 14
7 PM

une élève

Carol est élève dans une école américaine.

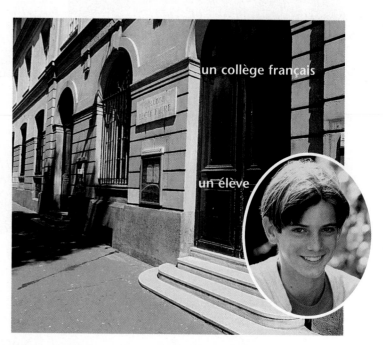

un collège français

un élève

Bruno est élève dans un collège français.
Un collège est une école secondaire en France.

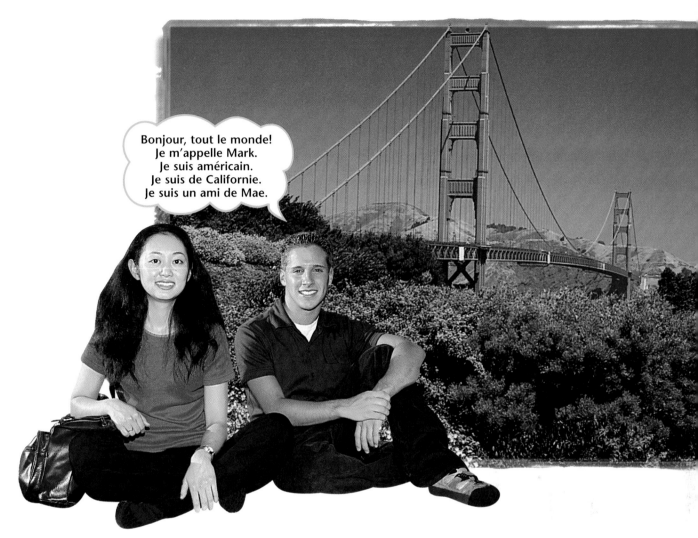

Bonjour, tout le monde!
Je m'appelle Mark.
Je suis américain.
Je suis de Californie.
Je suis un ami de Mae.

Mae est une amie de Mark.
Mae est très sympathique.
Mark est très sympa aussi.

**Note** 🎧

You can also use the following cognates to describe people.

| | |
|---|---|
| dynamique | égoïste |
| énergique | enthousiaste |
| populaire | sociable |
| timide | |

## Les nombres de 30 à 60

| | | |
|---|---|---|
| 30 trente | 35 trente-cinq | 40 quarante |
| 31 trente et un | 36 trente-six | 50 cinquante |
| 32 trente-deux | 37 trente-sept | 60 soixante |
| 33 trente-trois | 38 trente-huit | |
| 34 trente-quatre | 39 trente-neuf | |

# Quel est le mot?

**6** **Historiette** **Une élève française** Choisissez la bonne réponse.
*(Choose the right answer.)*

1. _____ est française.
   **a.** Céline Dupont **b.** Thomas Duhamel
2. Céline est élève dans _____.
   **a.** une école américaine **b.** un collège français
3. Elle est _____.
   **a.** de Paris **b.** de Miami
4. Céline est _____ de Karim.
   **a.** un ami **b.** une amie
5. Karim est _____ de Céline.
   **a.** un ami **b.** un élève
6. David est _____ de Céline.
   **a.** la sœur **b.** le frère
7. Céline est _____ de David.
   **a.** le frère **b.** la sœur

**7** **Qui est d'où?** Répondez d'après la carte.
*(Answer according to the map.)*

1. Qui est de Bordeaux?
2. D'où est Maïa?
3. Et Olivia, elle est d'où?
4. Et Ahmed, il est d'où?

Maïa

Paul

Paris

Strasbourg

Ahmed

Bordeaux

Cannes

Olivia

**8** **Historiette** **David Williams, un garçon américain**
Inventez une histoire. *(Make up a story.)*

1. Qui est américain, David Williams ou Serge Legrand?
2. D'où est David Williams? Il est de New York ou de Paris?
3. Il est de quelle nationalité? Il est français ou américain?
4. David est élève dans un collège français ou dans une école américaine?
5. Comment est David? Il est timide ou sociable?

**9** **Historiette** **Sophie est vraiment amusante.** Complétez. *(Complete.)*

Sophie Bellecour est de Lyon. Elle est __1__.
Elle n'est pas américaine. Sophie est blonde. Elle
n'est pas __2__. Elle n'est pas timide. Pas du tout!
Elle est très __3__. Elle est très sympa aussi.
Elle est __4__ dans un collège à Lyon.

Lyon, France

Pascal Denjean

**10** **Pascal Denjean** Here is a photo of Pascal Denjean. He is a student from Bordeaux. Say a few things about Pascal.

**11** **Élodie Denjean** The blonde girl in the photo is Élodie Denjean. She is Pascal's sister. She is also a student in Bordeaux. Say a few things about Élodie.

Élodie Denjean

**12** **Jeu** **Un nombre secret** Think of a number between 1 and 60. Your partner tries to guess the number you have in mind. Use a hand gesture to indicate whether the number you are thinking of is higher or lower. Continue until your partner guesses the correct number. Take turns.

*For more practice using words from **Mots 2**, do Activity 2 on page H3 at the end of this book.*

# Structure

## Les articles au singulier
### Talking about a person or a thing

**1.** A noun is the name of a person, place, or thing. In French, every noun has a gender, either masculine or feminine. Except for people, you cannot tell what the gender of a noun is by just looking at it. You need other clues.

**2.** Many words that accompany nouns can indicate gender. They are called "gender markers." **Une** and **un** are gender markers. They are indefinite articles and correspond to *a (an)* in English. **Une** accompanies a feminine noun and **un** accompanies a masculine noun.

### LES ARTICLES INDÉFINIS

| Féminin | Masculin |
|---------|----------|
| une amie | un ami |
| une sœur | un frère |
| une école | un collège |

**3.** **Le, la,** and **l'** are definite articles and often correspond to *the* in English.

### LES ARTICLES DÉFINIS

| Féminin | Masculin |
|---------|----------|
| la fille | le garçon |
| la sœur | le frère |
| l'amie | l'ami |

## Attention!

Note that the definite articles **le** and **la** are shortened to **l'** when they accompany a noun that begins with a vowel. When pronounced, the vowel sound is dropped. This is called "elision."

la amie → l'amie
le ami → l'ami

The **n** of the indefinite article **un** is pronounced when it accompanies a noun beginning with a vowel. This is called "liaison."

un ̲n̲ ami        un ̲n̲ élève

Une sœur et un frère

# Comment dit-on?

**13 Historiette** **Olivier et Marie** Complétez avec **un** ou **une.**
*(Complete with* un *or* une.)

Olivier est __1__ garçon très sympa. Olivier est __2__ ami de Christophe. Christophe est __3__ élève très intelligent. Il est élève dans __4__ école secondaire à New York.

Marie est __5__ amie de Christophe. Marie est __6__ élève intelligente aussi. Marie est __7__ fille vraiment amusante.

**14 Historiette** **Brendan Jones et Sabine Morel**
Complétez avec **le, la** ou **l'.** *(Complete with* le, la, *or* l'.)

__1__ garçon, Brendan Jones, est américain, mais __2__ fille, Sabine Morel, n'est pas américaine. Elle est française. Sabine est __3__ amie de Ludovic Girard et __4__ sœur de Luc Morel. Brendan n'est pas __5__ ami de Sabine; il est de Miami et Sabine est de Strasbourg. Brendan est __6__ ami de Karen Miller et __7__ frère de Melissa Jones. Brendan est élève et Sabine est élève aussi. __8__ école de Brendan est à Miami. __9__ collège de Sabine est à Strasbourg.

Strasbourg, France

# L'accord des adjectifs
## Describing a person or a thing

1. An adjective is a word that describes a noun. The highlighted words in the following sentences are adjectives.

> **La fille est blonde. Le garçon est blond aussi.**
> **Jeanne est française. Vincent aussi est français.**

2. In French, an adjective must agree with the noun it describes or modifies. Adjectives that end in a consonant such as **blond** and **français** have two forms in the singular. Study the following.

| Féminin | Masculin |
|---|---|
| La fille est blonde. | Le garçon est blond. |
| La fille est française. | Le garçon est français. |
| La fille est brune. | Le garçon est brun. |
| La fille est intelligente. | Le garçon est intelligent. |
| L'école est grande. | Le collège est grand. |

3. Adjectives that end in **e**, such as **énergique** and **sympathique**, are both feminine and masculine.

| Féminin | Masculin |
|---|---|
| Charlotte est très énergique. | Nicolas est très énergique. |
| Elle est sympathique. | Il est sympathique. |

La fille est blonde. Le garçon est brun.

## Attention!

When a final consonant is followed by an **e**, you pronounce the consonant. When a word ends in a consonant, you don't pronounce it.

| petite | petiṯ |
| française | françaiṣ |
| intéressante | intéressanṯ |

# Comment dit-on?

**15** **Historiette** **Chloé et Adrien Chancel** Répondez d'après le dessin. (*Answer according to the illustration.*)

1. Chloé est française ou américaine?
2. Elle est blonde ou brune?
3. Elle est grande ou petite?
4. Elle est amusante?
5. Adrien est le frère de Chloé?
6. Adrien est blond ou brun?
7. Il est grand ou petit?
8. Il est amusant?
9. Chloé est élève dans un collège français ou dans une école américaine?
10. Et le frère de Chloé, il est élève dans un collège français ou dans une école américaine?

**16** **Historiette** **Maïa, Emmanuel et moi** Complétez. (*Complete.*)

1. Maïa est une amie ＿＿ et ＿＿. (amusant, sympathique)
2. Emmanuel est le frère de Maïa. Il est ＿＿ aussi. Il est ＿＿ et très ＿＿! (sympathique, amusant, sociable)
3. Maïa est ＿＿. (français)
4. Et moi, je m'appelle ＿＿ (*your name*). Je suis ＿＿. Je ne suis pas ＿＿. (américain, français)
5. Je suis élève dans une école ＿＿ ＿＿. (secondaire, américain)
6. Je ne suis pas élève dans un collège ＿＿. (français)

**17** **Jeu** **Devinez.** You often hear French teenagers talk about their friends' younger siblings and say something like: «**Oh, la petite sœur de Corinne, elle est vraiment casse-pieds!**» (literally, *a foot-breaker*). Can you guess what expression we use in English?

**18** **Un ami idéal ou une amie idéale**

What are some qualities an ideal friend would have? With a classmate, discuss what you think an ideal friend is like.

**19** **C'est qui?** Work with a classmate. Say three things that describe someone in the class. First your partner will tell you whether you're describing a boy or a girl. Then, he or she will guess who it is. Take turns.

—brun, grand, amusant
—C'est un garçon. C'est Marc.

# Le verbe être au singulier
## Identifying people and things

**1.** The verb *to be* in French is **être.** Study the following forms.

| ÊTRE |
|------|
| je suis |
| tu es |
| il est |
| elle est |

**2.** You use **je** to talk about yourself.

You use **tu** to address a friend.

Je suis française.

Tu es américain?

You use **il** to talk about a boy or a man.

You use **elle** to talk about a girl or a woman.

Il est blond.

Elle est brune.

**3.** You also use **il/elle** when referring to things.

Le collège? Il est grand.
L'école? Elle est petite.

# Comment dit-on?

**20** **Historiette** **Sylvie Latour** Voici une photo de Sylvie Latour. Décrivez Sylvie d'après les indications. (*Here is a photo of Sylvie Latour. Describe Sylvie using the cues.*)

**1.** canadienne
**2.** blonde
**3.** amusante et intelligente
**4.** sociable
**5.** de Montréal

**21** **En France** Répétez la conversation. (*Repeat the conversation.*)

Salut! Tu es l'ami américain de Sandrine Valois, n'est-ce pas?

Oui, je m'appelle Matt, Matt Porter.

Tu es de New York?

Oui, je suis de New York.

**22** **Historiette** **Matt Porter** Parlez de Matt.
(*Say all you can about Matt.*)

**23** **Pardon!** Répondez d'après le modèle. (*Answer according to the model.*)

Je suis de Paris.

Pardon, tu es d'où?

**1.** Je suis de Nice.
**2.** Je suis d'Antibes.
**3.** Je suis de Lille.
**4.** Je suis de Strasbourg.

**24** **Je suis...** Donnez des réponses personnelles. *(Give your own answers.)*

Je m'appelle ___1___ *(name)*. Je suis de ___2___ *(place)*. Je suis ___3___ *(nationality)*. Je suis ___4___ *(occupation)*.

**25** **Une interview** Posez des questions à un(e) ami(e). *(Ask a friend the following questions.)*

1. Tu es français(e) ou américain(e)?
2. Tu es d'où?
3. Tu es élève dans une école secondaire?
4. Tu es sociable ou timide?

Rémi Tonon

**26** **Rémi** Voici une photo de Rémi Tonon. Il est de Nîmes. Posez des questions à Rémi d'après le modèle. *(Ask Rémi questions according to the model. Your partner will answer as Rémi.)*

**français ⟶**
**—Rémi, tu es français?**
**—Oui, je suis français.**

1. de Nîmes
2. élève dans un collège de Nîmes
3. sociable
4. intelligent

**27** **Historiette** **Antoine Delcourt** Complétez. *(Complete.)*

Voici Antoine Delcourt. Il ___1___ français. Il est de Marseille. Moi aussi, je ___2___ de Marseille. Marseille ___3___ un port important en France. Antoine ___4___ élève dans un collège à Marseille. Le collège est assez grand.

Et toi, tu ___5___ français(e) ou américain(e)? Tu ___6___ d'où? Tu ___7___ élève dans une école secondaire? L'école ___8___ petite?

Marseille, France

# La négation
## Making a sentence negative

To make a sentence negative in French, you put **ne... pas** around the verb.
Note that **ne** becomes **n'** before a vowel.

| Affirmatif | Négatif |
|---|---|
| Je suis américain. | Je ne suis pas français. |
| Tu es amusant. | Tu n'es pas timide. |
| Il est sociable. | Il n'est pas égoïste. |
| Elle est de Lyon. | Elle n'est pas de Paris. |

# Comment dit-on?

 **28** **Non, Justine n'est pas américaine.**
Mettez à la forme négative. *(Change to the negative.)*

1. Justine est américaine.
2. Elle est de San Francisco.
3. Et moi, je suis français(e).
4. Je suis de Paris.
5. Je suis élève dans un collège à Paris.

Lycée Henri IV, Paris

 **29** **Tu es français(e)?** Donnez des réponses
personnelles. *(Give your own answers.)*

1. Tu es français(e)?
2. Tu es de Lyon?
3. Tu es timide?
4. Tu es l'ami(e) de Justine?

 **30** **Un petit ami ou une petite amie** A classmate will
pretend that he or she has a new boyfriend or girlfriend.
Ask as many questions as you can to find out who it is.

 *For more practice using the verb **être**, do Activity 3
on page H4 at the end of this book.*

*Vous êtes sur le bon chemin. Allez-y!*

# Conversation

## Il est d'où, Luc?

**Sophie:** Luc, tu es de Paris, non?
**Luc:** Non. Je ne suis pas de Paris.
**Sophie:** Tu es d'où, alors?
**Luc:** Je suis de Cannes.
**Sophie:** Tu es de Cannes… sur la Côte d'Azur?
**Luc:** Oui.
**Sophie:** C'est super, la Côte d'Azur!

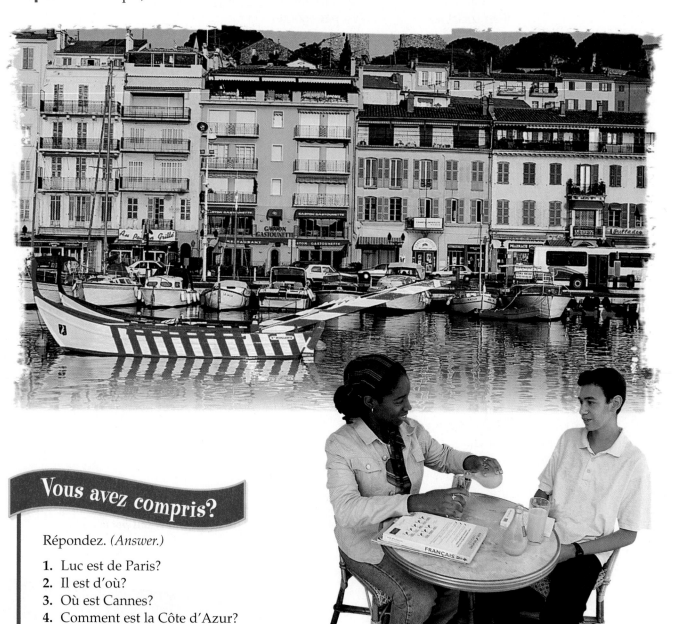

## Vous avez compris?

Répondez. (*Answer.*)

1. Luc est de Paris?
2. Il est d'où?
3. Où est Cannes?
4. Comment est la Côte d'Azur?

# Parlons un peu plus

**A**  **Au café** You've just met a student your own age at a café in Antibes, near Cannes. Have a conversation to get to know each other better.

**B**  **Tu es... !** Play a guessing game. Think of someone in the class. Pretend you are this person and describe yourself. Your classmates have to guess who you are.

Antibes, France

---

## Prononciation

### L'accent tonique 🎧

1. In English, you stress certain syllables more than others. In French, you pronounce each syllable evenly. Compare the following pairs of English and French words.

   *timid* / **timide**          *patient* / **patient**
   *popular* / **populaire**      *American* / **américain**
   *sociable* / **sociable**

2. Repeat the following sentences. Notice how each word is linked to the next so that the sentence sounds like one long word.

   **Élisabeth est l'amie de Nathalie.**
   **Paul est le frère de Nathalie.**
   **Il est très sympathique.**

# Lectures culturelles

## Un garçon et une fille

### Un Parisien

Nicolas Martin est français. Il est de Paris, la capitale de la France. Nicolas est un garçon sympa. Il est très intelligent aussi. Nicolas est élève dans un lycée à Paris, le lycée Henri IV. Un lycée est aussi une école secondaire en France, mais après[1] le collège. Le lycée Henri IV à Paris est une école excellente.

[1] après *after*

Lycée Henri IV, Paris

Haïti
La Martinique

## Une Martiniquaise

Valérie Boucher est française aussi. Elle est de Fort-de-France, la ville[2] principale de la Martinique. La Martinique est une île[3] française dans la mer des Caraïbes (la mer des Antilles). Valérie est élève dans un lycée à Fort-de-France—le lycée Bellevue. Le lycée Bellevue est une école excellente.

[2] ville *city*    [3] île *island*

Fort-de-France, Martinique

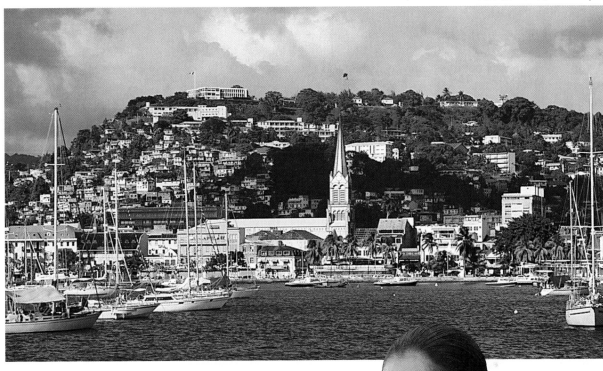

## Vous avez compris?

**A Un Parisien** Répondez. *(Answer.)*
1. Nicolas Martin est de quelle nationalité?
2. Il est d'où?
3. Quelle est la capitale de la France?
4. Comment est Nicolas?
5. Il est élève où?

**B Une Martiniquaise** Vrai ou faux? *(True or false?)*
1. Valérie Boucher est espagnole.
2. Elle est de Pointe-à-Pitre.
3. La Martinique est une île portugaise.
4. Valérie est élève dans une école américaine.

## Le français en Afrique

Bonjour! Je m'appelle Diane Koffi. Je suis d'Abidjan. Abidjan est la ville principale de la Côte d'Ivoire. La Côte d'Ivoire est un pays[1] d'Afrique Occidentale[2]. C'est un pays francophone[3].

Moi, je m'appelle Karim Ashour. Je suis tunisien. Je suis de Tunis, la capitale de la Tunisie. La Tunisie est un pays nord-africain sur la mer Méditerranée. La langue officielle de la Tunisie est l'arabe. Le français est la deuxième[4] langue.

[1] pays *country*
[2] Occidentale *Western*
[3] francophone *French-speaking*
[4] deuxième *second*

Abidjan, Côte d'Ivoire

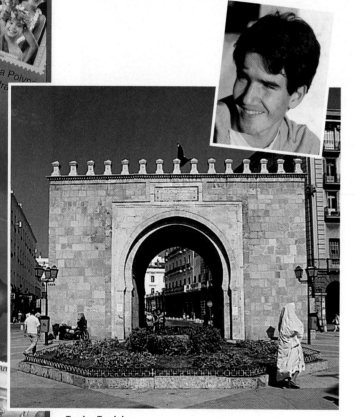

Tunis, Tunisie

## Vous avez compris?

**A Diane** Complétez. *(Complete.)*
1. Diane Koffi est d'_____.
2. Abidjan est la ville principale de la _____.
3. La Côte d'Ivoire est un pays d'_____ Occidentale.

**B Karim** Vrai ou faux? *(True or false?)*
1. Karim Ashour est une fille.
2. Karim est algérien.
3. Karim est de Tunis.
4. Tunis est la capitale de la Tunisie.
5. La Tunisie est en Europe.
6. La langue officielle de la Tunisie est le français.

## Un artiste français

Henri de Toulouse-Lautrec est un peintre français.
Il est d'Albi, une petite ville dans le sud de la France.
La famille d'Henri est noble et assez riche.

Le jeune Henri est très petit. Il est boiteux[1]. Le petit garçon
souffre de beaucoup de[2] fractures. Mais le jeune Henri possède
un grand talent. Il adore la peinture[3].

Un sujet favori de Toulouse-Lautrec est la vie[4] parisienne.

Un autre sujet favori de Toulouse-Lautrec est le
cirque. Le clown est très amusant, n'est-ce pas?

[1] boiteux *lame*
[2] beaucoup de *many*
[3] peinture *painting*
[4] vie *life*

La Belgique

La Tunisie

## Vous avez compris?

### A Un peintre français
Répondez. (*Answer.*)
1. Qui est Toulouse-Lautrec?
2. Il est d'où?
3. Comment est la famille Toulouse-Lautrec?
4. Comment est le jeune Henri?
5. Il souffre de beaucoup de fractures?
6. Il adore la peinture?
7. Il adore le cirque?

### B Stratégie de lecture
Trouvez les mots apparentés dans la lecture.
(*Find the following cognates in the reading.*)
1. family
2. talent
3. rich
4. subject
5. possess
6. favorite
7. circus
8. painter

Albi, France

Le Mali

# CONNEXIONS

## Les sciences sociales

### La géographie

Geography is the study of the earth. It deals with all the earth's features, such as mountains, rivers, and seas. It is also the study of where people live and how the earth's features affect their lives. It is a subject that has interested human beings since the earliest of times.

Look at the map of France. Notice how many geographical terms you are able to recognize in French. See how easy it is to read about geography in French.

Le Rhône à Avignon

La Seine à Paris

## La France

### Villes

La France est en Europe. La France est un pays important dans le monde[1]. La capitale, Paris, est une ville culturelle. Lille, dans le nord, est une ville industrielle. Marseille, dans le sud, est un port important sur la mer Méditerranée.

### Fleuves

Il y a[2] cinq fleuves[3] en France. La Seine passe à Paris. La Seine est un fleuve très calme. La Loire est un fleuve très long. Le Rhin forme une frontière naturelle entre la France et l'Allemagne. Le Rhône est un fleuve important: c'est une grande source d'énergie électrique. La Garonne est un fleuve assez violent.

[1] monde *world*    [2] Il y a *There are*    [3] fleuves *rivers*

Musée du Louvre, Paris

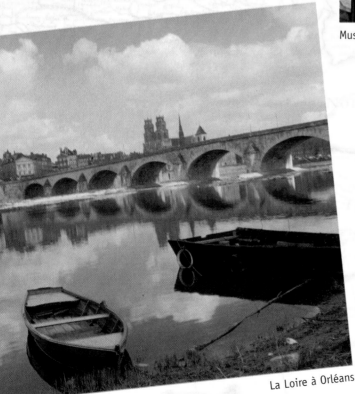

La Loire à Orléans

### Vous avez compris?

#### Un peu de géographie
Vrai ou faux? (*True or false?*)

1. La France est un continent.
2. Paris est une ville industrielle.
3. Lille est dans le sud de la France.
4. Marseille est un port.
5. La Seine est un fleuve violent.
6. La Loire est un fleuve très long.
7. Un fleuve forme une frontière naturelle entre la France et l'Allemagne.

# C'est à vous

## Use what you have learned

PARLER

**1**

### Un ami
✔ *Describe a male friend and answer questions about him*

Work with a classmate. Here's a picture of Vincent Terrier, a friend of yours from Paris, France. Say as much as you can about him. Answer any questions your partner may have about Vincent.

PARLER

**2**

### Une élève
✔ *Ask a female friend questions and tell her about yourself*

Jeanne Marin (a classmate) is a new girl in your school. She is from Montreal, Canada. You want to get to know her better and help her feel at home. Find out as much as you can about her. Tell Jeanne about yourself, too.

Jeanne Marin

Saint-Tropez, France

PARLER

**3**

### Dis donc, c'est qui?
✔ *Ask someone questions about another person*

You and a friend (a classmate) are at a sidewalk café in Saint-Tropez, on the French Riviera. You see an attractive girl or boy sitting a few tables away. It just so happens that your friend knows the person. Ask your friend as many questions as you can to find out about the boy or girl you're interested in.

ÉCRIRE

**4** **Un ami français**

✔ *Write a postcard to a friend about yourself*

Here's a postcard you just received from a new pen pal. First read his message. Then answer it. Give Christophe similar information about yourself.

Notre-Dame

PARIS

Salut !

Je m'appelle Christophe Legrand. Je suis de Paris, la capitale de la France. Je suis français. Je suis élève dans un collège à Paris— le collège Eugène Delacroix. C'est un collège excellent.

Je suis brun et assez grand. Je suis très sociable. Je ne suis pas timide. Pas du tout !

À bientôt,

Christophe

## Writing Strategy

**Freewriting** One of the easiest ways to begin any kind of personal writing is simply to begin—to let your thoughts flow and write the first thing that comes to mind. Sometimes as you think of one word, another word you know will come to mind. If you get stuck, take several minutes to think of another word or phrase you have already learned. Brainstorming and freewriting are often methods for generating ideas when writing about yourself.

ÉCRIRE

**5** **Moi**

On a piece of paper, write down as much as you can about yourself in French. Your teacher will collect the descriptions and choose students to read them to the class. You'll all try to guess who's being described.

# Assessment

Paris, France

## Vocabulaire

To review Mots 1, turn to pages 18–19.

**1 Répondez d'après la photo.**
*(Answer according to the photo.)*

1. Jeanne est française ou américaine?
2. Elle est de Paris ou de Boston?
3. Elle est blonde ou brune?

**2 Choisissez.** *(Choose.)*

4. Guillaume est _____ dans un collège français.
   **a.** ami      **b.** élève
5. Guillaume est _____ de Françoise.
   **a.** le frère      **b.** la sœur

To review Mots 2, turn to pages 22–23.

## Structure

**3 Complétez avec «un» ou «une».**
*(Complete with un or une.)*

6. Sylvie est élève dans _____ collège français.
7. Sylvie est _____ fille très sympa.
8. Paul est _____ ami de Sylvie.
9. Paul est _____ garçon sympa aussi.

To review these gender markers, turn to page 26.

**4 Complétez avec «le», «la» ou «l'».**
*(Complete with le, la, or l'.)*

10. _____ fille, Sylvie, est de Lyon.
11. Jean-Pierre est _____ frère de Sylvie.
12. _____ école de Sylvie est grande.

**5 Complétez.** *(Complete.)*

13. C'est une école assez _____. (petit)
14. Martine est une fille très _____. (dynamique)
15. Le garçon _____ est amusant. (américain)
16. Robert est un élève _____. (intelligent)

To review agreement of adjectives, turn to page 28.

**6  Complétez avec «être».**  *(Complete with* être.*)*

17. Dominique, tu ___ français?
18. Oui, je ___ de Bordeaux.
19. La fille blonde, elle ___ américaine?
20. Non, elle ___ canadienne.

To review the verb **être**, turn to page 30.

**7  Répondez au négatif.**  *(Answer in the negative.)*

21. Alain Gérard est américain?
22. Il est timide?
23. Alain est le frère de Julie?

To review making a sentence negative, turn to page 33.

# Culture

**8  Choisissez.**  *(Choose.)*

24. Un lycée est ___ secondaire en France.
    **a.** un collège     **b.** un élève          **c.** une école
25. La ville principale de la Martinique est ___.
    **a.** Bellevue      **b.** Fort-de-France    **c.** Paris

To review this cultural information, turn to pages 36–37.

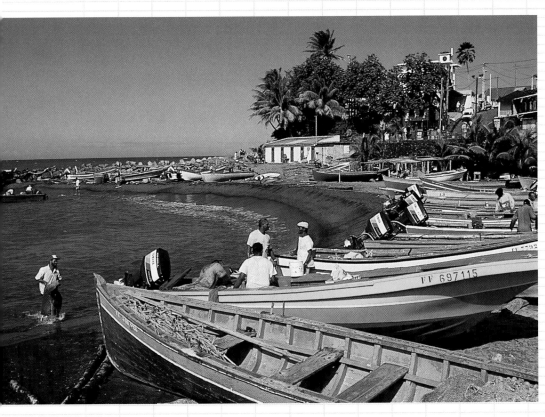

Grand-Rivière, Martinique

Tell all you can about this illustration.

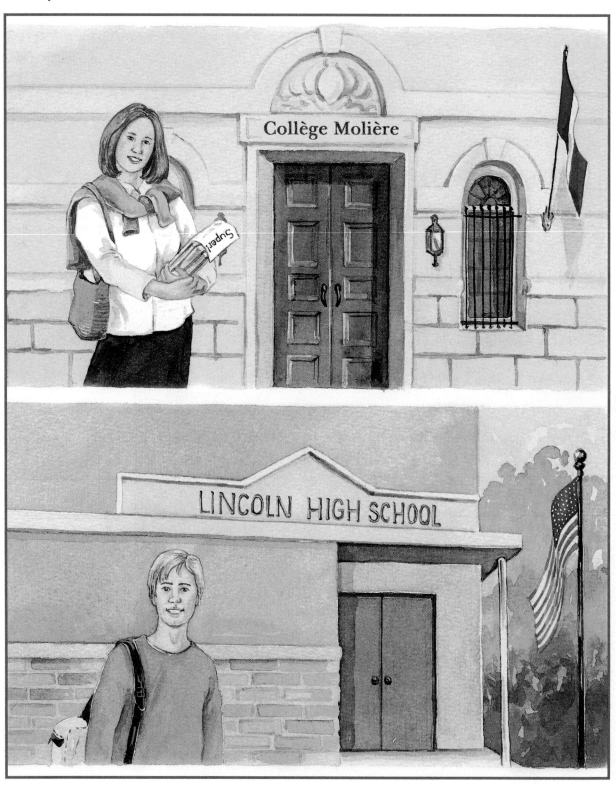

# Vocabulaire

## Identifying a person or thing

| | |
|---|---|
| un garçon | un frère |
| une fille | une sœur |
| un ami | une école |
| une amie | un collège |
| un(e) élève | être |

## Describing a person

| | |
|---|---|
| petit(e) | sympa(thique) |
| grand(e) | timide |
| brun(e) | énergique |
| blond(e) | égoïste |
| amusant(e) | dynamique |
| patient(e) | populaire |
| intelligent(e) | sociable |
| intéressant(e) | enthousiaste |

## Stating nationality

français(e)
américain(e)

## Finding out information

| | |
|---|---|
| Qui? | C'est qui? |
| D'où? | De quelle nationalité? |
| Comment? | |

## Expressing degrees

assez
très
vraiment

## Other useful words

voilà
aussi
secondaire

**How well do you know your vocabulary?**

• Choose five words that describe a good friend.

• Use these words to write several sentences about him or her.

**VIDÉOTOUR**

**Épisode 1**

In this video episode, Vincent and Chloé, each hoping to get a great shot of **le Sacré-Cœur**, bump into each other on the steps below the church. See page 526 for more information.

# Les cours et les profs

## Objectifs

In this chapter you will learn to:

- ✓ *describe people and things*
- ✓ *talk about more than one person or thing*
- ✓ *tell what subjects you take in school and express some opinions about them*
- ✓ *speak to people formally and informally*
- ✓ *talk about French-speaking people in the United States*

Pierre Bonnard *Écriture de fille*

# Vocabulaire

## Les élèves et les profs 🎧

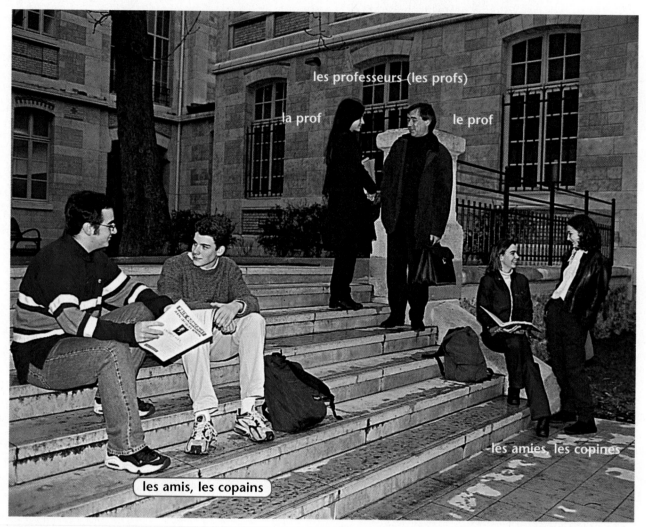

les professeurs (les profs)

la prof      le prof

les amies, les copines

les amis, les copains

Karine et Stéphanie sont françaises.
Pierre et Alexandre sont français aussi.

Les quatre copains sont de Rouen.
Ils sont élèves dans le même lycée.
Ils sont tous très sympathiques.

## Comment sont les cours? 🎧

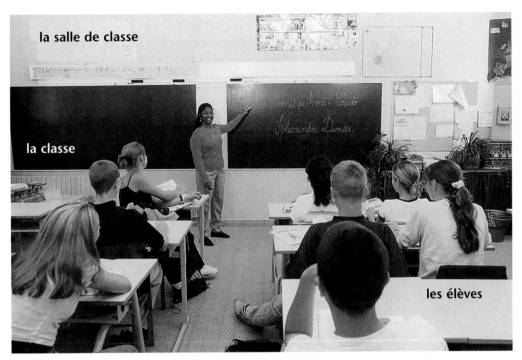

la salle de classe

la classe

les élèves

Le cours de français est facile.
La prof n'est pas trop stricte. Juste un peu.

Mais les cours de sciences sont vraiment difficiles. Toi, tu es d'accord ou pas?

Non, je ne suis pas d'accord. Pour moi, les cours de sciences sont très faciles.

# Quel est le mot?

Rennes, France

Des lycéens de Rennes

**1** **Historiette**
**Deux copines françaises**
Inventez une histoire. (*Make up a story.*)

1. Léa et Touria sont françaises
   ou américaines?
2. Elles sont copines?
3. Elles sont de Rennes?
4. Elles sont élèves dans le même lycée?
5. Le lycée est à Rennes?
6. Elles sont dans la salle de classe?

**2** **Historiette**
**Deux copains français**
Inventez une histoire. (*Make up a story.*)

1. Paul et Jamal sont français
   ou américains?
2. Ils sont copains?
3. Ils sont amusants?
4. Ils sont sympathiques?
5. Ils sont de Rennes?
6. Ils sont élèves dans le même lycée?

**FRENCH Online**

**For more information about Rennes and other cities in France, go to the Glencoe French Web site:** french.glencoe.com

**3** **Le cours de français** Donnez des réponses personnelles.
(*Give your own answers.*)

1. Qui est le/la prof de français?
2. Il/Elle est sympa?
3. Il/Elle est strict(e)?
4. Il/Elle est de quelle nationalité?
5. Le cours de français est facile ou difficile?
6. Pour toi, les cours de sciences sont faciles ou difficiles?

**4** **Le prof idéal ou la prof idéale** Work with a classmate. Share ideas as to what you look for in an ideal teacher. Let your classmate know whether you agree with him or her. You may want to use some of the following words.

 intéressant

 sympathique

 patient

 strict

 intelligent

 amusant

 enthousiaste

 dynamique

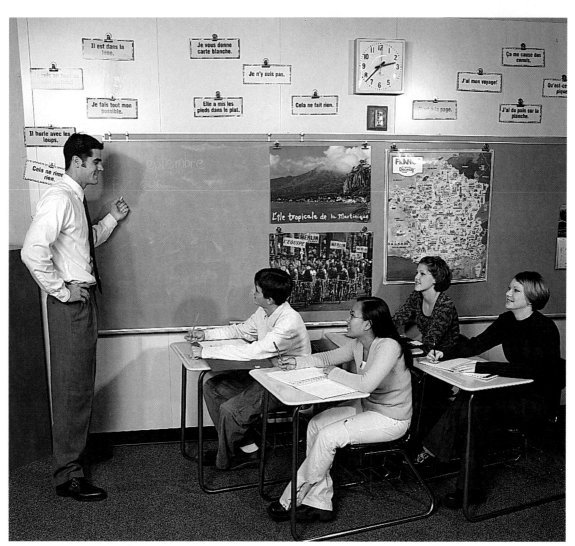

Un cours de français aux États-Unis

 **ENCORE PLUS** *For more practice using words from* **Mots 1,** *do Activity 4 on page H5 at the end of this book.*

# Vocabulaire

Les matières 🎧

## Les sciences naturelles

la biologie
la chimie
la physique

## Les mathématiques (Les maths)

l'algèbre
la géométrie
la trigonométrie
le calcul

## Les langues

le français
l'italien
l'espagnol
l'allemand
l'anglais
le latin

## Les sciences sociales

l'histoire
la géographie
l'économie

## D'autres matières

la littérature
l'informatique
la gymnastique
la musique
le dessin

# En cours de français 🎧

Salut les copains!
Nous sommes américains.
Nous sommes de New York.
Et vous, vous êtes américains
aussi, n'est-ce pas?

Nous sommes tous très
forts en français!

C'est pas vrai!
Vous êtes très mauvais!

M. Boursier est le prof de français.
Maintenant, nous sommes en
cours de français.

---

### Les nombres de 70 à 100

| | | |
|---|---|---|
| 70 soixante-dix | 80 quatre-vingts | 90 quatre-vingt-dix |
| 71 soixante et onze | 81 quatre-vingt-un | 91 quatre-vingt-onze |
| 72 soixante-douze | 82 quatre-vingt-deux | 92 quatre-vingt-douze |
| 73 soixante-treize | 83 quatre-vingt-trois | 93 quatre-vingt-treize |
| 74 soixante-quatorze | 84 quatre-vingt-quatre | 94 quatre-vingt-quatorze |
| 75 soixante-quinze | 85 quatre-vingt-cinq | 95 quatre-vingt-quinze |
| 76 soixante-seize | 86 quatre-vingt-six | 96 quatre-vingt-seize |
| 77 soixante-dix-sept | 87 quatre-vingt-sept | 97 quatre-vingt-dix-sept |
| 78 soixante-dix-huit | 88 quatre-vingt-huit | 98 quatre-vingt-dix-huit |
| 79 soixante-dix-neuf | 89 quatre-vingt-neuf | 99 quatre-vingt-dix-neuf |
| | | 100 cent |

# Quel est le mot?

**5** **Sciences ou langues?** Vrai ou faux?
*(True or false?)*

1. La chimie est une science.
2. L'histoire et la géographie sont des mathématiques.
3. Le calcul est une langue.
4. Le latin et l'espagnol sont des langues.
5. Pour vous, le français est un cours obligatoire.

Un cours de chimie à Paris

**6** **Des cours faciles et difficiles** Donnez des réponses personnelles. *(Give your own answers.)*

1. Le cours de français est facile ou difficile?
2. Pour toi, quels sont les cours faciles?
3. Quels sont les cours difficiles?
4. Tu es fort(e) en français?
5. Tu es fort(e) en sciences?
6. Tu es très fort(e) en quelle matière?
7. Tu es assez mauvais(e) en quelle matière?

**7** **Historiette** **Des élèves américains**
Inventez une histoire. *(Make up a story.)*

1. Les élèves sont de quelle nationalité?
2. Ils sont élèves dans une école secondaire américaine?
3. Ils sont en cours de français?
4. Le cours de français est facile ou difficile?
5. Les élèves sont forts en français?

**8** **C'est quel cours?** Identifiez le cours. *(Identify the course.)*

1. la littérature, la grammaire anglaise
2. la conversation, la culture française
3. un poème, une pièce de théâtre, une fable
4. un microbe, un animal, une plante, un microscope
5. un cercle, un rectangle, un triangle, un parallélogramme
6. un piano, un violon, un concert, un opéra
7. les montagnes, les villes, les villages, les capitales, les océans
8. la peinture, la sculpture, les statues, les artistes
9. une disquette, un moniteur, un microprocesseur, un bit

**Comment est la classe?** With a classmate, look at the illustration. Take turns asking each other questions about it. Use the following question words: **qui, où, quel cours, à quelle heure, comment.**

LUGAGNE-DELPON Olivier
257 r Lecourbe 15e ...............................01 45 58 96 30
LUGAGNE DELPON Paul
4 r Chevert 7e ...................................01 44 05 55 31
LUGAGNE-DELPONT Véronique
15 r Marie et Louise 10e ...................01 43 41 37 85
LUGAN Benoît
34 pl Marché St-Honoré 1e ........01 42 97 55 05
» **Bernard et Gabrielle**
5 bd Grenelle 15e ......................01 45 75 47 83
» **Bruno et Stéphanie** Bat A2
64 r Compans 19e ...................01 40 18 13 57
» **Hermann**
11 r Vasco de Gama 15e ...........01 45 55 44 35
» **Jacques** 75 av Ledru Rollin 12e ......01 43 47 84 57

 **Le numéro de téléphone** Look at this page from the Paris phone book with a classmate. Give a telephone number. Your classmate will tell whose number it is. Then reverse roles.

 **Jeu** **Quelle matière?**
Work with a classmate. Think of a school subject and use whatever means necessary (voice, hands, drawings) to help your partner guess which subject it is.

Un cours de dessin à Paris

 *For more practice using words from Mots 2, do Activity 5 on page H6 at the end of this book.*

# Structure

## Le pluriel: articles, noms et adjectifs
### Talking about more than one person or thing

**1.** The articles you know (**un/une, le/la/l'**) are singular markers. The plural forms of these articles are plural markers. Study the following.

### LES ARTICLES INDÉFINIS

| Masculin | | Féminin | |
|---|---|---|---|
| **Singulier** | **Pluriel** | **Singulier** | **Pluriel** |
| un garçon | des garçons | une fille | des filles |
| un ami | des amis | une amie | des amies |
| un collège | des collèges | une école | des écoles |

### LES ARTICLES DÉFINIS

| Masculin | | Féminin | |
|---|---|---|---|
| **Singulier** | **Pluriel** | **Singulier** | **Pluriel** |
| le garçon | les garçons | la fille | les filles |
| l'ami | les amis | l'amie | les amies |
| le collège | les collèges | l'école | les écoles |

**2.** In French, you form the plural of most nouns by adding an **s.** This **s,** however, is not pronounced. It is the article **les** or **des** that lets you know the noun is plural: **un prof ⟶ des profs; la prof ⟶ les profs.**

**3.** When a noun is plural, any adjective that describes or modifies it must also be in the plural. You form the plural of most adjectives in French by adding an **s.** The **s** is not pronounced.

| Singulier | Pluriel |
|---|---|
| La classe est petite. | Les classes sont petites. |
| La prof est patiente. | Les profs sont patientes. |
| Le lycée est grand. | Les lycées sont grands. |
| Le prof est intéressant. | Les profs sont intéressants. |

Note: You do not add an **s** if the word already ends in **s.**
    **un cours    des cours**

# Comment dit-on?

**12** **Ils sont comment?** Mettez au pluriel.
*(Put in the plural.)*

—**Le garçon est blond.**
—**Les garçons sont blonds.**

1. La fille est blonde.
2. Le garçon est brun.
3. La sœur de Valentin est amusante.
4. Le frère de Stéphane est égoïste.
5. Le prof est intéressant.
6. Le cours est assez difficile.
7. La salle de classe est petite.
8. L'ami de Paul est vraiment sympathique.
9. L'élève est très intelligent.
10. L'ami de Valérie est amusant.

*Deux lycéennes de Yerres, France*

**13** **Pour toi...** Citez... *(Name . . . )*

**Pour moi, deux matières très intéressantes sont \_\_\_\_ et \_\_\_\_.**

1. deux matières très intéressantes
2. deux cours très intéressants
3. deux écoles excellentes
4. deux élèves sociables
5. deux professeurs stricts
6. deux filles très intelligentes
7. deux garçons très sympas
8. deux élèves fort(e)s en géographie
9. deux élèves assez mauvais(es) en musique

**14** **En commun** Inventez des points communs.
*(Make up what these people have in common.)*

**Caroline et Marie** →
**Elles sont amusantes, fortes en algèbre…**

1. Laurent et Christian
2. Isabelle et Sandrine
3. Romain et Christophe
4. Marine et Nathalie
5. Loïc et Mathias

**15** **Comme moi** Work with a classmate. Tell your partner what you and your friends have in common. Your partner will agree or disagree.

Sue et Jennifer sont sociables… comme moi.

Moi, je ne suis pas d'accord. Elles ne sont pas sociables du tout!

*Les vrais amis sont amis pour la vie*

# Le verbe être au pluriel
## Talking about more than one

**1.** You have already learned the singular forms of the verb **être.** Now study the plural forms.

**ÊTRE**

| Singulier | Pluriel |
|---|---|
| je suis | nous sommes |
| tu es | vous $_z$ êtes |
| il/elle est | ils/elles sont |

**2.**

Nous sommes amis.

Vous êtes amusants.

You use **nous** when referring to yourself and another person or other people.

You use **vous** when talking to two or more people.

Ils sont sympas.

Ils sont sympas.

You use **ils** when referring to two or more males or to a group of males and females.

Elles sont copines.

You use **elles** when referring to two or more females.

**Savez-vous que... ?**

You also use **ils/elles** when referring to things.

**Les cours? Ils sont très faciles.**

**Les salles? Elles sont petites.**

LES COURS ET LES PROFS

# Comment dit-on?

**16** **Vous êtes d'où?** Répétez la conversation. *(Repeat the conversation.)*

**17** **Historiette** **Ils sont américains.** Complétez d'après la conversation. *(Complete according to the conversation.)*

Les deux garçons __1__ américains. Ils ne __2__ pas de New York. Ils __3__ de Boston. Boston __4__ une grande ville américaine.

Les deux filles ne __5__ pas américaines. Elles __6__ françaises. Elles __7__ de Toulouse. Toulouse __8__ une grande ville française.

**18** **À vous** Répondez en utilisant **nous.** *(Choose a partner and answer for both of you using* nous.*)*

1. Vous êtes américain(e)s?
2. Vous êtes d'où?
3. Vous êtes élèves dans une école secondaire?
4. Vous êtes dans la classe de quel professeur?
5. Vous êtes fort(e)s en français?

*For more practice using the verb* **être**, *do Activity 6 on page H7 at the end of this book.*

**19** **Des questions** Posez des questions et répondez d'après le modèle. *(Ask and answer questions according to the model.)*

américaine / française �le
—**Vous êtes américaines ou françaises?**
—**Nous sommes françaises.**

1. martiniquaise / américaine
2. petit / grand
3. sociable / timide
4. brune / blonde

**20**  **Historiette** **L'ami de Christophe**
Complétez en utilisant **être.** *(Complete with* être.*)*

Je __1__ un ami de Christophe. Christophe __2__ très sympa et très amusant. Nous __3__ français, Christophe et moi. Nous __4__ de Cancale, un petit village breton (en Bretagne). Cancale __5__ vraiment très pittoresque.

Nous __6__ élèves dans un collège. Où __7__ le collège? À Dinard. Tous les deux, nous __8__ forts en anglais. La prof d'anglais, Mlle Fielding, __9__ anglaise. Elle __10__ de Liverpool. Elle __11__ assez stricte et le cours d'anglais n'__12__ pas facile. Mais les élèves de Mlle Fielding __13__ très intelligents!

Dinard, Bretagne

**21** **Vous êtes américains?** Complétez la conversation. *(Complete the conversation.)*

—Vous __1__ américains, n'est-ce pas?
—Oui, nous __2__ américains. Nous __3__ de __4__.
—Vous __5__ élèves dans une école secondaire?
—Oui, et nous __6__ très forts en français.
—Vraiment? Qui __7__ le/la prof de français?
—C'est __8__.
—Il/Elle __9__ comment?
—Il/Elle __10__ __11__.

**22**  **Tous les deux** Work with a classmate. Discuss things you have in common.
—**Nous sommes sympathiques, intelligent(e)s, fort(e)s en...**

# Structure

## Tu et vous
### Talking to people formally or informally

**1.** As you already know, there are two ways to say *you* in French: **tu** and **vous.** You use **tu** when talking to a friend, a person your own age, or a family member.

Éric, tu es trop timide!

Maman, tu es d'accord?

**2.** You use **vous** when talking to two or more people.

**3.** You also use **vous** when talking to an older person, a person whom you do not know very well, or anyone to whom you wish to show respect.

Vous deux, vous êtes d'accord?

Monsieur, s'il vous plaît! Vous êtes le professeur de musique?

# Comment dit-on?

**23** **Vous êtes français?** Regardez les photos et posez la question.
*(Ask the people in the photographs if they are French.)*

1.

2.

3.

4.

5.

6.

**24** **D'autres questions** Ask the same people other questions.
You may want to use some of the following words or expressions:
**d'où, de quelle nationalité, d'accord, patient, fort en.**

*Vous êtes sur le bon chemin. Allez-y!*

# Conversation

## Quel prof?

**Paul:** Vous êtes dans la classe de Mme Martin?
**Anne:** Non, nous sommes dans la classe de M. Lepic.
**Paul:** M. Lepic?
**Anne:** Ben oui, le prof de maths.
**Paul:** Ah oui. Comment il est?
**Anne:** Un peu strict, mais sympa.
**Paul:** Oui, mais toi et Samuel, vous êtes forts en maths.
**Anne:** Ben, toi aussi.
**Paul:** Moi? Je suis très mauvais en maths. Je suis complètement nul!

## Vous avez compris?

Répondez. *(Answer.)*

1. Anne et Samuel sont dans la classe de Mme Martin?
2. Ils sont dans la classe de quel professeur?
3. Qui est M. Lepic?
4. Il est comment?
5. Samuel et Anne sont forts en maths?
6. Et Paul, il est fort en maths?

# Parlons un peu plus

  **A**  **D'accord ou pas?** Make a chart like the one below. List all your classes and rate them. Then compare your chart with that of a classmate.

—Pour moi, le cours de français n'est pas difficile. Tu es d'accord?

—Oui, je suis d'accord. / Non, je ne suis pas d'accord. Pour moi, le cours de français est très difficile.

| Cours | Pas difficile | Assez difficile | Très difficile |
|---|---|---|---|
| le français | ✓ | | |
| l'algèbre | | | ✓ |

**B**    **Quel cours?** Work with a classmate. He or she gives you one word about a class. Guess what class it is. If you're wrong, your partner will give you another hint until you can guess the class. Take turns.

## Prononciation

### Les consonnes finales 🎧

1. In French, you do not usually pronounce the final consonant you see at the end of a word. Repeat the following.

| | | | |
|---|---|---|---|
| petit | grand | intéressant | français |
| amusant | intelligent | patient | blond |

2. You also do not pronounce the final **s** you add to a word to make it plural. This is why a singular noun and its plural sound alike. Repeat the following pairs of words and then the sentences.

un copain → des copains   une copine → des copines
le garçon → les garçons   la fille → les filles

Tous les copains de Vincent sont sympathiques.
Les cours de maths sont très difficiles.

intelligent

# Lectures culturelles

Une plage près de Port-au-Prince, Haïti

Deux copains haïtiens

## Reading Strategy

### Using titles

Always look at titles and subtitles before you begin to read. They will help you figure out what a reading selection is about. Having an idea of what a reading is about will help you guess the meaning of unfamiliar words and therefore understand better as you read.

## Le français aux États-Unis

### L'influence haïtienne

Bonjour! Nous sommes Abélard Jean-Baptiste et Nicole Jolicœur. Nous sommes élèves dans une école secondaire à Miami. Et pour nous, le cours de français est vraiment très facile! Pour nous, le français n'est pas une langue étrangère[1]. Nous sommes haïtiens. Nous sommes de Port-au-Prince, la capitale d'Haïti. En Haïti, il y a[2] deux langues—le français et le créole. Le créole est une langue à base de français, d'espagnol et de divers dialectes africains.

### L'influence canadienne

Et nous? Nous sommes Antonine Gagnon et Donald Maillet. Nous sommes de Montpelier dans le Vermont. Comme beaucoup de personnes de la Nouvelle-Angleterre[3], nous sommes d'origine canadienne. Et pour nous, le français n'est pas une langue étrangère. Le français est la langue maternelle des Canadiens français.

Deux amis de Montpelier

Tahiti

[1] étrangère  *foreign*
[2] il y a  *there are*
[3] Nouvelle-Angleterre  *New England*

Haïti

La Martinique

### L'influence «cajun»

Bonjour! Ici Alice Richard et Pierre Doucet. Nous sommes de Louisiane. Nous sommes cajuns. Nous les Cajuns, nous sommes des descendants des Acadiens. Les Acadiens sont les Français expulsés[4] de l'est du Canada par les Anglais.

L'influence cajun est assez forte en Louisiane. Il y a même[5] deux langues officielles en Louisiane—l'anglais et le français.

[4] expulsés *expelled*   [5] même *even*

Deux élèves de Louisiane

## Vous avez compris?

### A Les Haïtiens
Répondez. *(Answer.)*
1. Abélard Jean-Baptiste et Nicole Jolicœur sont d'où?
2. Pour Abélard et Nicole, le français est facile?
3. Ils sont de quelle nationalité?
4. Le créole est à base de quelles langues?

### B Les descendants des Canadiens français Répondez. *(Answer.)*
1. D'où sont Antonine et Donald?
2. Montpelier est dans quel état?
3. Il y a beaucoup de personnes d'origine canadienne en Nouvelle-Angleterre?
4. Quelle est la langue maternelle des Canadiens français?

### C Les Cajuns Répondez. *(Answer.)*
1. Qui sont les Cajuns?
2. Quelles sont les deux langues officielles en Louisiane?

La France
La Suisse
BELGIQUE-BELGIE
BELGIE
1949 1999
La Belgique
La Tunisie
Le Maroc
Le Mali
Le Sénégal
REPUBLIQUE DE CÔTE D'IVOIRE

# La scolarité en France

Le collège en France est une école secondaire. Les élèves sont des collégiens. Le collège est obligatoire pour quatre ans.

Après[1] le collège, le lycée est aussi une école secondaire, mais pour trois ans. Les élèves sont des lycéens. Il y a[2] deux diplômes d'études secondaires—un diplôme professionnel après deux ans et le baccalauréat après trois ans. Le baccalauréat ou «le bac» est nécessaire pour entrer à l'université.

Voici l'emploi du temps de Louise Belleroche. Elle est en troisième, l'équivalent de *ninth grade*. Il y a combien de[3] cours en troisième en France?

[1] Après  *After*        [2] Il y a  *There are*        [3] combien de  *how many*

Lycée Pasteur, Neuilly, France

## Vous avez compris?

**A La scolarité**  Vrai ou faux?
*(True or false?)*
1. En France un collège est une petite université.
2. Le collège n'est pas obligatoire.
3. Le lycée est une école secondaire.
4. Le «bac» est un diplôme universitaire.
5. Le «bac» est nécessaire pour entrer à l'université.

**B L'emploi du temps de Louise**  Répondez. *(Answer.)*
1. Il y a combien de cours?
2. Le cours de maths est quels jours? À quelle heure?
3. Et le cours d'anglais?
4. Et le cours de français?
5. Et le cours de biologie?
6. Et le cours d'histoire/géographie?
7. Et le cours de dessin?

La Polynésie française

Tahiti

## Un message

Salut! Je m'appelle Nicolas Vidal. Je suis de Versailles, une ville[1] dans la banlieue[2] parisienne. Je suis élève dans un lycée. Mais maintenant, je ne suis pas à Versailles. Je suis à Biarritz avec la famille de Guillaume Cartier. Guillaume et moi, nous sommes copains. Nous sommes élèves dans le même lycée. Mais maintenant, pas de profs, pas de cours! Nous sommes libres[3]! Nous sommes en vacances à Biarritz. Biarritz est une petite ville très pittoresque à la frontière espagnole. Pour moi, les vacances, c'est toujours super. Tu es d'accord?

¹ ville *town*    ² banlieue *suburbs*    ³ libres *free*

Biarritz, France

Versailles, France

## Vous avez compris?

### A Deux copains  Répondez. *(Answer.)*

1. D'où est Nicolas?
2. Où est Versailles?
3. Où est Nicolas maintenant?
4. Il est à Biarritz avec qui?
5. Les deux garçons sont copains?
6. Les deux copains sont en vacances? Où?

### B Un peu de géographie

Vrai ou faux? *(True or false?)*

1. Versailles est sur la Côte d'Azur.
2. Versailles est dans la banlieue parisienne.
3. Biarritz est aussi dans la banlieue parisienne.
4. Biarritz est à la frontière espagnole.
5. Biarritz est en Espagne.
6. Biarritz est en France.

La Belgique

La Tunisie

Maroc

Le Mali

# CONNEXIONS

## Les sciences naturelles
### La biologie, la physique et la chimie

Sciences are an important part of the school curriculum. If you like science, it would be fun to be able to read some scientific material in French. You will see how easy it is. It's easy because you already have some background in science from your science courses. In addition, many scientific terms are cognates.

### La biologie

La biologie est l'étude des organismes vivants. En biologie, il y a trois catégories importantes: l'anatomie, la zoologie et la botanique. L'anatomie est l'étude du corps humain. La zoologie est l'étude des animaux et la botanique est l'étude des plantes.

La botanique est l'étude des plantes.

La zoologie est l'étude des animaux.

## La physique et la chimie

La physique est l'étude de la matière et de l'énergie. La chimie est l'étude des caractéristiques des éléments.

## Les savants

Dans un laboratoire, le savant (le biologiste, le chimiste ou le physicien) observe et analyse des phénomènes scientifiques. Le biologiste, par exemple, observe et analyse des microbes[1], des cellules, des bactéries et des virus à l'aide d'un microscope.

[1] microbes *germs*

Une biologiste

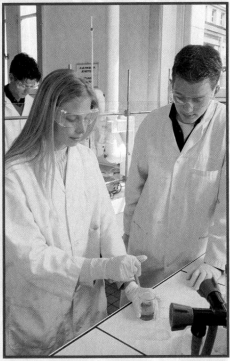

Des élèves dans un laboratoire à Paris

## Vous avez compris?

**A Des termes scientifiques**
Préparez une liste. *(Make a list of scientific terms you recognize in the reading.)*

**B C'est quelle science?** Répondez. *(Answer.)*

1. l'étude des animaux
2. l'étude des plantes
3. l'étude de la matière et de l'énergie
4. l'étude du corps humain

**C Stratégie de lecture** Note that the words in each of the following groups are all related to one another. If you know the meaning of one word, you can guess the meanings of the others. Can you figure them all out?

1. la biologie, un(e) biologiste, biologique
2. analyser, une analyse, analytique
3. un microbe, microbien
4. une bactérie, bactérien
5. un virus, viral

# C'est à vous

## Use what you have learned

L'école internationale de Paris

PARLER
**1**

### Nous
✔ *Describe yourself and someone else*

Work with a classmate. You are at an international student gathering in France. You and your partner introduce yourselves to the other students. Try to get to know one another better. You may use the following as a guide:

- say who you are
- give your nationality
- tell where you're from
- give the name of your school
- describe some of your qualities or faults

PARLER
**2**

### L'école idéale
✔ *Talk about school*

Work with a classmate. Describe what for each of you is an ideal school. Say as much as you can about the teachers, classes, and students. Determine whether or not you share the same opinions.

Lycée Janson de Sailly, Paris

# 3 Un message
## ✔ Write about your classes and friends

You answer an e-mail message from a student in France who wants to know about your life in the United States. Give him or her as many details as possible about your classes and your friends.

Collège de Montois, Noyen-sur-Seine

## Writing Strategy

**Keeping a journal** There are many kinds of journals you can keep, each having a different purpose. One type of journal is the kind in which you write about daily events and record your thoughts and impressions about these events. It's almost like "thinking aloud." By keeping such a journal, you may find that you discover something new that you were not aware of.

# 4 Les cours et les professeurs

You've been in school for about a month. You've had a chance to get to know what your courses are like and to become familiar with your teachers. Create a journal entry about school. Try to write about your classes, the days and times of each, what the class is like, who the teacher is, and what he or she is like. When you have finished, reread your journal entry. Did you discover anything about your courses or your teachers that you hadn't thought of before?

# Assessment

## Vocabulaire

*To review **Mots 1,** turn to pages 50–51.*

**1 Choisissez.** *(Choose.)*

1. Christophe et Julien sont amis. Ils sont ____.
   **a.** frères     **b.** sœurs     **c.** copains

2. Les deux garçons sont ____ dans un lycée français.
   **a.** élèves     **b.** profs     **c.** cours

3. Le cours de français n'est pas difficile. Le cours de français est ____.
   **a.** strict     **b.** facile     **c.** comique

4. La prof n'est pas très stricte. Juste ____.
   **a.** difficile     **b.** d'accord     **c.** un peu

*To review **Mots 2,** turn to pages 54–55.*

**2 Vrai ou faux?** *(True or false?)*

5. L'algèbre et la musique sont des sciences naturelles.

6. L'économie est une langue.

7. Pour les élèves américains, l'anglais est un cours obligatoire.

8. L'allemand est une science sociale.

## Structure

*To review plural articles, nouns, and adjectives, turn to page 58.*

**3 Mettez au pluriel.** *(Put in the plural.)*

9. Le copain de Lucie est amusant.
   ____ copain__ de Lucie sont amusant__.

10. La sœur de Monique est intelligente.
    ____ sœur__ de Monique sont intelligente__.

11. L'ami de Frédéric est français.
    ____ ami__ de Frédéric sont français__.

12. Le prof de biologie est strict.
    ____ prof__ de biologie sont strict__.

13. La fille brune est américaine.
    ____ fille__ brune__ sont américaine__.

**4** **Complétez avec «être».**
*(Complete with* être.*)*

14. Nous _____ élèves dans une école secondaire américaine.
15. Ils _____ élèves dans un lycée français.
16. Vous _____ élèves où?
17. Les élèves de Madame Fauvet _____ intelligents.
18. Qui _____ le prof de géométrie?

To review the verb **être**, turn to page 60.

# Culture

**5** **Choisissez.** *(Choose.)*

19. En Haïti, il y a deux langues—le français et _____.
    **a.** l'anglais      **b.** le créole      **c.** l'espagnol
20. Il y a beaucoup d'influence «cajun» en _____.
    **a.** Nouvelle-Angleterre      **b.** Haïti      **c.** Louisiane

To review this cultural information, turn to pages 68–69.

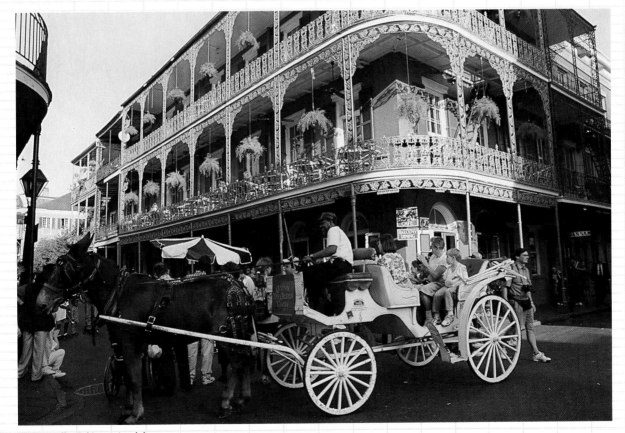

La Nouvelle-Orléans, Louisiane

# On parle super bien!

Tell all you can about this illustration.

# Vocabulaire

## Identifying a person or thing

| | | |
|---|---|---|
| un professeur | une copine | un cours |
| un(e) prof | un lycée | une classe |
| un copain | une salle de classe | une matière |

## Identifying school subjects

| | | | |
|---|---|---|---|
| les sciences naturelles | les langues *(f. pl.)* | les sciences sociales | d'autres matières |
| la biologie | le français | l'histoire *(f.)* | la littérature |
| la chimie | l'espagnol *(m.)* | la géographie | l'informatique *(f.)* |
| la physique | l'italien *(m.)* | l'économie *(f.)* | la gymnastique |
| les mathématiques, | l'allemand *(m.)* | | la musique |
| les maths *(f. pl.)* | l'anglais *(m.)* | | le dessin |
| l'algèbre *(f.)* | le latin | | |
| la géométrie | | | |
| la trigonométrie | | | |
| le calcul | | | |

## Describing teachers, students, and courses

| | | |
|---|---|---|
| facile | strict(e) | fort(e) |
| difficile | intéressant(e) | mauvais(e) |

## Agreeing and disagreeing

Tu es d'accord?
Oui, je suis d'accord.
Non, je ne suis pas d'accord.
C'est vrai.
Ce n'est pas vrai. C'est pas vrai.

## Other useful words and expressions

en cours de (français, maths, etc.)
même
tous
trop
juste un peu

### How well do you know your vocabulary?

- Choose your favorite school subject. Choose words to describe this subject.
- Use these words to describe the subject and your teacher.

### VIDÉOTOUR

**Épisode 2**

In this video episode, you will see Vincent at the lycée Louis-le-Grand, interviewing students about their teachers and courses. See page 527 for more information.

# CHAPITRE 3

# Pendant et après les cours

## Objectifs

In this chapter you will learn to:

- ✓ talk about what you do in school
- ✓ talk about what you and your friends do after school
- ✓ identify and shop for school supplies
- ✓ talk about what you don't do
- ✓ tell what you and others like and don't like to do
- ✓ discuss schools in France

Pierre Auguste Renoir *La lecture*

# Vocabulaire

## Une journée à l'école 🎧

une maison

une rue

quitter

arriver

Patrick habite près de Paris.
Il habite rue Saint-Paul.
Patrick quitte la maison.

Le matin, Patrick arrive à l'école.
À quelle heure?
Il arrive à l'école à huit heures.
Il passe la journée à l'école.

parler

un CD

écouter

Le prof parle.
Les élèves écoutent bien.
Les élèves étudient.

Les élèves regardent une vidéo (un DVD).
Deux élèves écoutent des CD.

la main

Moi, je n'aime pas du tout les examens. Je déteste les examens.

Sophie lève la main.
Elle pose une question.

## Note

The expression **passer un examen** is an example of a false cognate (**un faux ami**). It means "to take an exam," not "to pass an exam."

Vincent passe un examen.
Il n'aime pas les examens.

la cantine

Les élèves déjeunent à la cantine.
Ils déjeunent à midi (12 h).

jouer

la cour

Pendant la récré(ation) les élèves jouent dans la cour.
Il y a beaucoup d'élèves dans la cour.
Ils rigolent.
Ils parlent entre les cours.

## Note

The popular word **rigoler** means "to joke around." **Tu rigoles!** means "You don't mean it!" or "You're joking!"

# Quel est le mot?

**1** **Historiette** **Un élève parisien**
Inventez une histoire. *(Make up a story.)*

1. Fabien est de Paris?
2. Il habite rue Jacob?
3. Il quitte la maison à quelle heure?
4. Il passe la journée où?
5. Il déjeune à la cantine?

**2** **Toujours des questions** Répondez.
*(Answer.)*

**Le matin, les élèves arrivent à l'école à huit heures.**

1. Qui arrive à l'école?
2. Ils arrivent où?
3. Ils arrivent à quelle heure?
4. Ils arrivent à l'école le matin ou à midi?

**Les élèves déjeunent à la cantine à midi.**

5. Qui déjeune?
6. Les élèves déjeunent où?
7. Ils déjeunent à la cantine à quelle heure?

Un lycéen français

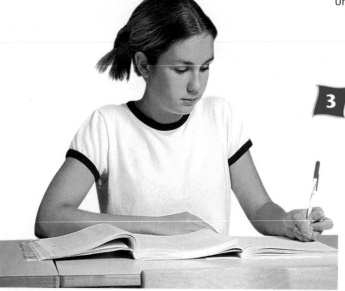

**3** **Historiette** **En classe** Complétez.
*(Complete.)*

En classe la prof __1__ et les élèves __2__.
Anne est une élève excellente. Elle __3__
beaucoup. Sophie est dans la même classe.
Elle __4__ la main et __5__ une question.

Vincent __6__ un examen. Les examens
sont difficiles. Vincent n' __7__ pas les
examens. Il __8__ les examens.

**4** **Pardon!** Préparez une petite conversation d'après le modèle.
*(Prepare a short conversation according to the model.)*

> Sandrine regarde un DVD.

> Pardon? Qu'est-ce qu'elle regarde?

1. Sandrine regarde une vidéo.
2. Sandrine écoute un CD.
3. Sandrine lève la main.
4. Sandrine pose une question.
5. Sandrine passe un examen.
6. Sandrine adore les vidéos.

**5** **Historiette** **Dans la cour** Répondez. *(Answer.)*

1. Les élèves sont dans la cour?
2. Ils sont dans la cour pendant la récréation?
3. Ils parlent entre les cours?
4. Ils jouent où?
5. Ils rigolent avec les copains?
6. Ils déjeunent dans la cour?

**6** **En classe** With a classmate, look at the illustration. Take turns saying as much as you can about it.

*For more practice using words from* **Mots 1***, do Activity 7 on page H8 at the end of this book.*

# Vocabulaire

## Des fournitures scolaires

un bloc-notes

un sac à dos

un classeur

une feuille de papier

un stylo-bille

une règle

un feutre

un cahier

un crayon

un livre

une calculatrice

une gomme

Qu'est-ce que c'est?
C'est un cahier.

## Après les cours 🎧

**Le sac à dos, c'est combien, s'il vous plaît?**

**Vingt dollars cinquante.**

la caisse

payer

un magasin

Lucette travaille après les cours.
Elle travaille dans une papeterie.
Combien d'heures par semaine?
Dix heures.

Sylvain regarde un sac à dos.
Il demande combien coûte le sac à dos.
Il achète le sac à dos.
Il paie à la caisse.

### Les nombres de 100 à 1 000

| | | |
|---|---|---|
| 100 cent | 400 quatre cents | |
| 101 cent un | 500 cinq cents | |
| 102 cent deux | 600 six cents | |
| 200 deux cents | 700 sept cents | |
| 220 deux cent vingt | 800 huit cents | |
| 300 trois cents | 900 neuf cents | |
| 350 trois cent cinquante | 1 000 mille | |

Après les cours, Patrick ne travaille pas.
Il rentre à la maison l'après-midi.
Il rentre chez lui.

Il écoute la radio.
Il parle un peu au téléphone.

# Quel est le mot?

**7** **Des fournitures scolaires** Préparez une liste de fournitures scolaires. *(Make a list of school supplies.)*

**8** **Historiette** **Loïc est français.**
Répondez d'après l'indication.
*(Answer according to the cues.)*

1. Loïc est français ou américain? (français)
2. Il habite où? (près de Paris)
3. Il travaille après les cours? (non)
4. Il rentre chez lui après les cours? (oui)
5. Qu'est-ce qu'il écoute? (la radio)
6. Qu'est-ce qu'il regarde? (une vidéo)
7. Il parle au téléphone? (oui)
8. Avec qui? (les copains)

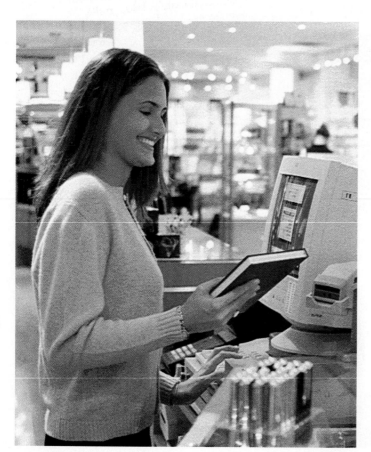

Une papeterie,
Montréal, Canada

**9** **Historiette** **Dans une papeterie** Inventez une histoire.
*(Make up a story.)*

1. Catherine est canadienne?
2. Elle travaille après les cours?
3. Elle travaille combien d'heures par semaine?
4. Elle travaille dans une papeterie?
5. Où est la papeterie?
6. Qu'est-ce qu'il y a dans une papeterie?
7. Il y a beaucoup d'élèves dans la papeterie?
8. Un garçon paie à la caisse?
9. Un cahier coûte combien?

**10** **Historiette** **À la papeterie** Choisissez la bonne réponse. *(Choose the correct completion.)*

1. Sandrine _____ dans une papeterie.
   **a.** étudie **b.** habite **c.** travaille
2. Elle _____ à un client au téléphone.
   **a.** écoute **b.** parle **c.** paie
3. Les élèves _____ des fournitures scolaires dans la papeterie.
   **a.** travaillent **b.** rentrent **c.** regardent
4. Un garçon _____ un cahier.
   **a.** regarde **b.** joue **c.** rentre
5. Il _____ une calculatrice pour le cours de maths.
   **a.** passe **b.** quitte **c.** achète
6. La calculatrice _____ six dollars canadiens.
   **a.** paie **b.** habite **c.** coûte
7. Le garçon _____ à la caisse.
   **a.** quitte **b.** coûte **c.** paie

**11**  **Pour la rentrée des classes** Work with a classmate. It's back-to-school time and you're buying the school supplies below. Take turns being the customer and the salesperson.

**12** **Jeu** **Qu'est-ce que c'est?** Work with a classmate. Have your partner close his or her eyes. Hand your partner a school supply. Have your partner guess what it is. Take turns.

 **ENCORE PLUS** *For more practice using words from Mots 2, do Activity 8 on page H9 at the end of this book.*

# Structure

## Les verbes réguliers en -er au présent
### Talking about people's activities

**1.** A word that expresses an action or a state is a verb. **Parler** (*to speak*), **écouter** (*to listen to*), and **aimer** (*to like*) are verbs in the infinitive form. They are called regular verbs because they all follow a regular pattern. Their infinitives end in **-er.**

**2.** French verbs change endings with each subject. To form the stem to which the endings are added, you drop the **-er** from the infinitive.

| Infinitive | Stem |
|---|---|
| parler | parl- |
| écouter | écout- |
| aimer | aim- |

**3.** You add the ending for each subject to the stem. Note that, although the endings for the **je, tu, il,** and **ils** forms are spelled differently, they are pronounced the same.

| | | | PARLER | | AIMER |
|---|---|---|---|---|---|
| je | parl | -e | je parle | | j' aime |
| tu | parl | -es | tu parles | | tu aimes |
| il/elle | parl | -e | il/elle parle | | il/elle aime |
| nous | parl | -ons | nous parlons | | nous‿aimons |
| vous | parl | -ez | vous parlez | | vous‿aimez |
| ils/elles | parl | -ent | ils/elles parlent | | ils‿/elles‿aiment |

**4.** You will see and hear the word **on** a great deal. **On** has several meanings, such as "we," "they," and "people." **On** always takes the **il/elle** form of the verb. In spoken French, people use **on** more often than **nous.**

> On parle français en France.
> On travaille beaucoup.
> On‿arrive à l'école le matin.

## Attention!

There is elision when **je** or **ne** is followed by a verb that begins with a vowel or silent **h.**
**J'habite à Paris.**    **Je n'habite pas à Lyon.**
**J'aime les maths.**    **Je n'aime pas les sciences.**

There is a liaison with all plural subject pronouns and a verb that begins with a vowel or silent **h.** The **s** on the pronoun is pronounced as a **z.**
**nous‿étudions**    **vous‿aimez**    **ils‿habitent**

# Comment dit-on?

## 13 Historiette Un Américain

Inventez une histoire. *(Make up a story.)*

1. Kevin est français ou américain?
2. Il habite à Paris ou à Chicago?
3. Il parle anglais ou français?
4. Il étudie quelle langue?
5. Il parle beaucoup en classe?
6. Il travaille bien à l'école?

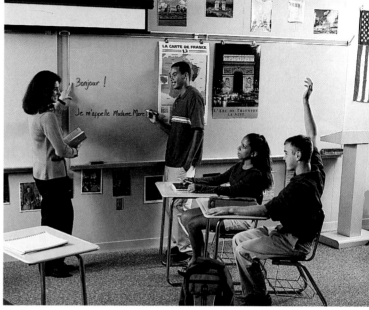

Un cours de français aux États-Unis

## 14 Historiette Les élèves ou les profs? Suivez le modèle.
*(Follow the model.)*

—**Qui arrive à l'école le matin?**
—**Les élèves et les profs arrivent à l'école.**

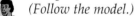

1. Qui parle en classe?
2. Qui écoute quand le prof parle?
3. Qui écoute des cassettes?
4. Qui passe des examens?

5. Qui étudie beaucoup?
6. Qui lève la main?
7. Qui pose des questions?
8. Qui rigole dans la cour?

## 15 Aux États-Unis Un(e) élève français(e) pose des questions à un(e) élève américain(e). *(You are a French student. Ask a classmate about life in the United States.)*

On arrive à l'école à quelle heure?

On arrive à l'école à huit heures.

1. On arrive à l'école à quelle heure?
2. On quitte l'école à quelle heure?
3. On travaille beaucoup à l'école?
4. On aime beaucoup les examens?

5. On travaille après les cours?
6. On écoute des CD?
7. On regarde la télé?
8. On parle au téléphone?

**16** **Tu parles français?** Répétez la conversation.
*(Repeat the conversation.)*

**Sue:** Tu n'es pas français, toi?

**Luc:** Non, je ne suis pas français.

**Sue:** Mais tu parles français!

**Luc:** Bien sûr que je parle français.

**Sue:** Et comment ça, si tu n'es pas français?

**Luc:** Mais je suis belge.

**Sue:** Ah, c'est vrai. On parle français en Belgique.

**17** **Historiette** **À votre tour!** Donnez des
réponses personnelles. *(Give your own answers.)*

1. Tu habites dans quelle ville?
2. Tu quittes la maison à quelle heure le matin?
3. Tu arrives à l'école à quelle heure?
4. Est-ce que tu parles français avec les copains?
5. Tu aimes quelles matières?
6. Tu aimes quels profs?
7. Tu détestes quelles matières?
8. Tu travailles après les cours?
9. Tu parles beaucoup avec les copains au téléphone?
10. Tu regardes la télé?

Bruxelles, Belgique

**18** **Pardon?** Posez des questions d'après
le modèle. *(Ask questions according to the model.)*

Nous écoutons des CD.

Pardon? Qu'est-ce que vous écoutez?

1. Nous détestons les examens.
2. Nous regardons la télé.
3. Nous regardons des magazines.
4. Nous écoutons la radio.
5. Nous aimons l'école.
6. Nous étudions l'espagnol.

**19** **Nous tous** Donnez des réponses personnelles en utilisant **nous.** (*Give answers about you and your classmates. Use* nous.)

1. Vous arrivez à l'école à quelle heure le matin?
2. Vous quittez l'école à quelle heure l'après-midi?
3. Vous passez combien d'heures à l'école?
4. Vous aimez les cours?
5. Vous écoutez bien quand le professeur parle en classe?
6. Vous aimez ou vous détestez les examens?

**20** **Historiette** **À l'école** Complétez. (*Complete.*)

Nous __1__ (arriver) à l'école à sept heures et demie. Et vous, vous __2__ (arriver) à quelle heure? Avant les cours, j'__3__ (aimer) parler un peu avec les copains. On __4__ (rigoler). Mais en classe, non! On __5__ (travailler) beaucoup. Moi, j'__6__ (écouter) bien quand les profs __7__ (parler). Et toi, tu __8__ (travailler) beaucoup aussi? Tu __9__ (passer) des examens? Tu __10__ (aimer) les examens ou pas?

**21** **Une journée typique** Work with a classmate. Tell each other about a typical school day. Find out what activities you have in common.

**22** **Tu travailles ou pas?** Get together in small groups and find out who works after school in your group. Find out where, how many hours a week, etc. Here are some words you may want to use.

*For more practice using **-er** verbs in the present, do Activity 9 on page H10 at the end of this book.*

## La négation des articles indéfinis
### Talking about what you don't do

In the negative, the indefinite articles **un, une,** and **des** change to **de** (or **d'**).

| Affirmatif | Négatif |
|---|---|
| Julie regarde un CD. | Éric ne regarde pas de CD. |
| Julie regarde une vidéo. | Éric ne regarde pas de vidéo. |
| Julie regarde des photos. | Éric ne regarde pas de photos. |

**Attention!**

Note the elision with **de**.
**Je suis content: pas d'examen aujourd'hui!**

## Comment dit-on?

**23** **En classe** Répondez que non. (*Answer with* non.)

1. Tu écoutes un CD?
2. Tu regardes une vidéo?
3. Tu poses des questions?
4. Tu écoutes des cassettes?
5. Tu passes un examen aujourd'hui?

**24** **Historiette** **Dans une papeterie**

Répondez d'après les indications. (*Answer according to the cues.*)

1. René est dans une papeterie? (oui)
2. Il regarde un feutre et un cahier? (oui)
3. Il achète un stylo-bille? (non)
4. Il achète un feutre? (oui)
5. Il achète un DVD? (non)
6. Il achète une vidéo? (oui)

**25** **J'achète ou je n'achète pas.** Work with a classmate.

Take turns telling what you buy or don't buy.

## Verbe + infinitif
### Discussing likes and dislikes

**1.** In French when the verbs **aimer, adorer,** and **détester** are followed by another verb, the second verb is in the infinitive form.

> Il aime **rigoler.**
> J'adore **écouter la radio.**
> On déteste **travailler.**

**2.** In a negative sentence, the **ne… pas** goes around the first verb.

> Vous **n'aimez pas** travailler?

## Comment dit-on?

**26**  **Tu aimes travailler?** Posez les questions suivantes à un copain ou une copine. *(Ask a classmate the following questions.)*

—**Tu aimes travailler?**
—**Bien sûr. J'aime beaucoup travailler./**
  **Non, pas du tout. Je déteste travailler.**

1. Tu aimes regarder la télé?
2. Tu aimes écouter la musique?
3. Tu aimes étudier?
4. Tu aimes rigoler?
5. Tu aimes parler au téléphone?

**27**  **On aime ou on n'aime pas!**
Work with a classmate. Tell some things you like and don't like to do.

*Vous êtes sur le bon chemin. Allez-y!*

# Conversation

## Un élève français aux États-Unis

**Carol:** En France, tu arrives à quelle heure à l'école le matin?

**Cédric:** Moi, j'arrive à l'école vers sept heures et demie.

**Carol:** Et les cours commencent à quelle heure?

**Cédric:** À huit heures. J'aime parler un peu avec les copains avant la classe.

**Carol:** Et tu quittes l'école à trois heures?

**Cédric:** À trois heures! Tu rigoles! En France on quitte l'école à cinq heures.

**Carol:** À cinq heures! C'est pas vrai!

**Cédric:** Si, c'est vrai.

### Vous avez compris?

Répondez. *(Answer.)*

1. En France, Cédric arrive à l'école à quelle heure?
2. Cédric parle avec une amie américaine ou française?
3. Les cours de Cédric commencent à quelle heure?
4. Cédric quitte l'école à quelle heure?
5. Et Carol, elle quitte l'école à quelle heure?

# Parlons un peu plus

**A** **Comparaisons** With a classmate, look at the illustrations. Then compare your own daily school habits with those of the students in the illustrations.

1.

2.

3.

4.

5.

**B** **Jeu** **Les nombres** Give some numbers in a mathematical pattern but leave one out. Your partner will guess what the missing number is. Take turns. Use the model as a guide.

—**deux cents, quatre cents, _____, huit cents**
—**six cents**

## Prononciation

### Les sons /é/ et /è/ 🎧

élève

1. There is an important difference in the way French and English vowels are pronounced. When you say the French word **des,** your mouth is tense, in one position. You can repeat the sound /é/ many times without moving your mouth at all. But when you pronounce the English word *day*, your mouth is relaxed and you actually say two vowel sounds.

2. Listen to the word **élève.** It has two distinct vowel sounds. The sound /é/ is "closed" and the sound /è/ is "open." This describes the positions of the mouth for each sound. Repeat the following.

Le son /é/: **la télé**   **l'école**   **la journée**   **parler**   **écoutez**
Le son /è/: **après**   **la cassette**   **vous êtes**   **le collège**

**Après l'école, les élèves aiment écouter des cassettes.**
**Elles aiment regarder la télé.**

# Lectures culturelles

## Une journée avec Jacqueline 🔄 🎧

Jacqueline est une élève française. Elle habite rue Jacob à Paris. La rue Jacob est dans le Quartier latin, tout près de[1] la Sorbonne. La Sorbonne est une université célèbre[2] à Paris. Le Quartier latin est un quartier très fréquenté par les étudiants d'université et les lycéens.

[1] tout près de  *very near*
[2] célèbre  *famous*

Une librairie, boulevard Saint-Michel, Paris

La Sorbonne, Paris

Jacqueline est élève au lycée Louis-le-Grand. Le matin, elle quitte la maison à sept heures et demie. Les cours commencent à huit heures. Jacqueline passe la journée au lycée. Comme tous[3] les lycéens, Jacqueline travaille beaucoup, à Louis-le-Grand et à la maison. À la récréation, Jacqueline retrouve[4] des copains dans la cour. Ils parlent et ils rigolent un peu. À midi, ils déjeunent à la cantine. Ils ne rentrent pas à la maison pour déjeuner.

Jacqueline quitte le lycée à cinq heures de l'après-midi. Et vous, vous quittez l'école à quelle heure?

[3] Comme tous  *Like all*
[4] retrouve  *meets, gets together with*

Lycée Louis-le-Grand, Paris

## Vous avez compris?

**A** **Une élève française**  Répondez. *(Answer.)*
1. Qui est Jacqueline?
2. Elle habite où?
3. Jacqueline quitte la maison à quelle heure?
4. Les cours commencent à quelle heure?
5. Elle retrouve des copains où?
6. À midi, elle rentre chez elle pour déjeuner?
7. Elle déjeune avec qui?
8. Elle quitte le lycée à quelle heure?

**B** **Paris**  Trouvez les informations dans la lecture.
*(Find the information in the reading.)*
1. la rue où Jacqueline habite
2. le nom d'une université célèbre à Paris
3. un quartier de Paris fréquenté par les étudiants et les lycéens
4. le nom du lycée de Jacqueline

La France

La Suisse

La Belgique

La Tunisie

Le Maroc

Le Mali

Le Sénégal

## Qui travaille?

Le centre commercial
«Place de la Cathédrale»

Antoine est canadien. Il est québécois. Il est de Montréal, la deuxième ville francophone du monde après Paris. Après les cours, il travaille dans une papeterie pour gagner un peu d'argent[1]. Il travaille dix heures par semaine. La papeterie où il travaille est dans le centre commercial[2] «Place de la Cathédrale». C'est un très grand centre commercial souterrain[3].

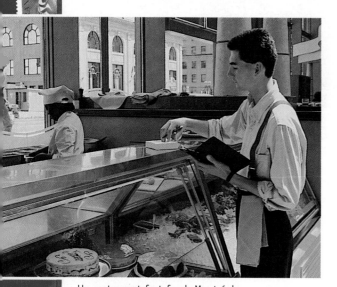

Un restaurant fast-food, Montréal

Aux États-Unis et au Québec aussi, un grand nombre d'élèves travaillent après les cours. Ils travaillent dans un magasin, dans un supermarché ou dans un restaurant fast-food (de restauration rapide). Ils gagnent de l'argent pour acheter des CD, des cassettes, un blue jean. En France, non. Très peu de collégiens ou de lycéens travaillent après les cours. C'est assez rare. Certains travaillent, mais seulement pendant les vacances. Mais… ils sont à l'école jusqu'à cinq heures de l'après-midi!

[1] gagner un peu d'argent *to earn a little money*
[2] centre commercial *mall*
[3] souterrain *underground*

## *V*ous *avez* compris?

**Au Québec** Exprimez d'une autre façon.
(*Express another way.*)
1. Antoine est *du Canada*.
2. Montréal est la *seconde* ville francophone du monde.
3. Antoine travaille après *l'école*.
4. C'est un *immense* centre commercial.
5. Aux États-Unis, *beaucoup* d'élèves travaillent.
6. *Pas beaucoup* de lycéens français travaillent après les cours.

GRAFFITI

• SITUÉ AU CŒUR DE LA VILLE ET DE LA VIE DES GENS DE QUÉBEC

• FINE CUISINE DU MARCHÉ ITALO-FRANÇAISE

• DÉJEUNER-DÎNER LE DIMANCHE
• DÉCOR CHALEUREUX, VERRIÈRE ET SALON PRIVÉ

• STATIONNEMENT

RESTO·CITÉ

Tahiti

# Un groupe de rap-Manau

Quand les collégiens ou les lycéens français rentrent à la maison l'après-midi, qu'est-ce qu'ils écoutent? Eh bien, ils écoutent la même musique que les élèves américains. Ils écoutent du rap, par exemple.

Manau, c'est un groupe de rap très populaire chez les collégiens français. Et Manau n'est pas un groupe de rap ordinaire. C'est un groupe de rap «celtique». Les instruments de musique sont la cornemuse[1], le violon, la harpe… Les chansons[2] de Manau parlent de mythes et légendes celtes avec des druides et des dolmens.

Les deux garçons du groupe, Cédric et Martial, sont copains. Le musicien, c'est Cédric: Cédric est le compositeur de la musique. Et le texte, c'est Martial: Martial est l'auteur des paroles[3].

Les deux garçons sont de la région parisienne. Mais les mères[4] de Cédric et Martial sont de Bretagne. Comme beaucoup de Bretons, elles sont d'origine celtique. Le nom du premier[5] album de Manau? *Panique Celtique!*

[1] cornemuse *bagpipes*    [3] paroles *words*    [5] premier *first*
[2] chansons *songs*        [4] mères *mothers*

**FRENCH Online**

**For more information about music in the Francophone world, go to the Glencoe French Web site:** french.glencoe.com

Un dolmen près de Carnac, Bretagne

## Vous avez compris?

**Un groupe de rap** Vrai ou faux? (*True or false?*)
1. Les collégiens français n'écoutent pas la même musique que les élèves américains.
2. Manau, c'est un groupe de rap ordinaire.
3. Les chansons de Manau parlent de l'école.
4. Cédric et Martial sont de Bretagne.

# CONNEXIONS

## *La technologie*

### L'ordinateur

Some years ago computers began to revolutionize the way people conduct their lives. They have changed the way we view the world. Computers have a place in our homes, in our schools, and in the world of business.

If you are interested in computers, you may want to familiarize yourself with some basic computer vocabulary in French. Then read the information about computers on the next page.

un ordinateur

un écran

un clavier

un CD-ROM

une souris

une disquette

une imprimante

# L'ordinateur travaille!

### Le hardware et le software

Un ordinateur exécute très rapidement les instructions d'un programme. Le hardware, c'est la partie électronique de l'ordinateur. Le software, c'est la partie programmation de l'ordinateur. Les logiciels sont des programmes. Un programme ou un logiciel est un groupe d'instructions. Un document est un fichier. L'ordinateur stocke des données[1]. On sauvegarde les documents importants sur une disquette ou un CD.

### Internet

Quand on est connecté à Internet par cable ou satellite, la connexion est pratiquement instantanée. Les satellites transmettent l'information vingt fois plus vite que le modem. Et l'ADSL transmet l'information de cinquante à cent cinquante fois plus vite que le modem. De jour en jour, grâce aux progrès de la technologie, les communications deviennent[2] plus faciles et plus rapides. C'est un fait, le monde[3] entier est connecté! Le nombre des sites est infini. On télécharge[4] des informations sur l'histoire, l'économie, l'art, la musique et toutes sortes de domaines intéressants. Quand on navigue sur Internet, on est capable d'envoyer[5] un e-mail, parler avec des amis sur d'autres continents… Il n'y a pas de limites!

[1] données *data*
[2] deviennent *become*
[3] monde *world*
[4] télécharge *download*
[5] envoyer *to send*

## Vous avez compris?

### A En français, s'il vous plaît.
Trouvez les mots suivants dans la lecture.
*(Find the following words in the reading.)*

1. hardware
2. software
3. program
4. file
5. modem
6. surf the net
7. e-mail
8. connection
9. site
10. save

### B Une page Web
Look at the monitor on page 102. If you have access to the Internet either at home or at school, go to **french.glencoe.com**

# C'est à vous

## Use what you have learned

PARLER
**1**

### Dans une papeterie
✔ *Identify and shop for school supplies*

With a classmate, take turns playing the parts of a student and a salesperson in a stationery store. Here are a few exchanges you may want to use.

—Où sont les _____, s'il vous plaît?

—Là-bas.

—Merci.

—_____, c'est combien?

—_____ euros.

—On paie à la caisse?

—Non, ici.

Une papeterie, Évry, France

## 2 Au café
**PARLER**

✔ *Talk about school life in the United States*

You're seated at a café in Provins. You're chatting with a French student (your partner). He or she has some questions about school life in the United States. Have a conversation. Be sure to answer his or her questions.

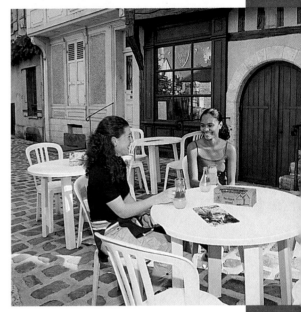

Un café, Provins, France

## 3 Une journée typique
**ÉCRIRE**

✔ *Write about a typical school day*

You can now go back to the e-mail you sent your new friend on page 75 and add more details about what a typical school day is like in the United States.

D'où?

À quelle heure?

Comment?

Où?

Qui?

### Writing Strategy

**Preparing for an interview** An interview is one way to gather information for a story or a report. A good interviewer should think about what he or she hopes to learn from the interview and prepare the questions ahead of time. The interview questions should be open-ended. Open-ended questions cannot be answered by "yes" or "no." They give the person being interviewed more opportunity to "open up" and speak freely.

## 4 Interview avec Charles Bauchart
**PARLER ÉCRIRE**

Your first assignment for the school newspaper is to write an article about a new exchange student, Charles Bauchart, from Fort-de-France in Martinique. To prepare for your interview with him, write down as many questions as you can. Ask him about himself, his school, and his friends in Martinique. After you have prepared your questions, conduct the interview with a partner who plays the role of Charles. Write down your partner's answers. Then organize your notes and write your article.

# Assessment

## Vocabulaire

### 1 Choisissez. *(Choose.)*

To review **Mots 1,**
turn to pages
82–83.

**1.** Sandrine ＿＿＿ la maison à sept heures et demie.
   **a.** quitte       **b.** arrive       **c.** habite

**2.** Les élèves passent ＿＿＿ à l'école.
   **a.** la cantine       **b.** la prof       **c.** la journée

**3.** Leïla pose une ＿＿＿.
   **a.** rue       **b.** question       **c.** maison

**4.** Vincent ＿＿＿ des cassettes.
   **a.** écoute       **b.** quitte       **c.** passe

**5.** Le prof ＿＿＿ et les élèves écoutent bien.
   **a.** travaille       **b.** regarde       **c.** parle

### 2 Identifiez. *(Identify.)*

To review
**Mots 2,** turn to
pages 86–87.

**6.**       **7.**       **8.**

**9.**       **10.**

## Structure

### 3 Complétez. *(Complete.)*

To review **-er** verbs
in the present tense,
turn to page 90.

**11.** Les élèves ＿＿＿ à l'école le matin. (arriver)

**12.** Nous ＿＿＿ entre les cours. (parler)

**13.** Je ＿＿＿ à la cantine avec les copains. (déjeuner)

**14.** Luc ＿＿＿ la télé après les cours. (regarder)

**15.** Tu ＿＿＿ beaucoup à la maison? (travailler)

**16.** On ＿＿＿ français en France. (parler)

**4 Mettez à la forme négative.**
*(Make each sentence negative.)*

17. Sandrine achète un crayon à la papeterie.
18. Elle regarde une calculatrice.
19. Ils achètent des livres.
20. Les élèves passent un examen aujourd'hui.

To review indefinite articles in the negative, turn to page 94.

**5 Choisissez.** *(Choose.)*

21. On aime _____ la télé.
    **a.** regardent    **b.** regarder    **c.** regarde
22. Je déteste _____.
    **a.** travailler    **b.** travaille    **c.** travaillons

To review the use of verbs with infinitives, turn to page 95.

# Culture

**6 Vrai ou faux?** *(True or false?)*

Une rue du Quartier latin, Paris

To review this cultural information, turn to pages 98–99.

23. La Sorbonne est une université célèbre à Paris.
24. La Sorbonne est dans le Quartier latin.
25. En France, les élèves quittent le lycée à trois heures de l'après-midi.

# On parle super bien!

Tell all you can about this illustration.

# Vocabulaire

## Getting to school

une maison
une rue
quitter

habiter
arriver

## Discussing classroom activities

passer la journée
parler
écouter
regarder

étudier
lever la main
poser une question
passer un examen

## Discussing recess and lunch activities

la récré(ation)
la cour
la cantine

jouer
rigoler
déjeuner

## Discussing afterschool activities

rentrer à la maison
écouter la radio

parler au téléphone
travailler

**How well do you know your vocabulary?**

- Identify the words and expressions that describe what you do at school and after school. Make two lists.
- Use as many words as you can from one of your lists to write a story about either your school activities or what you do after school.

## Identifying school supplies

Qu'est-ce que c'est?
des fournitures (f. pl.)
   scolaires
un cahier
un bloc-notes
un crayon

un stylo-bille
un feutre
une gomme
une règle
un livre
un classeur

une calculatrice
une feuille de papier
un sac à dos
une cassette
une vidéo, un DVD
un CD

## Shopping for school supplies

un magasin
une papeterie
la caisse

acheter
payer
demander

coûter
C'est combien?
Ça coûte combien?

## Other useful words and expressions

aimer
détester
après
pendant
entre
chez
le matin
l'après-midi
À quelle heure?

combien de (d')

beaucoup de (d')

**VIDÉOTOUR**

**Épisode 3**

In this video episode, you will join Amadou and Christine after school. See page 528 for more information.

# La famille et la maison

## Objectifs

**In this chapter you will learn to:**

- talk about your family

- describe your home and neighborhood

- tell your age and find out someone else's age

- tell what belongs to you and others

- describe more people and things

- talk about families and homes in French-speaking countries

Bonne Fête Maman
POSTES

Pierre Auguste Renoir *Madame Charpentier et ses enfants*

.32 PB ·11

# Vocabulaire

## Mots 1

### La famille Morel 🎧

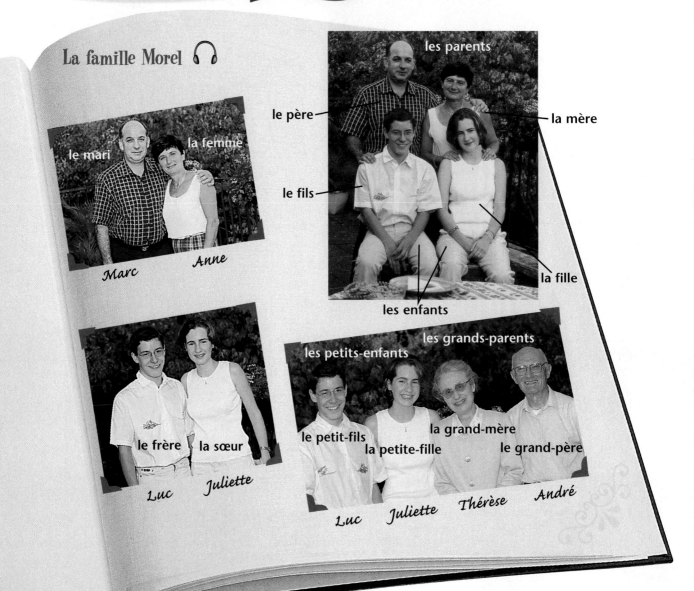

les parents

le mari — Marc
la femme — Anne

le père
la mère
le fils
la fille
les enfants

le frère — Luc
la sœur — Juliette

les grands-parents
les petits-enfants
le petit-fils — Luc
la petite-fille — Juliette
la grand-mère — Thérèse
le grand-père — André

Médor

le chien

Voici la famille Morel.
M. et Mme Morel ont deux enfants—un fils et une fille.
Les Morel ont un chien.
Leur chien est adorable.
La famille Morel n'a pas de chat.

Lucie

le chat

## L'anniversaire de Marie 🎧

Tu as quel âge, Marie?

une bougie    un gâteau    un cadeau

Moi? J'ai quinze ans. Aujourd'hui, c'est mon anniversaire.

C'est quand, l'anniversaire de Marie?
C'est le deux août.
Tout le monde a un cadeau pour Marie.
Il y a beaucoup de cadeaux.

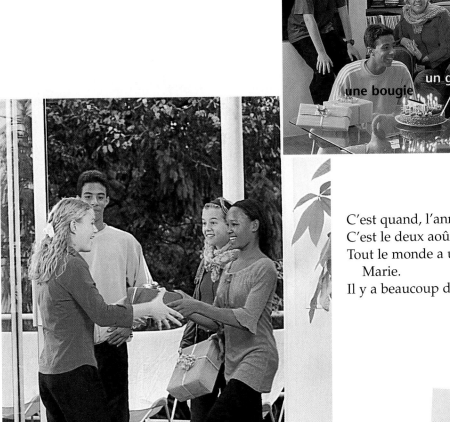

Marie donne une fête pour son anniversaire.
Elle invite ses amis et ses cousins.

### Note 🎧

In French, some of the words for family members are cognates. Can you guess who these family members are?

| | |
|---|---|
| une tante | un oncle |
| une cousine | un cousin |
| une nièce | un neveu |

Here are some words for other family members.

**une belle-mère** *stepmother*
**un beau-père** *stepfather*
**une demi-sœur** *half sister*
**un demi-frère** *half brother*

# Quel est le mot?

**1** **Historiette** **La famille Senghor**

Inventez une histoire. *(Make up a story.)*

1. Madame Senghor est la femme de Monsieur Senghor?
2. Monsieur Senghor est le mari de Madame Senghor?
3. La famille Senghor est française?
4. M. et Mme Senghor ont deux enfants? Ils ont un fils et une fille?
5. Les enfants ont quel âge?
6. Quelle est la date de l'anniversaire de la fille?
7. Il y a combien de personnes dans la famille Senghor?
8. Les Senghor ont un chien ou un chat?

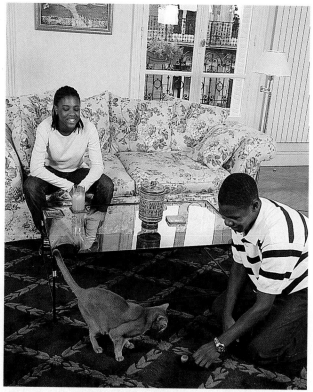

Marie et Blaise Senghor habitent à Paris.

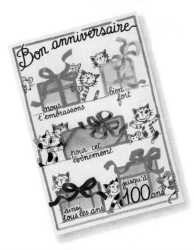

**2** **Historiette** **L'anniversaire de Francine** Répondez

 d'après les indications. *(Answer according to the cues.)*

1. Elle a quel âge, Francine? (quinze ans)
2. C'est quand, son anniversaire? (aujourd'hui)
3. Quelle est la date aujourd'hui? (le deux août)
4. Qu'est-ce que Francine donne pour son anniversaire? (une fête)
5. Elle invite qui à la fête? (ses amis et ses cousins)
6. Qu'est-ce que tout le monde a pour Francine? (beaucoup de cadeaux)
7. Il y a un gâteau pour Francine? (oui)
8. Le gâteau a des bougies? (oui, quinze)

**3** **La famille** Complétez. *(Complete.)*

1. Le frère de mon père est mon _____.
2. La sœur de mon père est ma _____.
3. Le frère de ma mère est mon _____.
4. La sœur de ma mère est ma _____.
5. Le fils de mon oncle et de ma tante est mon _____.
6. La fille de mon oncle et de ma tante est ma _____.
7. Le père de ma mère est mon _____.
8. Et la mère de mon père est ma _____.

Ma grand-mère habite à Paris.

**4** **Moi** Choisissez la bonne réponse.
*(Choose the correct answer.)*

1. Moi, je suis _____ de mes grands-parents.
   **a.** le petit-fils   **b.** la petite-fille
2. Je suis _____ de mes parents.
   **a.** le fils   **b.** la fille
3. Je suis _____ de mon oncle.
   **a.** le neveu   **b.** la nièce
4. Je suis _____ de mes cousins.
   **a.** le cousin   **b.** la cousine

 **5** **Une famille** This country wedding, *Une noce à la campagne,* was painted by le Douanier Rousseau in 1905. Give the people names and decide who they are in relation to one another.

*Une noce à la campagne*

   **6** **Une fête d'anniversaire**
With a classmate describe some things that take place at a typical birthday party. You may want to use some of the following words.

 arriver

 écouter

 donner

 préparer

 danser

 inviter

regarder

 For more practice using words from *Mots 1*, do Activity 10 on page H11 at the end of this book.

# Vocabulaire

## La maison 🎧

une vieille maison

une fleur

un arbre

un garage

une voiture

un jardin

une terrasse

La vieille maison est très belle.
Il y a un jardin autour de la maison.
De la terrasse on a une vue du jardin.

## L'immeuble 🎧

un immeuble    un appartement

un quartier

le troisième étage

le deuxième étage

le premier étage

le rez-de-chaussée

une entrée

une station de métro    un balcon

un code:
B0275

Le balcon donne sur la rue.
Les Briand ont un très joli appartement.
Il est dans un très beau quartier de Paris.
Leur immeuble est (tout) près d'une station de métro.
L'immeuble n'est pas loin d'une station de métro.

Attention! Il y a
un nouveau code!

Les voisins sont dans la cour.

Les Briand montent toujours en ascenseur.
Ils montent au troisième étage.

## Les pièces de la maison 🎧

# Quel est le mot?

La maison de Claude Monet, Giverny

**7** **Historiette** **La maison de Monet** Répondez que **oui**. (*Answer* oui.)

1. Monet est un artiste célèbre?
2. Il a une jolie maison?
3. Sa maison est grande?
4. Il y a un jardin autour de sa maison?
5. C'est un très beau jardin?
6. Il y a des arbres et des fleurs dans le jardin?

**8** **Historiette** **L'appartement des Lapeyre**
Inventez une histoire. (*Make up a story.*)

1. La famille Lapeyre a un appartement dans un vieil immeuble à Paris?
2. Leur appartement est dans un beau quartier de Paris?
3. L'appartement est au rez-de-chaussée ou au troisième étage?
4. Leur balcon donne sur la rue ou sur la cour?
5. Il y a six pièces dans l'appartement de la famille Lapeyre?
6. Quelles pièces?
7. Les Lapeyre montent toujours à pied ou en ascenseur?
8. L'immeuble est près d'une station de métro ou loin d'une station de métro?
9. Il y a un code pour entrer dans l'immeuble?

**FRENCH Online**

For more information about French painters, go to the Glencoe French Web site: french.glencoe.com

**9** **Quelle pièce?** Choisissez la bonne réponse. (*Choose the correct answer.*)

1. On regarde la télé dans _____.
   **a.** la salle de bains   **b.** la salle à manger   **c.** la salle de séjour
2. On prépare le dîner dans _____.
   **a.** la salle à manger   **b.** la cuisine   **c.** la chambre à coucher
3. On parle avec ses voisins dans _____.
   **a.** la salle de bains   **b.** la cour   **c.** la chambre à coucher
4. On dîne dans _____.
   **a.** la salle à manger   **b.** la salle de séjour   **c.** la chambre à coucher
5. On a une belle vue _____.
   **a.** du balcon   **b.** de l'étage   **c.** de l'ascenseur

**10** **Historiette** **Chez moi** Donnez des réponses personnelles. *(Give your own answers.)*

1. Tu habites quelle rue?
2. Tu habites dans un appartement ou dans une maison privée?
3. Il y a combien de pièces dans l'appartement ou la maison?
4. Il y a combien de chambres à coucher?
5. Il y a un jardin ou un balcon?
6. La maison ou l'immeuble a un garage?
7. Il y a une voiture dans le garage?

**11** **Quelle maison pour nous?** Work with a classmate. Your families plan to spend a month in France. Read the following real estate ads and discuss which house or apartment is good for your family.

**Appartement**

dans un bel immeuble, cinq pièces, deux chambres à coucher, une grande cuisine moderne, bien situé au centre-ville, près d'une station de métro

**Très jolie villa**

avec jardin et terrasse, vue sur l'océan, huit pièces, quatre chambres à coucher, garage pour deux voitures, située dans une rue très calme, loin de la ville

**Petit bungalow**

dans un vieux quartier, beaucoup de charme, trois pièces, une chambre à coucher, vingt minutes de la ville de Caen.

*For more practice using words from* ***Mots 2,*** *do Activity 11 on page H12 at the end of this book.*

# Structure

## Le verbe avoir au présent
### Telling what you and others have

**1.** Study the following forms of the irregular verb **avoir** *(to have).*

| AVOIR | |
|---|---|
| j' ai | nous‿avons |
| tu as | vous‿avez |
| il/elle/on‿a | ils‿/elles‿ont |

**2.** You also use the verb **avoir** to express age.

> **Tu as quel âge?**
> **Moi? J'ai quatorze ans.**

**3.** The expression **il y a** means "there is" or "there are."

> **Il y a un jardin autour de la maison.**
> **Il n'y a pas de fleurs dans le jardin.**

> **Rappelez-vous que...**
>
> Un, une, and des become de (d') after a negative.
> J'ai une sœur mais Marc n'a pas de sœur.

## Comment dit-on?

**12** 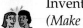 **Historiette** Les Binand
Inventez une histoire.
*(Make up a story.)*

1. Suzanne Binand a un frère?
2. Guillaume a une sœur?
3. Monsieur et Madame Binand ont deux enfants?
4. La famille Binand a un appartement à Paris?
5. Ils ont un chat?

Deux amis, Narbonne, France

 **13** **Tu as un frère?** Répétez la conversation. *(Repeat the conversation.)*

**Flore:** Tu as un frère?
**Rémi:** Non, je n'ai pas de frère, mais j'ai une sœur.
**Flore:** Tu as une sœur? Elle a quel âge?
**Rémi:** Elle a quatorze ans.
**Flore:** Et toi, tu as quel âge?
**Rémi:** Moi, j'ai seize ans.
**Flore:** Et… vous avez un chien?
**Rémi:** Non, on n'a pas de chien. Mais on a un petit chat.

**14** **Rémi** Complétez d'après la conversation. *(Complete according to the conversation.)*

1. Rémi n'___ pas ___ frère.
2. Il ___ une sœur.
3. Sa sœur ___ quatorze ans.
4. Rémi ___ seize ans.
5. Rémi et sa sœur n'___ pas ___ chien.
6. Mais ils ___ un petit chat adorable.

 **15** **Historiette** **Ma famille** Donnez des réponses personnelles. *(Give your own answers.)*

1. Tu as des frères? Tu as combien de frères?
2. Tu as des sœurs? Tu as combien de sœurs?
3. Tu as un chien ou un chat?
4. Tu as des amis?
5. Tu as des cousins?
6. Tu as combien de cousins?
7. Tu as une grande famille ou une petite famille?
8. Tu as quel âge?

Un père et son fils

LA FAMILLE ET LA MAISON

**16** **Dans mon sac à dos** Préparez une conversation d'après le modèle. *(Make up a conversation according to the model.)*

—Tu as des livres dans ton sac à dos?
—Oui, j'ai des livres dans mon sac à dos. /
    Non, je n'ai pas de livres dans mon sac à dos.

**17** **Qu'est-ce que vous avez?** Préparez une conversation d'après le modèle. *(Make up a conversation according to the model.)*

une maison ou un appartement →
—Vous avez une maison ou un appartement?
—Nous avons _____.

1. une grande famille ou une petite famille
2. une grande voiture ou une petite voiture
3. un chien ou un chat
4. un PC ou un Mac

**18** **Historiette** **La famille Ghez** Complétez avec **avoir.**
*(Complete with* avoir.*)*

La famille Ghez __1__ un bel appartement à Nice. Leur appartement __2__ six pièces. Leur appartement __3__ un balcon. Le balcon donne sur la mer Méditerranée. Du balcon les Ghez __4__ une très belle vue sur la mer.

Il y a quatre personnes dans la famille Ghez. Halima a dix-sept ans et son frère, Ahmed, __5__ quinze ans. Halima et Ahmed __6__ un petit chat adorable.

Et toi, tu __7__ un chien ou un chat? Tu __8__ une petite ou une grande famille? Vous __9__ un appartement ou une maison?

Moi, j'__10__ quinze ans et j'__11__ un chien adorable. J'adore mon petit chien.

# Les adjectifs possessifs
## Telling what belongs to you and others

1. You use a possessive adjective to show possession or ownership. Like other adjectives, a possessive adjective must agree with the noun it modifies.

2. The adjectives **mon** (*my*), **ton** (*your*), and **son** (*his/her*) each have three forms. The adjectives **notre** (*our*), **votre** (*your*), and **leur** (*their*) each have two forms.

| SINGULIER | | PLURIEL | |
|---|---|---|---|
| **Masculin** | **Féminin** | **Masculin** | **Féminin** |
| mon frère | ma sœur | mes frères | mes sœurs |
| ton frère | ta sœur | tes frères | tes sœurs |
| son frère | sa sœur | ses frères | ses sœurs |
| notre frère | notre sœur | nos frères | nos sœurs |
| votre frère | votre sœur | vos frères | vos sœurs |
| leur frère | leur sœur | leurs frères | leurs sœurs |

3. **Son, sa,** and **ses** can mean "his" or "her." The adjective agrees with the item owned, not the owner.

   **C'est le chien de Paul.**  **C'est son chien.**
   **C'est le chien de Marie.**  **C'est son chien.**

4. You use **mon, ton,** or **son** before a feminine singular noun that begins with a vowel or silent **h.**

   **son‿amie et mon‿amie**

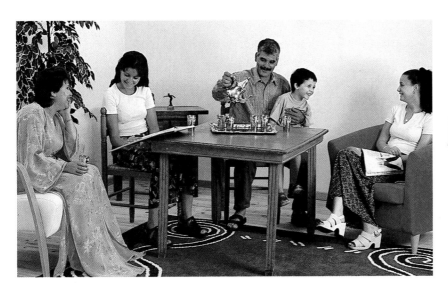

Une famille d'origine marocaine, Saint-André, France

## Attention!

Liaison occurs with **mon, ton,** and **son,** as well as with all plural possessive adjectives.

**mon‿oncle**  **nos‿amis**
**ton‿ami**  **vos‿amis**
**son‿école**  **leurs‿amis**

# Comment dit-on?

**19** **Historiette** **Ta famille et chez toi** Donnez des réponses personnelles. *(Give your own answers.)*

1. Où est ta maison ou ton appartement?
2. Ta maison ou ton appartement a combien de pièces?
3. Ta maison est grande ou petite? Ton appartement est grand ou petit?
4. C'est quand, ton anniversaire? Tu as quel âge?
5. Quel âge a ton frère, si tu as un frère?
6. Quel âge a ta sœur, si tu as une sœur?

Un beau chalet, Suisse

**20** **J'ai une question pour toi.**
Suivez le modèle. *(Follow the model.)*

—Où est __ta__ maison?
—Ma maison est dans la rue Jacob.

1. Qui est _____ amie?
2. Qui est _____ ami?
3. Où habitent _____ grands-parents?
4. _____ frère a quel âge?
5. _____ sœur a quel âge?
6. Où est _____ maison ou _____ appartement?
7. Tu aimes _____ cours de français?
8. _____ prof est sympa?

**21** **Oui!** Suivez le modèle. *(Follow the model.)*

—Le frère de Marine est dans sa chambre?
—Oui, son frère est dans sa chambre.

1. Le père de Marine est dans la cuisine?
2. La sœur de Marine est blonde?
3. La sœur de Thomas est à Paris?
4. La maison de Thomas est jolie?
5. L'appartement de Marine est beau?
6. Les cousins de Thomas sont élèves?
7. Les grands-parents de Thomas ont un chien?

## 22 Historiette  Notre école

Donnez des réponses personnelles.
*(Give your own answers.)*

1. Votre école est grande ou petite?
2. Votre école est près ou loin de votre maison?
3. Votre école a combien d'élèves?
4. Vos cours sont faciles ou difficiles?
5. Vos profs sont intéressants ou pas?
6. Vos classes sont grandes ou petites?

La Techno Parade, Paris

## 23 Historiette  Leur maison

Complétez. *(Complete.)*

Fabien et Christophe sont frères. Ils sont dans __1__ chambre. Ils écoutent __2__ disques. __3__ collection de CD est surtout de la techno. __4__ amies, Catherine et Émilie, aiment aussi la techno. Fabien et Christophe, __5__ deux amies et __6__ copains écoutent souvent de la techno. Mais __7__ parents n'aiment pas du tout la techno.

## 24 Votre famille
Draw your own family tree and say as many things as you can about your family to your classmates.

*For more practice using **avoir** and possessive adjectives, do Activity 12 on page H13 at the end of this book.*

## D'autres adjectifs
### Describing more people and things

**1.** Most French adjectives follow the noun. Some common ones, such as **petit** and **grand,** come before the noun. The adjectives **beau** *(beautiful)*, **nouveau** *(new)*, and **vieux** *(old)* also come before the noun. These adjectives have several forms. Pay careful attention to both the spelling and the pronunciation of these adjectives.

### SINGULIER

| Féminin | Masculin (Voyelle) | Masculin (Consonne) |
|---|---|---|
| une belle maison | un bel appartement | un beau quartier |
| une nouvelle maison | un nouvel appartement | un nouveau quartier |
| une vieille maison | un vieil appartement | un vieux quartier |

### PLURIEL

| Féminin | Masculin (Voyelle) | Masculin (Consonne) |
|---|---|---|
| de belles maisons | de beaux‿appartements | de beaux quartiers |
| de nouvelles maisons | de nouveaux‿appartements | de nouveaux quartiers |
| de vieilles maisons | de vieux‿appartements | de vieux quartiers |

**2.** In formal French, **de** is used instead of **des** with a plural adjective that precedes the noun. In informal French, people use **des.**

### Attention!

Liaison occurs with **beaux, nouveaux,** and **vieux** when they come before a word beginning with a vowel or silent **h.** The **x** is pronounced as a **z.**
mes nouveaux‿amis
les vieux‿appartements

De belles maisons,
Montréal, Canada

# Comment dit-on?

**25** **Historiette** **Le bel appartement des Texier** Complétez. *(Complete.)*

1. Les Texier ont un _____ appartement dans un _____ immeuble dans un _____ quartier de la ville. (beau, vieux, beau)
2. Il y a de _____ et de _____ quartiers à Montréal. (nouveau, vieux)
3. L'appartement des Texier a de très _____ pièces. (beau)
4. Il a de _____ pièces et un très _____ balcon. (grand, beau)
5. De l'appartement il y a une très _____ vue sur la ville. (beau)
6. Les Texier ont une _____ voiture. (nouveau)
7. Leur _____ voiture est _____. (nouveau, beau)

## Attention!

You have just learned that the plural of **beau** and **nouveau** is spelled with an **x**. Almost all words in French that end in **(e)au** or **eu** are spelled with **x**, not **s**, in the plural.

| | |
|---|---|
| **un cadeau** | **des cadeaux** |
| **un beau château** | **de beaux châteaux** |
| **mon neveu** | **mes neveux** |

Mettez au pluriel. *(Write in the plural.)*

1. Il a un très beau cadeau pour son neveu.
   Il a de très _____ _____ pour ses _____.
2. Le beau gâteau est aussi pour son neveu.
   Les _____ _____ sont aussi pour ses _____.
3. Il visite un beau château avec son neveu.
   Il visite de _____ _____ avec ses _____.

**26** **Comme qui?** Work with a classmate. Take turns saying whom you and your family members take after. You may wish to use the following words.

**Je suis intelligent(e) comme ma mère.**
**Mon frère est enthousiaste comme notre père.**

petit

amusant     blond          sympa

grand              beau              brun

*Vous êtes sur le bon chemin. Allez-y!*

# Conversation

## Ma nouvelle adresse

| | |
|---|---|
| **Vincent:** | Tu as ma nouvelle adresse? |
| **Charlotte:** | Ta nouvelle adresse? Non! Tu habites où maintenant? |
| **Vincent:** | 21, avenue de la Bourdonnais. |
| **Charlotte:** | Ah, avenue de la Bourdonnais. C'est dans le 7$^e$ tout près de la tour Eiffel, non? |
| **Vincent:** | Oui. De notre balcon on a une très belle vue sur la tour Eiffel. |
| **Charlotte:** | Génial! |

## Vous avez compris?

Répondez. (*Answer.*)

1. Vincent parle à qui?
2. Charlotte a la nouvelle adresse de Vincent?
3. Quelle est sa nouvelle adresse?
4. Où est l'avenue de la Bourdonnais?
5. Est-ce que l'appartement de Vincent a un balcon?
6. De son balcon il a une vue sur la tour Eiffel?

# Parlons un peu plus

**A** **Appartement ou maison?** Work with a classmate. Pretend you live in Rouen. One of you lives in a house, the other lives in an apartment. Decide who lives where. Then describe your house or apartment.

**B** **Jeu** **Qui est qui?** Work with a classmate. Write down the first names of some of your family members. Exchange lists and then ask each other who's who.

C'est qui, Paul?

C'est mon oncle. C'est le frère de ma mère.

## Prononciation

Le son /ã/

1. There are three nasal vowel sounds in French: /ã/ as in **cent**, /õ/ as in **sont**, and /ẽ/ as in **cinq**. They are called "nasal" because some air passes through the nose when they are pronounced. In this chapter, you will practice only the sound /ã/ as in **cent**.

2. Repeat the following. Notice that there is no /n/ sound after the nasal vowel.

| | | | |
|---|---|---|---|
| **Jean** | **cent** | **grand** | **amusant** |
| **français** | **parent** | **fantastique** | |

**Voilà les grands-parents, les parents et les enfants.**
**Jean-François est fantastique. Il est français, grand, amusant.**

les parents et les enfants

# Lectures culturelles

## Où habitent les Français?

### Maisons et appartements

Beaucoup de Français qui habitent en ville habitent dans un appartement. Il y a des appartements de toutes sortes: des studios, de petits appartements, de grands appartements. Pour les gens qui n'ont pas beaucoup d'argent il y a des H.L.M.[1] (Habitations à Loyer Modéré). Les H.L.M. sont généralement à l'extérieur des villes, à la périphérie ou en banlieue[2]. En banlieue, il y a aussi de petites maisons individuelles—des pavillons.

[1] H.L.M.  *low-income housing*
[2] en banlieue  *in the suburbs*

Des H.L.M.

Des pavillons de la banlieue parisienne

Haïti

La Martinique

### La famille Duval

Les Duval habitent à Paris. Leur appartement est dans un vieil immeuble dans le premier arrondissement. Les Duval habitent dans un très beau quartier.

L'immeuble où habitent les Duval a six étages. Les Duval habitent au cinquième. Ils ont un appartement de quatre pièces: une salle de séjour, une salle à manger et deux chambres à coucher. Il y a aussi, bien sûr, une cuisine, une salle de bains, des toilettes et même une petite entrée. La salle de séjour et la salle à manger donnent sur la rue. La cuisine et les chambres à coucher donnent sur la cour. De leur balcon, les Duval ont une très belle vue sur le musée du Louvre.

Un bel appartement à Paris

## Vous avez compris?

### A Le logement Vrai ou faux? (*True or false?*)
1. Beaucoup de Français habitent dans des appartements.
2. Il y a beaucoup de maisons individuelles dans les villes françaises.
3. Les H.L.M. sont pour les gens qui n'ont pas beaucoup d'argent, qui ne sont pas très riches.
4. Les H.L.M. sont toujours au centre-ville.
5. Le Louvre est dans le deuxième arrondissement.

### B La famille Duval Répondez. (*Answer.*)
1. Où habitent les Duval?
2. Où est leur appartement?
3. Il y a combien d'étages dans l'immeuble?
4. Ils habitent au cinquième?
5. Quelles pièces donnent sur la rue?
6. Quelles pièces donnent sur la cour?
7. Du balcon de l'appartement, il y a une vue sur quel musée parisien?

# Le logement dans d'autres pays

Dakar, Sénégal

Une maison avec un toit de chaume, Sénégal

## En Afrique

Dans les grandes villes modernes de l'Afrique Occidentale comme Abidjan ou Dakar il y a beaucoup de grands immeubles où les Ivoiriens et les Sénégalais habitent dans de très beaux appartements de grand standing. Mais dans les petits villages de la brousse[1], les gens habitent dans des petites maisons avec un toit de chaume. Voilà une maison typique de la brousse.

## À la Martinique

La Martinique est une belle île francophone dans la mer des Antilles (la mer des Caraïbes). La Martinique est un département français d'outre-mer[2]. Beaucoup de Martiniquais habitent dans des maisons en bois[3]. Les couleurs des maisons martiniquaises sont très belles.

[1] brousse *bush*
[2] d'outre-mer *overseas*
[3] en bois *wooden*

## Vous avez compris?

**Le monde francophone** Donnez les informations suivantes. (*Give the following information.*)
1. deux grandes villes africaines
2. une région rurale dans beaucoup de pays africains
3. un département français d'outre-mer
4. une île où il y a beaucoup de maisons multicolores en bois

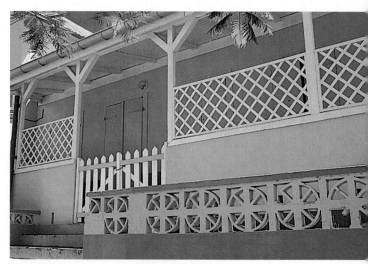

Une maison en bois, Pointe-à-Pitre, Guadeloupe

## Les noms de famille

En France les noms de famille ont des origines très variées. Certains évoquent une caractéristique physique: **Legrand, Lebrun, Petit.**

D'autres sont des noms de profession.

Médecin    Boucher    Charpentier

D'autres sont des noms d'endroits.

Lacour

Dujardin

Delarue

D'autres encore sont des termes géographiques.

Dumont

Duval

Dubois

Quel est votre nom de famille?
Il signifie quelque chose de spécial?

### Vous avez compris?

**Noms de famille américains**  Can you think of some American family names for each of the above categories? Can you think of any other categories for American family names?

La Belgique

La Tunisie

Le Maroc

Le Mali

# CONNEXIONS

## Les Beaux-Arts

### Art et histoire

Art and history are often closely connected. Looking at a beautiful painting brings us much enjoyment. It can also teach us a great deal about the period in which the artist produced it. A portrait, for example, shows us how people looked and dressed at the time.

Today many families keep a photo album. Prior to the invention of photography many families had a portrait done. This was particularly true of the royal families, and King Louis XVI and his queen, Marie-Antoinette, were no exception.

*Marie-Antoinette à la rose*

### La portraitiste de Marie-Antoinette

Élisabeth Vigée-Lebrun est née[1] à Paris en 1775 (mille sept cent soixante-quinze). Elle étudie l'art auprès de son père, l'artiste Louis Vigée. La jeune Élisabeth a beaucoup de talent et en très peu de temps[2] elle a du succès. Élisabeth Vigée-Lebrun est la portraitiste de Marie-Antoinette.

### Marie-Antoinette

Voici un portrait de Marie-Antoinette avec ses quatre enfants. La reine est une mère dévouée. Elle adore ses enfants.

[1] née  *born*
[2] en très peu de temps  *in a short time*

*Marie-Antoinette et ses enfants*

### Versailles

La famille royale habite dans le grand palais à Versailles. Mais Marie-Antoinette n'aime pas beaucoup la vie[3] au grand palais. Elle a un petit palais—le Petit Trianon. Pas loin du Petit Trianon Marie-Antoinette a un petit hameau où elle aime passer du temps. Le hameau est un petit village avec des maisonnettes (petites maisons) avec un toit de chaume. Là, Marie-Antoinette aime passer du temps avec les gens[4] simples.

### La Révolution

Pendant la Révolution la famille royale est séparée et emprisonnée. Louis XVI et Marie-Antoinette sont guillotinés. *Les adieux de Louis XVI* est un tableau de l'artiste J.-J. Hauer de l'époque révolutionnaire.

[3] vie *life*    [4] gens *folks, people*

Le hameau de Marie-Antoinette

*Les adieux de Louis XVI*

## Vous avez compris?

**La famille royale** Donnez les informations suivantes. (*Give the following information.*)

1. le nom de la portraitiste de Marie-Antoinette
2. le nom du mari de Marie-Antoinette
3. la résidence officielle de la famille royale
4. le nom du petit palais de Marie-Antoinette
5. la destinée de la famille royale

# C'est à vous

## Use what you have learned

PARLER
**1**

### Belle résidence

✔ *Describe a home or apartment*

You are trying to sell one of the apartments or houses listed in the ads. Say as much as you can to convince your client (your classmate) to buy one.

CHAUSSON IMMOBILIER IMMO*Plus*
• 33, av. de Foix - 09120 VARILHE
Tél. : 05.61.60.79.80 - Fax : 05.61.60.86

**Région PAMIERS :** (09) **NID D'AIGLE** rénové, cuisine campagnarde, séjour-salon cheminée 65 m², bureau, 4 chambres, salle de bains, wc. Tout confort. Grande dépendance. Site isolé avec très bel environnement.

**Près VARILHES :** (09) **MAISON** campagne, 5 pièces, salle d'eau, wc, grandes dépendances (bergerie, étable, chai) aménageables. Cour, jardin. Proximité toutes commodités.

PARLER
**2**

### L'immeuble

✔ *Talk about families and where they live*

With a classmate, look at the apartment building. A different family lives on each floor. University students live in the garrets under the roof. Give each family and student a name. Say as much as you can about them and their lodgings.

Dans station thermale des **PYRÉNÉES :** près station de ski, **MAISON** de maître, 12 pièces, bon état, maison de gardien, garage, boxes à chevaux. Terrain 8 ha. Situation exceptionnelle.

### 3 Quinze ans

✔ *Invite a friend to a birthday party*

A good friend will soon be fifteen. Write an invitation to his or her birthday party. You may wish to use the well-known French expression R.S.V.P.— **Répondez, s'il vous plaît.**

### 4 Ma famille et moi

✔ *Describe yourself and your family*

You plan to spend next year as an exchange student in Toulouse, France. You have to write a letter about yourself and your family to the agency in your community that selects the exchange students. Your letter must be in French. Make your description as complete as possible.

---

**Writing Strategy**

**Ordering details** There are several ways to order details when writing. The one you choose depends upon your purpose for writing. When describing a physical place, it is sometimes best to use spatial ordering. This means describing things as they actually appear—from left to right, from back to front, from top to bottom, or any other logical order that works.

---

### 5 La maison de mes rêves

Write a description of your dream house. Be as complete as you can.

Un château à Rocamadour, France

# Assessment

## Vocabulaire

**1 Complétez.** *(Complete.)*

To review **Mots 1,** turn to pages 112–113.

1. Mes parents sont ma _____ et mon _____.
2. Les parents de mes parents sont mes _____.
3. La sœur de ma mère est ma _____.
4. Le frère de mon père est mon _____.
5. Les enfants de mes oncles et de mes tantes sont mes _____ et mes _____.

**2 Identifiez.** *(Identify.)*

To review **Mots 2,** turn to pages 116–117.

## Structure

To review the verb *avoir,* turn to page 120.

**3 Complétez avec «avoir».** *(Complete with* avoir.*)*

11. J'_____ une petite famille.
12. Marc aussi _____ une petite famille.
13. Sa sœur _____ seize ans.
14. Les parents de Marc et sa sœur _____ un appartement à Paris.
15. Vous _____ une maison ou un appartement?
16. Et toi, tu _____ une petite ou une grande famille?

**4** **Choisissez.** *(Choose.)*

17. Où est la voiture de Serge? _____ voiture est dans le garage?

    **a.** Sa    **b.** Son    **c.** Ses

18. Où est _____ maison?

    **a.** ta    **b.** ton    **c.** tes

19. _____ anniversaire est le 4 novembre.

    **a.** Ma    **b.** Mon    **c.** Mes

20. Paul et Marc sont les frères de Sandrine? Oui, ce sont _____ frères.

    **a.** leurs    **b.** son    **c.** ses

To review possessive adjectives, turn to page 123.

**5** **Complétez.** *(Complete.)*

21. Il y a de très _____ maisons dans notre _____ quartier. (vieux, beau)

22. Nous avons un _____ appartement avec de _____ pièces. (nouveau, beau)

To review these adjectives, turn to page 126.

# Culture

**6** **Vrai ou faux?** *(True or false?)*

23. Les pavillons sont de petites maisons en banlieue.

24. Les H.L.M. sont généralement à l'extérieur des villes.

25. Beaucoup de Français qui habitent en ville habitent dans une maison privée.

To review this cultural information, turn to pages 130–131.

Des H.L.M.

Tell all you can about this illustration.

# Vocabulaire

### Identifying family members

| | | |
|---|---|---|
| la famille | le frère | la petite-fille |
| les parents *(m. pl.)* | la sœur | l'oncle |
| le père | les grands-parents | la tante |
| la mère | *(m. pl.)* | le neveu |
| le mari | le grand-père | la nièce |
| la femme | la grand-mère | le/la cousin(e) |
| le fils | les petits-enfants | un chat |
| la fille | *(m. pl.)* | un chien |
| l'enfant *(m. et f.)* | le petit-fils | |

### Talking about family affairs or events

| | |
|---|---|
| un anniversaire | donner |
| un cadeau | inviter |
| un gâteau | avoir… ans |
| une bougie | Quel âge… ? |
| une fête | |

**How well do you know your vocabulary?**
- Find the sixteen cognates.
- Use as many of them as you can to write a story.

### Identifying the rooms of a house

| | |
|---|---|
| une pièce | une chambre à coucher |
| une salle de séjour | une salle de bains |
| une cuisine | des toilettes *(f. pl.)* |
| une salle à manger | |

### Talking about a home and the neighborhood

| | | | |
|---|---|---|---|
| une maison | un garage | un code | (tout) près de |
| un appartement | une voiture | une cour | loin de |
| un immeuble | un balcon | un(e) voisin(e) | donner sur |
| un quartier | une vue | beau, belle | monter |
| une station de métro | le rez-de-chaussée | nouveau, nouvelle | à pied |
| une terrasse | un étage | vieux, vieille | en ascenseur |
| un jardin | un escalier | premier, première | |
| un arbre | un ascenseur | deuxième | |
| une fleur | une entrée | troisième | |

### Other useful words and expressions

| | |
|---|---|
| une journée | il y a |
| tout le monde | C'est (pas) rigolo. |
| autour de (d') | |

**VIDÉOTOUR**

**Épisode 4**

In this video episode, you will accompany Christine and Madame Séguin on a trip to Giverny. See page 529 for more information.

# Révision

## Conversation

### Un anniversaire

**Sandrine:** Bonjour, Christophe. Ça va?

**Christophe:** Oui, ça va. Et toi?

**Sandrine:** Pas mal. Qu'est-ce que tu as dans ton sac?

**Christophe:** J'ai un cadeau pour ma sœur. C'est son anniversaire aujourd'hui.

**Sandrine:** Ta sœur Mélanie? Elle a quel âge?

**Christophe:** Elle a seize ans. Et Sandrine, tu as ma nouvelle adresse?

**Sandrine:** Ta nouvelle adresse? Tu n'habites pas rue de l'Odéon?

**Christophe:** Non, maintenant on habite dans le 5ᵉ, tout près de la station de métro Maubert-Mutualité.

Le boulevard Haussmann, Paris

La station de métro Maubert-Mutualité

## Vous avez compris?

Répondez. *(Answer.)*

1. Sandrine parle à qui?
2. Qu'est-ce qu'il y a dans son sac?
3. C'est l'anniversaire de qui?
4. C'est quand, son anniversaire?
5. Elle a quel âge?
6. Qui a une nouvelle adresse?
7. Il habite où maintenant?
8. Il habite près de quelle station de métro?

# Structure

## Les verbes au présent

**1.** Review the forms of regular **-er** verbs.

| PARLER | je parle, tu parles, il/elle/on parle, nous parlons, vous parlez, ils/elles parlent |
|---|---|
| AIMER | j'aime, tu aimes, il/elle/on aime, nous aimons, vous aimez, ils/elles aiment |

**2.** Review the irregular verbs you have learned so far.

| ÊTRE | je suis, tu es, il/elle/on est, nous sommes, vous êtes, ils/elles sont |
|---|---|
| AVOIR | j'ai, tu as, il/elle/on a, nous avons, vous avez, ils/elles ont |

**3.** Review the placement of **ne (n')... pas** when expressing a negative idea.

**Je ne travaille pas.**
**Il n'habite pas à Paris.**

**1** **Historiette** **Flore habite à Paris.**
Inventez une histoire. *(Make up a story.)*

1. Flore habite à Paris?
2. Elle quitte la maison à quelle heure le matin?
3. Et toi, tu habites où?
4. Le matin, tu arrives à l'école à quelle heure?
5. Tu parles français ou anglais à l'école?
6. Et Flore, qu'est-ce qu'elle parle?
7. Flore quitte le collège à cinq heures de l'après-midi?
8. Tes copains et toi, vous quittez l'école à quelle heure?
9. Vous travaillez après les cours?
10. Les élèves français travaillent après les cours?

**2** **Historiette** **Une famille**
Complétez. *(Complete.)*

1. Bonjour. Moi, je _____ français. Je
   _____ de Paris. (être)
2. Ma famille n'_____ pas très grande.
   Nous _____ quatre. (être)
3. J'_____ une sœur. (avoir)
4. Ma sœur _____ dix ans et moi, j'_____
   dix-sept ans. (avoir)
5. Et vous, vous _____ quel âge? (avoir)
6. Vous _____ américain(e) ou
   français(e)? (être)

Une famille française avec leur chat

# Les articles et les adjectifs

1. Review the following forms of the indefinite and
   definite articles.

   | | |
   |---|---|
   | **un garçon** | **une fille** |
   | **des copains** | **des<sub>z</sub> écoles** |

   | | | |
   |---|---|---|
   | **le garçon** | **la fille** | **l'ami(e)** |
   | **les copains** | **les<sub>z</sub> écoles** | **les<sub>z</sub> ami(e)s** |

2. Adjectives that end in a consonant have four forms.

   **Le garçon est brun.** **Les garçons sont bruns.**
   **La fille est brune.** **Les filles sont brunes.**

3. Adjectives that end in **e** have only two forms,
   singular and plural.

   **un ami sympathique** **des amis sympathiques**
   **une amie sympathique** **des amies sympathiques**

Deux copains sympathiques à Paris

**3** **Historiette** **La famille de Valentin** Complétez avec **un, une** ou **des.** *(Complete with* un, une, *or* des.*)*

Valentin a une grande famille. Il a __1__ père et __2__ mère. Il a __3__ frères et __4__ sœurs? Oui, il a trois frères et quatre sœurs. Il a aussi sept cousins, mais __5__ seule cousine. Il a __6__ chien, Tifou, et __7__ chat, Pompon.

Valentin et sa famille habitent dans __8__ grande maison à Pontchartrain. Valentin est élève dans __9__ lycée de la région. Valentin est __10__ élève excellent.

**4** **C'est qui?** Complétez avec **le, la, l'** ou **les.**
*(Complete with* le, la, l', *or* les.*)*

1. Guillaume est _____ ami de Loïc.
2. Joanne est _____ sœur de Guillaume.
3. Mais Joanne n'est pas _____ amie de Loïc.
4. Justine et Mélanie sont _____ amies de Joanne et Guillaume.
5. Marc et Jean-Paul aussi sont _____ amis de Joanne et Guillaume.
6. Guillaume est _____ frère de Joanne et Christelle.
7. Christelle est _____ cousine de Loïc.

**5** **Sa sœur aussi** Répondez d'après le modèle.
*(Answer according to the model.)*

—Il est très intelligent.

—Sa sœur aussi est très intelligente.

1. Il est content.
2. Il est amusant.
3. Il est sympathique.
4. Il est énergique.
5. Il est très intéressant.
6. Il est brun.

# Les adjectifs possessifs

**1.** Review the forms of the possessive adjectives. The adjectives
**mon, ton,** and **son** have three forms.

| | | | |
|---|---|---|---|
| mon ₙappartement | ma maison | mes ᵤappartements | mes maisons |
| ton ₙappartement | ta maison | tes ᵤappartements | tes maisons |
| son ₙappartement | sa maison | ses ᵤappartements | ses maisons |

**2.** The adjectives **notre, votre,** and **leur** have two forms—singular
and plural.

| | | | |
|---|---|---|---|
| notre appartement | notre maison | nos ᵤappartements | nos maisons |
| votre appartement | votre maison | vos ᵤappartements | vos maisons |
| leur appartement | leur maison | leurs ᵤappartements | leurs maisons |

**3.** Remember that you use **mon, ton, son** before a feminine singular
noun that begins with a vowel or silent **h: mon**ₙ**adresse,
mon**ₙ**amie.**

La salle à manger de
la maison de Monet
à Giverny

**6  Qui?**  Complétez. *(Complete.)*

Julien a un frère, Paul, et une sœur, Magali. __1__ parents ont donc trois enfants. __2__ trois enfants sont Julien, __3__ frère et __4__ sœur.

—Julien, __5__ frère a quel âge?

—Euh… __6__ frère a quinze ans et __7__ sœur a neuf ans.

—Julien et Paul, comment est __8__ prof de musique?

—Qui? __9__ prof de musique? Il est très sympa. Beaucoup de __10__ profs sont sympas.

École nationale de musique et de danse, Yerres

**7  Un(e) ami(e)**  Work with a classmate. Each of you will tell about a friend. Describe your friend, some things he or she does, and where he or she lives.

**8  Une conversation**  Have a conversation with a classmate. Talk about your school, classes, family, and house.

**LITERARY COMPANION** *You may wish to read the adaptation of* **La petite Fadette,** *a novel by George Sand. You will find this literary selection on page 504.*

1. Champ de coquelicots en Provence
2. Quart de finale de la coupe de l'UEFA à Lens, dans le Nord
3. La cité médiévale de Carcassonne, dans le Languedoc
4. La Promenade des Anglais et l'hôtel Negresco à Nice, sur la Côte d'Azur
5. Fillette musulmane à Marseille
6. L'Hôtel du Palais à Biarritz, au Pays Basque
7. Homme en costume traditionnel de l'Auvergne

6

NATIONAL GEOGRAPHIC

# REFLETS
### de la France

7

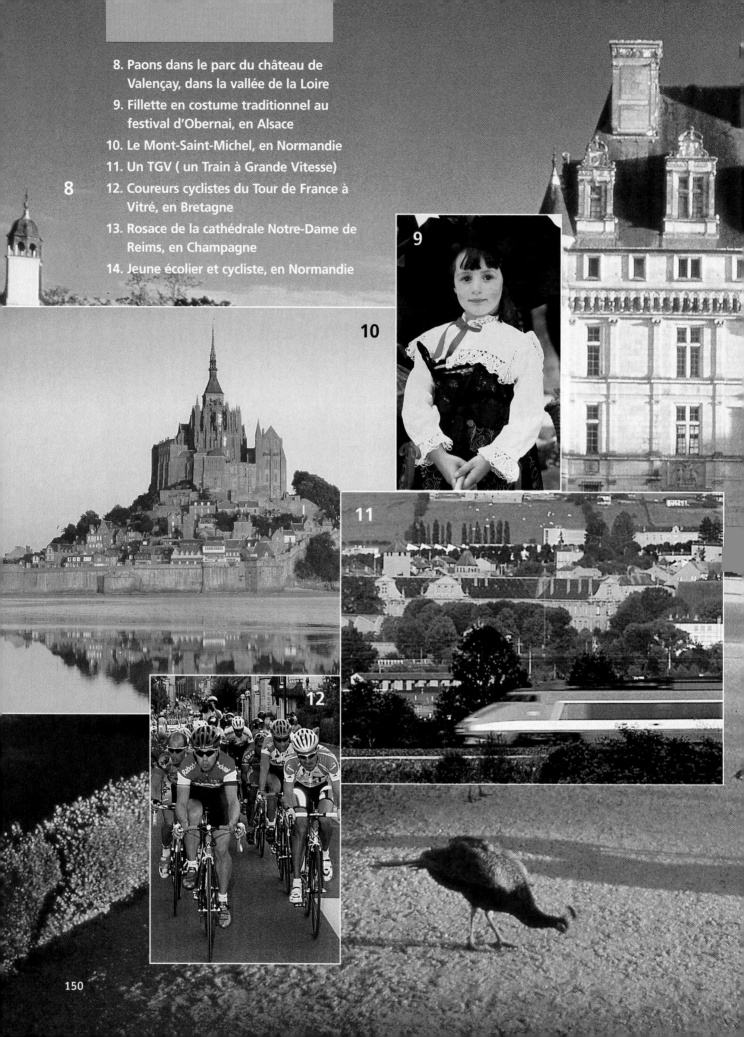

8. Paons dans le parc du château de Valençay, dans la vallée de la Loire

9. Fillette en costume traditionnel au festival d'Obernai, en Alsace

10. Le Mont-Saint-Michel, en Normandie

11. Un TGV ( un Train à Grande Vitesse)

12. Coureurs cyclistes du Tour de France à Vitré, en Bretagne

13. Rosace de la cathédrale Notre-Dame de Reims, en Champagne

14. Jeune écolier et cycliste, en Normandie

# REFLETS
## de la France

**13**

**14**

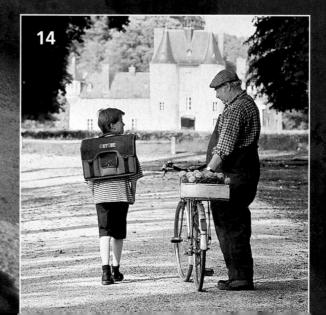

# Au café et au restaurant

## Objectifs

**In this chapter you will learn to:**

- order food or a beverage at a café or restaurant

- tell where you and others go

- tell what you and others are going to do

- give locations

- tell what belongs to you and others

- describe more activities

- compare eating habits in the United States and in the French-speaking world

Vincent Van Gogh *Terrasse du café le soir*

# Vocabulaire

## À la terrasse d'un café 🎧

trouver une table

une serveuse

une table occupée

une table libre

Karim va au café avec Maïa.
Les deux copains y vont ensemble.
Ils trouvent une table libre.

un serveur

la carte

Le serveur arrive.
Il donne la carte à Karim.
Maïa regarde la carte.

Vous désirez?

Un coca, s'il vous plaît.

Et pour moi, une limonade.

Karim prend un coca.
Maïa prend une limonade.
Ils commandent une boisson (une consommation).

J'ai soif. Je voudrais quelque chose à boire.

un citron pressé

un café (un express)

un jus d'orange

un jus de pomme

un crème

des tartines de pain beurré

un croissant

une omelette nature

une omelette aux fines herbes

un sandwich au jambon

un croque-monsieur

un sandwich au fromage

une salade verte

des frites

une soupe à l'oignon

une saucisse de Francfort, un hot-dog

J'ai faim. Je voudrais quelque chose à manger.

une crêpe

une glace au chocolat

une glace à la vanille

# Quel est le mot?

**1** **Historiette** **On va au café.**

Répondez d'après les indications.
(*Answer according to the cues.*)

1. Pierre va où? (au café)
2. Il va au café avec qui? (Chantal)
3. Ils vont au café quand? (après les cours)
4. Les deux copains y vont ensemble? (oui)
5. Qu'est-ce qu'ils trouvent?
   (une table libre)
6. Qui arrive? (le serveur)
7. Il donne la carte à qui? (à Chantal)
8. Qu'est-ce que les amis commandent?
   (une boisson)
9. Chantal prend une limonade? (oui)
10. Qu'est-ce que Pierre prend? (un coca)

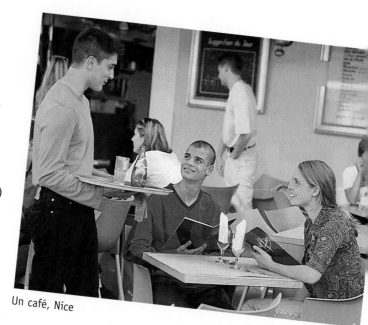
Un café, Nice

**2** **Tu as faim ou soif?** Suivez les modèles.
(*Follow the models.*)

une salade →
**Moi, j'ai faim. Je voudrais quelque chose à manger.**

un coca →
**Moi, j'ai soif. Je voudrais quelque chose à boire.**

1. un citron pressé
2. un petit crème
3. une omelette nature
4. une limonade
5. une glace à la vanille
6. un jus d'orange
7. un croque-monsieur
8. une crêpe

**3** **Historiette** **Un beau café**

Répondez d'après le dessin.
(*Answer according to the illustration.*)

1. C'est la terrasse d'un café ou l'intérieur
   d'un café?
2. Il y a beaucoup de tables occupées?
3. Il y a une table libre?
4. Qui travaille dans le café?
5. Magali a soif. Qu'est-ce qu'elle commande?
6. Rémi a faim. Qu'est-ce qu'il commande?

**4** **À la terrasse d'un café** Suivez le modèle.
*(Follow the model.)*

**Client:** Monsieur, s'il vous plaît!
**Serveur:** Oui, vous désirez?
**Client:** Une glace au chocolat, s'il vous plaît.

1.
2.
3.
4.

5.
6.
7.

**5** **J'aime ça.** Work with a classmate. Tell what snack foods and beverages you like or don't like.

**6** **Au café** Work in small groups. You're in a café in Honfleur, in Normandy. One of you will be the server. Have a conversation from the time you enter the café until you leave. You will get a table, order, and talk about your friends, family, and school. The waiter will have to interrupt once in a while.

Honfleur, Normandie

**7** **Jeu** **Devinette** French people often tell you: **J'ai une faim de loup!** Can you guess whether it means they are very hungry or not? You also hear: **Elle mange comme un oiseau.** Can you guess whether it means she eats a lot or very little? Are there similar expressions in English? What are they?

*For more practice using words from **Mots 1**, do Activity 13 on page H14 at the end of this book.*

# Vocabulaire

## Mots 2

## Le couvert 🎧

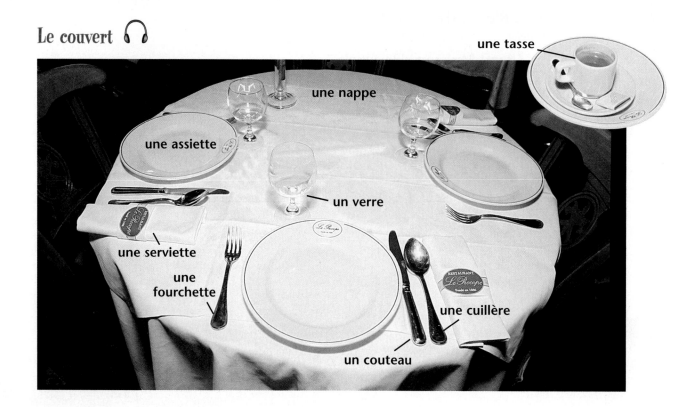

une tasse

une nappe

une assiette

un verre

une serviette

une fourchette

une cuillère

un couteau

## Au restaurant 🎧

Alexandre va au restaurant.
Il ne va pas au restaurant tout seul.
Il y va avec des copains.
Ils n'y vont pas en voiture.
Ils ne prennent pas le bus.
Ils y vont à pied.

Vous aimez votre steak comment?

À point, s'il vous plaît.

Monsieur, s'il vous plaît! Je n'ai pas de serviette.

Alexandre prend un steak frites.

saignant

à point

bien cuit

Alexandre n'invite pas ses copains.
Chacun paie pour soi.

**un pourboire**

**de l'argent**

Le service est compris.
Mais Alexandre laisse tout de même un petit pourboire.
Il laisse un peu d'argent pour le serveur.

**Note** 🎧
Here are some common time expressions. They range from "always" to "very seldom."

Au café…
Il y va toujours.
Il y va souvent.
Il y va quelquefois.
Il y va très peu.

## Les trois repas de la journée 🎧

| le petit déjeuner | le déjeuner | le dîner |

On prend le petit déjeuner
le matin.

On déjeune entre midi
et deux heures.

On dîne le soir.

# Quel est le mot?

**8 Historiette** **Au restaurant** Inventez une histoire. (*Make up a story.*)

1. Laurène va au restaurant?
2. Elle prend le bus pour aller au restaurant?
3. Elle a faim?
4. Elle regarde la carte?
5. Elle commande un steak frites?
6. Elle aime son steak comment?
7. Pour le dessert, elle prend une glace? À quel parfum? Au chocolat ou à la vanille?
8. Après le déjeuner, Laurène demande l'addition?
9. Le service est compris ou pas?
10. Laurène laisse un pourboire pour le serveur?
11. Elle laisse un peu d'argent ou beaucoup d'argent?

Laurène regarde la carte.

Un serveur

**9 Historiette** **Un dîner au resto** Choisissez. (*Choose.*)

1. Loïc ne va pas au restaurant _____. Il y va avec des copains.
   **a.** ensemble  **b.** au cinquième  **c.** tout seul
2. Ils n'y vont pas en voiture. Ils ne prennent pas le métro. Ils y vont _____.
   **a.** ensemble  **b.** à pied  **c.** après les cours
3. Loïc _____ un steak frites.
   **a.** prend  **b.** laisse  **c.** prépare
4. Après le dîner, Loïc demande _____.
   **a.** la carte  **b.** le pourboire  **c.** l'addition
5. Dans les restaurants en France, le service est _____.
   **a.** occupé  **b.** compris  **c.** libre
6. Le service est excellent et Loïc _____ un pourboire.
   **a.** laisse  **b.** prend  **c.** commande
7. Mais Loïc n'invite pas ses copains. _____ paie pour soi.
   **a.** L'addition  **b.** Chacun  **c.** Le serveur

**Madame, s'il vous plaît!** Demandez à la serveuse.
*(Tell the waitress what you need.)*

**Une serviette, s'il vous plaît, madame!**

1.    2.    3.    4.    5.

 **Les repas** Vrai ou faux? *(True or false?)*

1. On dîne le matin.
2. En France, on déjeune entre midi et deux heures.
3. On prend une tartine et un grand crème pour le dîner.
4. On prend un croque-monsieur pour le déjeuner.
5. On prend une soupe à l'oignon pour le dessert.
6. Une fourchette, c'est pour la soupe.
7. Une assiette, c'est pour le café.
8. Une nappe, c'est pour la soupe.

 **Au restaurant** Work with a classmate. Take turns asking each other questions about the illustration. Answer each other's questions.

 **Qu'est-ce que tu manges?** With a classmate, take turns finding out what each of you eats for breakfast and lunch.

*For more practice using words from Mots 2, do Activity 14 on page H15 at the end of this book.*

# Structure

## Le verbe aller au présent
### Telling and finding out where people go

**1.** The verb **aller** *(to go)* is an irregular verb. Study the following forms.

| ALLER | |
|---|---|
| je vais | nous_z_allons |
| tu vas | vous_z_allez |
| il/elle/on va | ils/elles vont |

> **Je vais au café, mais mes parents vont au restaurant.**
> **Tu vas au restaurant avec des copains?**
> **Vous y allez en bus?**

**Savez-vous que... ?**

The expression **On y va!** means "Let's get going." As a question, it means "Should we go?"

**2.** If you do not mention the place you are going to, you must put the word **y** before the verb **aller. Y** refers to a place already mentioned. **Aller** cannot stand alone.

> **Tu vas au café?**
> **Oui, j'y vais et Laurent y va aussi.**

**3.** As you already know, the verb **aller** is also used to express how you feel.

| | |
|---|---|
| **Ça va?** | **Oui, ça va bien, merci.** |
| **Comment tu vas?** | **Très bien, merci. Et toi?** |
| **Vous allez bien?** | **Oui, je vais bien, merci. Et vous?** |

Café de Flore, Paris

# Comment dit-on?

**14** **Au restaurant!** Répétez la conversation avec un copain ou une copine.
*(Repeat the conversation with a classmate.)*

**15** **On va au Flore.** Complétez d'après la conversation.
*(Complete according to the conversation.)*

1. Marie _____ bien.
2. Où _____ Paul?
3. Il _____ au Café de Flore.
4. Il n'y _____ pas tout seul.
5. Son amie Marie y _____ aussi.
6. Les deux copains y _____ ensemble.
7. Ils n'y _____ pas en voiture.
8. Ils y _____ à pied.

**16** **Historiette** **Oui, j'y vais.** Donnez des réponses personnelles.
*(Give your own answers.)*

1. Tu vas souvent ou très peu au restaurant?
2. Tu y vas seul(e) ou avec ta famille?
3. Tu vas quelquefois dans un restaurant chinois ou italien?
4. Tu vas toujours dans le même restaurant?
5. Tu vas quelquefois au restaurant avec des copains?

**17** **Historiette** **À l'école** Donnez des réponses personnelles.
*(Give your own answers.)*

1. Tes copains et toi, vous allez à l'école?
2. Vous allez à quelle école?
3. Vous allez à l'école à quelle heure?
4. Vous y allez comment—à pied, en car scolaire ou en voiture?
5. Après les cours, vous allez au café?

Honfleur, Normandie

**18** **On dîne au restaurant.** Complétez la conversation. *(Complete the conversation.)*

**Anne:** Ce soir, je dîne au restaurant.
**Jean:** Ah oui? Où est-ce que tu __1__?
**Anne:** Au Vieux Honfleur.
**Jean:** Excellente idée! On y __2__ ensemble.
**Anne:** Mais, euh… je n'y __3__ pas toute seule.
**Jean:** Ah bon, tu y __4__ avec qui?
**Anne:** Euh… avec Olivier.
**Jean:** Vous y __5__ à quelle heure?
**Anne:** Mais tu es bien indiscret!

# **A**ller + infinitif
## Telling what's going to happen

**1.** You use **aller** + an infinitive to express what is going to take place in the near future.

> **Demain on va avoir un examen.**
> **Les élèves vont étudier.**
> **Je vais passer l'examen.**
> **L'examen va être difficile, c'est sûr!**

**2.** To make a sentence negative, you put **ne… pas** around the conjugated form of **aller.**

> **Tu ne vas pas aller au café?**
> **Moi, je ne vais pas regarder la télé.**

# **C**omment dit-on?

**19** **Ce soir!** Donnez des réponses personnelles. *(Give your own answers.)*

1. Ce soir, tu vas regarder la télé?
2. Tu vas téléphoner à un copain ou une copine?
3. Tu vas préparer le dîner?
4. Tu vas aller en classe?
5. Tu vas inviter tes professeurs au restaurant?

**20** **Absurdités** Mettez à la forme négative.
*(Make the sentences negative.)*

1. Nous allons en classe pendant le week-end.
2. Les chiens et les chats vont à l'école.
3. Demain le prof de maths va parler français.
4. Vous allez déjeuner pendant le cours de géographie.
5. Ce soir, je vais parler au téléphone avec Elvis Presley.

**21** **Quand?** Work with a classmate. Tell each other some things you like to do. Then tell when you are going to do them—**ce soir, demain, demain matin, la semaine prochaine.**

# Les contractions avec à et de
## Expressing direction and possession

1. The preposition **à** can mean "to," "in," or "at." **À** is contracted with **le** and **les** to form one word—**au, aux.** Note that liaison occurs when **aux** is followed by a vowel.

| | | |
|---|---|---|
| à + le | = au | Je vais au lycée. |
| à + les | = aux | Le prof parle aux‿élèves. |
| à + la | = à la | Tu vas à la cantine? |
| à + l' | = à l' | Vous allez à l'école à pied? |

*Savez-vous que... ?*

**À** is used in many food expressions.

une soupe à l'oignon
une omelette aux fines herbes

2. The preposition **de** can mean "of," "from," or "about." **De** contracts with **le** and **les** to form one word—**du, des.** Liaison occurs when **des** is followed by a vowel.

| | | |
|---|---|---|
| de + le | = du | Il y a une belle vue du balcon. |
| de + les | = des | On parle toujours des‿amis. |
| de + la | = de la | Il arrive de la cantine. |
| de + l' | = de l' | Je rentre de l'école. |

3. The preposition **de** also indicates possession or ownership.

> **Le lycée de Vincent est à Paris.**
> **C'est la voiture du professeur de Vincent.**
> **Minou est le chat des voisins de Vincent.**

# Comment dit-on?

**22** **Tu vas où?** Donnez des réponses personnelles. *(Give your own answers.)*

1. Quel est le nom de ton école?
2. Tu vas à l'école à quelle heure?
3. Tu vas au cours de français le matin ou l'après-midi?
4. Tu vas au cours d'anglais à quelle heure?
5. Tu aimes parler aux profs?
6. Tu aimes parler des profs aussi?
7. Tu habites près de l'école ou loin de l'école?
8. Tu rentres de l'école à quelle heure?
9. Comment est-ce que tu rentres de l'école?

**23** **Historiette** **Je n'y vais pas.** Complétez avec **à**. *(Complete with à.)*

Ce soir, je ne vais pas __1__ (le concert). Je ne vais pas __2__ (le parc). Je ne vais pas __3__ (le collège). Je ne vais pas __4__ (le restaurant). Je ne vais pas parler __5__ (les copains). Je ne vais pas __6__ (l'anniversaire) de Julie. Je vais aller où, alors? Je vais rentrer __7__ (la maison). Pourquoi? Je suis fatigué(e)!

**24** **Au café** Suivez le modèle. *(Follow the model.)*

**une tarte aux fruits / une tarte aux pommes** →
—Qu'est-ce que tu vas prendre?
—Je vais prendre une tarte.
—Une tarte aux fruits ou une tarte aux pommes?
—Oh, je vais prendre une tarte ____.

1. un sandwich au jambon / un sandwich au fromage
2. une omelette au fromage / une omelette aux fines herbes
3. une soupe à la tomate / une soupe à l'oignon
4. une glace au chocolat / une glace à la vanille
5. une crêpe au chocolat / une crêpe aux fruits

**25** **Le dîner des copains** Combinez d'après le modèle. *(Combine according to the model.)*

**c'est la voiture / les parents de Vincent** →
**C'est la voiture des parents de Vincent.**

1. je vais à la table / les amis de Marc
2. ils sont à la terrasse / le café
3. nous regardons la carte / le restaurant
4. c'est le coca / l'amie de Marc
5. voilà le pourboire / la serveuse

Cellia Saubry *Coin de rue*

# Le verbe prendre au présent
## Describing more activities

**1.** The verb **prendre**, "to take," also means "to have" when used with foods. It is an irregular verb. Pay particular attention to both its spelling and pronunciation.

| PRENDRE | | | |
|---|---|---|---|
| je | prends | nous | prenons |
| tu | prends | vous | prenez |
| il/elle/on | prend | ils/elles | prennent |

**Je prends le car scolaire pour aller à l'école.**
**Les voisins ne prennent pas l'ascenseur.**
**Je vais prendre un coca.**

**2.** The verbs **apprendre** *(to learn)* and **comprendre** *(to understand)* are conjugated the same way as **prendre**.

**On apprend beaucoup à l'école.**
**Vous comprenez le français, n'est-ce pas?**

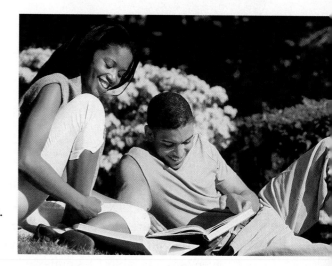

Les deux amis apprennent l'anglais.

# Comment dit-on?

**26** **Historiette** **Alexandre** Inventez une histoire.
*(Make up a story.)*

**1.** Alexandre prend le car scolaire pour aller à l'école?
**2.** En classe, il prend des notes quand le professeur parle?
**3.** Il comprend bien le français?
**4.** Il apprend beaucoup de choses au cours de français?

**27** **À l'école** Donnez des réponses personnelles. *(Give your own answers.)*

1. Tu prends ton petit déjeuner à la maison ou à la cafétéria de l'école?
2. À l'école, tu prends l'escalier ou l'ascenseur pour monter au premier étage?
3. À la cafétéria de l'école, qu'est-ce que tu prends quand tu as soif?
4. Qu'est-ce que tu prends quand tu as faim?

Ils prennent leur petit déjeuner.

**28**  **Toujours à l'école** Répondez. *(Answer.)*

1. La majorité des élèves prennent le car scolaire pour aller à l'école?
2. Les élèves prennent l'escalier ou l'ascenseur pour monter au premier étage?
3. En cours de français, tout le monde comprend bien quand le professeur parle?
4. Vous apprenez beaucoup de choses en cours de français?

**29**  **Au pluriel!** Mettez au pluriel. *(Make the sentences plural.)*

1. Je prends le car scolaire pour aller à l'école.
2. Je prends l'ascenseur pour monter au quatrième étage.
3. Tu prends le bus, le métro ou la voiture?
4. Tu prends beaucoup de notes en classe?
5. L'élève est très intelligent et il apprend beaucoup de choses.
6. Elle comprend bien la leçon.
7. Son copain prend un coca au café.
8. Et moi, je prends une glace au chocolat.

*For more practice using the verbs **aller** and **prendre**, do Activity 15 on page H16 at the end of this book.*

Vous êtes sur le bon chemin. Allez-y!

# Conversation

## Au restaurant

**Claire:** Tu as faim?

**Loïc:** Oui. J'ai hyper faim! Je vais prendre un bon steak frites.

**Serveur:** Vous désirez?

**Loïc:** Un steak frites, s'il vous plaît. Saignant.

**Serveur:** Et pour vous, mademoiselle?

**Claire:** Ben, un steak aussi, mais pas de frites. Une salade verte.

**Serveur:** Et vous aimez votre steak comment?

**Claire:** À point, s'il vous plaît.
*(Après le dîner)*

**Loïc:** L'addition, s'il vous plaît!

**Serveur:** Oui, monsieur, j'arrive!

**Claire:** On laisse quelque chose? Il est sympa, le serveur.

**Loïc:** Oh, écoute, le service est compris.

## Vous avez compris?

Répondez. *(Answer.)*

1. Où sont Claire et Loïc?
2. Loïc a faim?
3. Qu'est-ce qu'il va prendre?
4. Et Claire, qu'est-ce qu'elle va prendre?
5. Qu'est-ce qu'elle commande avec le steak?
6. Claire et Loïc prennent leur steak comment?
7. Après le dîner, qui demande l'addition?
8. À votre avis *(In your opinion)*, est-ce qu'ils vont laisser un pourboire?

# Parlons un peu plus

**On commande?** You and your friend are at a restaurant. Look at the menu and try to decide what to order. Then order. Another one of your classmates will be the server.

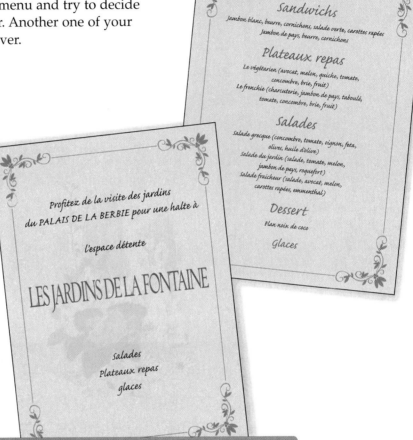

*sandwichs*

Jambon blanc, beurre, cornichons, salade verte, carottes rapées
Jambon de pays, beurre, cornichons

*Plateaux repas*

Le végétarien (avocat, melon, quiche, tomate, concombre, brie, fruit)
Le frenchie (charcuterie, jambon de pays, taboulé, tomate, concombre, brie, fruit)

*salades*

salade grecque (concombre, tomate, oignon, feta, olives, huile d'olive)
salade du jardin (salade, tomate, melon, jambon de pays, roquefort)
salade fraîcheur (salade, avocat, melon, carottes rapées, emmenthal)

*Dessert*

Flan noix de coco

*Glaces*

Profitez de la visite des jardins
du PALAIS DE LA BERBIE pour une halte à

l'espace détente

LES JARDINS DE LA FONTAINE

salades
Plateaux repas
glaces

## Prononciation

### Le son /**r**/ 🎧

The French sound /**r**/ is very different from the American /r/. When you say /**r**/, the back of your tongue should almost completely block the air going through the back of your throat. Repeat the following words and sentences.

| | | | |
|---|---|---|---|
| le verre | toujours | la voiture | le pourboire |
| la carte | la tartine | la cuillère | la fourchette |
| pour | les crêpes | le serveur | le croque-monsieur |
| boire | les frites | le croissant | |

Le serveur arrive avec un verre de jus d'orange.
Je voudrais laisser un pourboire pour la serveuse.

**verre**

# Lectures culturelles

## Au restaurant? Vraiment?

Ce soir, Valentin va dîner dans un petit restaurant du coin[1]. Il invite ses deux amis Ahmed et Julie. Ils vont aller tous ensemble au restaurant.

Les copains arrivent au restaurant. Ils trouvent une table libre et ils prennent leur place. Tango prend sa place aussi, sous[2] la table. Sous la table? Oui. Mais qui est Tango? C'est le chien de Julie. Il est très bien élevé[3], Tango. Julie ne laisse pas Tango seul à la maison. Tango accompagne Julie partout, même au restaurant. Pourquoi pas? Un chien bien élevé est toujours le bienvenu[4]!

[1] du coin *local*
[2] sous *under*
[3] bien élevé *well-behaved*
[4] le bienvenu *welcome*

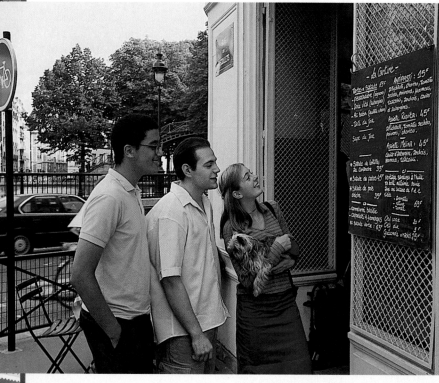

Haïti

La Martinique

Le serveur arrive. Les amis regardent la carte et ils commandent. Après le dîner, Valentin demande l'addition. Le serveur arrive et donne l'addition à Valentin. Valentin regarde l'addition et paie. D'habitude chacun paie pour soi, mais aujourd'hui, c'est exceptionnel. Valentin paie pour tout le monde parce qu'il invite ses copains. En France, «inviter», c'est «payer»!

## Vous avez compris?

**A Valentin va au restaurant?** Vrai ou faux? *(True or false?)*

1. Valentin va au restaurant tout seul.
2. Les copains entrent dans le restaurant et demandent une table au serveur.
3. Tango est un chien bien élevé.
4. Tango aussi va au restaurant.
5. Ahmed et Julie demandent l'addition.
6. Les trois amis paient l'addition.

**B Des différences culturelles** In this reading, there are some interesting cultural differences between France and the United States. What are they?

# Les repas en France

La façon de manger en France change assez vite[1]. Pour le petit déjeuner, ça ne change pas vraiment; on prend toujours le petit déjeuner à la maison. C'est toujours un petit déjeuner rapide et frugal: une tartine de pain beurré et un bol de café, de thé ou de chocolat. Quelquefois, les enfants mangent des céréales.

On déjeune entre midi et deux heures. Mais le déjeuner n'est plus[2] le repas principal parce que les enfants déjeunent à la cantine de l'école. Les parents déjeunent à la cafétéria de leur entreprise[3] ou dans un restaurant près de l'entreprise.

Le dîner est maintenant le repas principal pour beaucoup de Français. Un des parents (ou les deux) prépare le dîner dans la cuisine et la famille dîne ensemble. Souvent on mange des produits surgelés[4]. En France, il y a des plats surgelés excellents. Le dîner est un moment important pour la famille; c'est le seul moment de la journée où on est ensemble.

[1] vite *fast*
[2] n'est plus *is no longer*
[3] entreprise *firm*
[4] surgelés *frozen*

Un restaurant aux Champs-Élysées

## Vous avez compris?

**Les repas** Répondez. *(Answer.)*
1. En France, comment est le petit déjeuner?
2. Qu'est-ce qu'on prend pour le petit déjeuner?
3. On déjeune à quelle heure?
4. On déjeune où?
5. Quel est le repas principal?
6. Qu'est-ce qu'on prépare souvent pour le dîner?
7. Le dîner est un moment important pour la famille? Pourquoi?

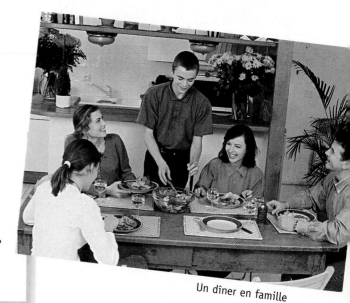

Un dîner en famille

# Les goûts changent.

Beaucoup de Français sont de vrais gourmets. Ils aiment manger bien. La cuisine française est excellente. Elle est célèbre dans le monde entier. Les Français continuent à apprécier leur cuisine mais ils apprécient aussi les plats d'autres pays[1]. La cuisine asiatique est très populaire: la cuisine chinoise, la cuisine thaïlandaise et aussi la cuisine vietnamienne. En France, il y a beaucoup de restaurants vietnamiens. La cuisine vietnamienne ressemble un peu à la cuisine chinoise. Il y a aussi beaucoup de restaurants algériens, tunisiens et marocains où la spécialité est toujours le couscous.

Comme aux États-Unis, il existe en France des chaînes de restaurants et des chaînes de fast-food. Certaines sont américaines, d'autres sont européennes. Elles sont françaises ou belges, par exemple, comme *Léon de Bruxelles.* Sa spécialité: les moules[2] frites, c'est-à-dire[3] des moules avec toutes sortes de sauces et des frites. C'est un plat traditionnel en Belgique.

Et la pizza? La pizza est très appréciée en France! Tout le monde aime la pizza!

Au restaurant *Léon de Bruxelles*

[1] pays *countries*
[2] moules *mussels*
[3] c'est-à-dire *that is to say*

> **Les aliments préférés des jeunes de 7 à 14 ans sont:**
> le steak frites (51%), les hamburgers (51%), la pizza (49%), les gâteaux (37%), les spaghettis ou raviolis (32%), les sandwichs (17%).
> 71% des Français indiquent qu'ils préfèrent la cuisine française aux cuisines étrangères.

## Vous avez compris?

**Au restaurant en France** Vrai ou faux? *(True or false?)*
1. Les Français aiment manger bien.
2. Les Français n'apprécient pas leur cuisine.
3. La cuisine asiatique est très populaire en France.
4. Les restaurants asiatiques en France sont toujours des restaurants chinois.
5. Le couscous est une spécialité vietnamienne.
6. *Léon de Bruxelles* est une chaîne de restaurants belge en France.
7. Les Français n'aiment pas du tout la pizza.

# CONNEXIONS

## Les mathématiques

### L'arithmétique

When we go shopping or out to eat, it is often necessary to do some arithmetic. We either have to add up the bill ourselves or check the figures someone else has done for us. In a café or restaurant we may want to figure out what we should leave for a tip, even if **le service est compris.**

We almost never do arithmetic in a foreign language. We normally do arithmetic in the language in which we learned it. However, it is fun to know some basic arithmetical terms in case we have to discuss a problem concerning a bill, for example, with a French-speaking person.

Before we learn some of these arithmetical terms in French, let's look at some differences in numbers. Note how the numbers 1 and 7 are written in French.

Note also that the thousands are indicated by a space or a period and the decimals are indicated by a comma.

```
1 000   2 000   3 000   4 000
1.000   2.000   3.000   4.000
            210,75
```

```
1   7
```

---

### L'arithmétique

| additionner | + | soustraire | − |
|---|---|---|---|
| multiplier | × | diviser | ÷ |

Pour additionner:
  Deux plus deux, ça fait quatre.
  $2 + 2 = 4$
Pour soustraire:
  Quatre moins deux, ça fait deux.
  $4 - 2 = 2$
Pour multiplier:
  Deux fois deux, ça fait quatre.
  $2 \times 2 = 4$
Pour diviser:
  Quatre divisé par deux, ça fait deux.
  $4 \div 2 = 2$
Dix pour cent (%) de 200 euros, c'est 20 euros.

---

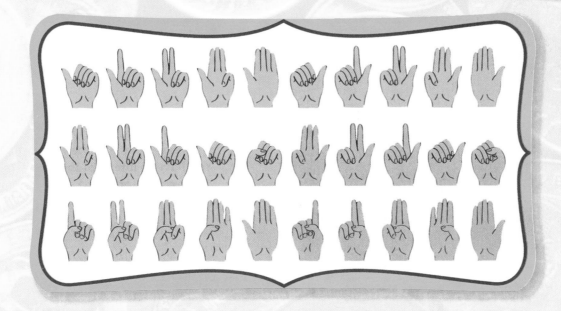

## Vous avez compris?

**A** **Ça fait combien?** Faites les opérations suivantes à voix haute. *(Solve the following problems aloud.)*

1. $2 + 2 =$
2. $14 + 6 =$
3. $30 - 8 =$
4. $20 - 4 =$

5. $4 \times 4 =$
6. $8 \times 3 =$
7. $27 \div 9 =$
8. $80 \div 10 =$

**B** **L'addition, s'il vous plaît!** You went out to a restaurant with three friends. This is your bill. Do the following.

1. Add up to see if the total is correct.
2. Add 10 percent, even though the tip is included.
3. Calculate how much each of you owes.

**C** **Comment compter sur ses doigts** Here are three different ways people count on their fingers. Which one is yours? With a classmate, choose a way that is not yours and show each other numbers. Take turns figuring out which number it is.

```
LE BAR À HUÎTRES
112, Bd du Montparnasse
75014 PARIS
TEL: 01 . 43 . 20 . 71 . 01

        6 Thomas

Tbl 16/1      Fct 9919        Cts 5
        25 Jul   20:19
        *** Réimprimée ***

3 Salade de Thon            25.00
1 M. FRAICH                 19.00
3 Terrine Volaille          23.00
3 SOLE MEUNIÈRE             78.00
1 Tout café                  3.00
1 Café Colombie              2.00
1 Café Crème                 3.00

    T. V. A.  19.6%
    Service  15%
      Total du   153.00


Toute l'équipe
Bar À Huîtres Montparnasse
vous remercie de votre visite.
À BIENTÔT
```

# C'est à vous

## Use what you have learned

**1** **Au café**

✔ *Order something to eat or drink in a café*

Work with a classmate. One of you is the customer and the other is the server. You order from the menu provided.

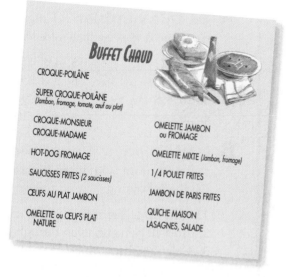

**BUFFET CHAUD**

CROQUE-POILÂNE

SUPER CROQUE-POILÂNE
*(Jambon, fromage, tomate, œuf au plat)*

CROQUE-MONSIEUR
CROQUE-MADAME

HOT-DOG FROMAGE

SAUCISSES FRITES *(2 saucisses)*

ŒUFS AU PLAT JAMBON

OMELETTE ou ŒUFS PLAT NATURE

OMELETTE JAMBON ou FROMAGE

OMELETTE MIXTE *(Jambon, fromage)*

1/4 POULET FRITES

JAMBON DE PARIS FRITES

QUICHE MAISON
LASAGNES, SALADE

PARLER
ÉCRIRE

**2** **À la terrasse des Deux Magots**

✔ *Talk about school and teachers as you order food and drinks*

Work in groups of three or four. You're all friends sitting on the **terrasse** of the famous café **Les Deux Magots** in Paris, watching the world go by. You talk about many things—school, teachers, friends, etc. One of you will play the role of the waiter. You have to interrupt the conversation once in a while to take the orders and serve.

## 3 La carte
✔ *Plan a menu*

Write a menu in French for your school cafeteria.

Élodie prend le déjeuner
à la cantine.

### Writing Strategy

**Visualizing** Many writers have a mental picture of what they want to write before they actually begin to write. The mental picture helps organize what they want to say. It also helps them visualize what they want to describe in their writing. Closing your eyes and visualizing what you want to write can make the writing experience more pleasant. When writing in a foreign language, you also have to restrict your mental picture to what you know how to say.

## 4 Un restaurant

You have been asked to write a short article about a visit to a restaurant. Look at this illustration. Pretend this is the mental picture you have of the restaurant you are going to write about. Look at it for several minutes and then write a paragraph about it.

# Assessment

## Vocabulaire

**1 Choisissez.** *(Choose.)*

To review **Mots 1,**
turn to pages
154–155.

**1.** Après les cours, Michel et Chantal vont au _____.
   **a.** café                     **b.** ensemble

**2.** Ils trouvent _____ à la terrasse.
   **a.** une table libre       **b.** une tartine

**3.** Le serveur _____ la carte à Chantal.
   **a.** regarde               **b.** donne

**4.** Chantal a soif. Elle commande quelque chose à _____.
   **a.** manger               **b.** boire

**5.** Michel a faim. Il prend _____.
   **a.** un jus d'orange       **b.** une tartine de pain beurré

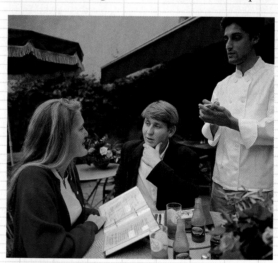

Deux amis au café

**2 Choisissez.** *(Choose.)*

To review **Mots 2,**
turn to pages
158–159.

**6.** À midi, Henri va _____ au restaurant.
   **a.** dîner        **b.** déjeuner        **c.** payer

**7.** Il _____ le métro.
   **a.** prend        **b.** commande      **c.** laisse

**8.** Henri aime son steak _____.
   **a.** à pied        **b.** à point        **c.** ensemble

**9.** Après le déjeuner, Henri _____ l'addition.
   **a.** demande     **b.** invite       **c.** laisse

**10.** Dans les restaurants en France _____ est compris.
   **a.** le verre      **b.** l'addition     **c.** le service

# Structure

**3 Complétez avec «aller».**
*(Complete with the verb aller.)*

11. Nous _____ à l'école en voiture?
12. Laurent, tu _____ au café?
13. Vous _____ bien, madame?

Au centre de Paris, près de l'Opéra
Angle 14, rue Favart - 9, rue d'Amboise
75002 - Paris - France
Tél : 01 42 96 36 89 - Fax : 01 47 03 97 31
Métro - Richelieu-Drouot

To review the verb **aller**, turn to page 162.

**4 Choisissez.** *(Choose.)*

14. Je vais _____ au café avec mes copains.
    **a.** déjeune    **b.** déjeuner
15. Ils vont _____ un pourboire pour le serveur.
    **a.** laisser    **b.** laissent

To review the use of **aller** + an infinitive, turn to page 165.

**5 Complétez avec «à» ou «de».**
*(Complete with à or de.)*

16. Les amis vont _____ café.
17. Vincent rentre _____ école à cinq heures.
18. C'est la voiture _____ père de Marie.
19. Le prof donne un examen _____ élèves.

To review the forms of à and **de**, turn to page 166.

**6 Complétez avec «prendre».**
*(Complete with the verb prendre.)*

20. Les copains _____ le métro.
21. Vous _____ le petit déjeuner à la maison?
22. Pour monter à l'appartement, on _____ l'ascenseur.
23. Tu _____ un sandwich à midi?

To review the verb **prendre**, turn to page 168.

# Culture

**7 Complétez.** *(Complete.)*

24. Les copains _____ une table libre au restaurant.
25. Claire paie pour tout le monde. Elle _____ ses copains.

To review this cultural information, turn to pages 172–173.

# On parle super bien!

Tell all you can about this illustration.

# Vocabulaire

## Getting along in a café or restaurant

| | | | |
|---|---|---|---|
| un café | la carte | inviter | avoir soif |
| la terrasse d'un café | l'addition (f.) | payer | Vous désirez? |
| une table | l'argent (m.) | laisser | je voudrais |
|   occupée | le pourboire | prendre | quelque chose |
|   libre | aller | déjeuner |   à manger |
| un serveur | trouver une table | dîner |   à boire |
| une serveuse | commander | avoir faim | Le service est compris. |

## Identifying snacks and beverages

| | | | |
|---|---|---|---|
| une boisson | un jus d'orange | un steak | une saucisse de |
| une consommation | une tartine de pain |   saignant |   Francfort, un |
| un coca |   beurré |   à point |   hot-dog |
| une limonade | un croissant |   bien cuit | une salade verte |
| un café | un sandwich | des frites (f. pl.) | une glace |
| un express |   au jambon | une soupe à l'oignon | À quel parfum? |
| un crème |   au fromage | une omelette |   au chocolat |
| un citron pressé | un croque-monsieur |   nature |   à la vanille |
| un jus de pomme | |   aux fines herbes | une crêpe |

## Identifying a place setting

| | | |
|---|---|---|
| le couvert | une fourchette | une assiette |
| un verre | un couteau | une nappe |
| une tasse | une cuillère | une serviette |

## Identifying meals

un repas
le petit déjeuner
le déjeuner
le dîner

> **How well do you know your vocabulary?**
> - Choose words for specific foods you enjoy.
> - Create a menu using these words.

## Other useful words and expressions

| | |
|---|---|
| tout(e) seul(e) | quelquefois |
| toujours | peu |
| souvent | |

**VIDÉOTOUR**

**Épisode 5**

In this video episode, you will join Chloé and Christine at a café. See page 530 for more information.

# La nourriture et les courses

RÉPUBLIQUE FRANÇAISE
LA POSTE 1992  3,40
*Pain et Céréales*
CONGRÈS INTERNATIONAL
O. BAILLAIS

## Objectifs

**In this chapter you will learn to:**

✔ *identify more foods*

✔ *shop for food*

✔ *tell what you or others are doing*

✔ *ask for the quantity you want*

✔ *talk about what you or others don't have*

✔ *tell what you or others are able to do or want to do*

✔ *talk about French food-shopping customs*

Paul Cézanne *Nature morte au panier*

# Vocabulaire

## Mots 1

### À la boulangerie-pâtisserie

un gâteau

une tarte aux pommes

du pain

un pain complet

une baguette

un croissant

### À la crémerie

de la crème

du lait

un œuf

du fromage

un yaourt

du beurre

### À la boucherie

un poulet

de la viande

du porc

du bœuf

de l'agneau

### À la poissonnerie

une crevette

un crabe

un poisson

### À la charcuterie

du saucisson

du jambon

### À l'épicerie

de l'huile

du vinaigre

du poivre

du sel

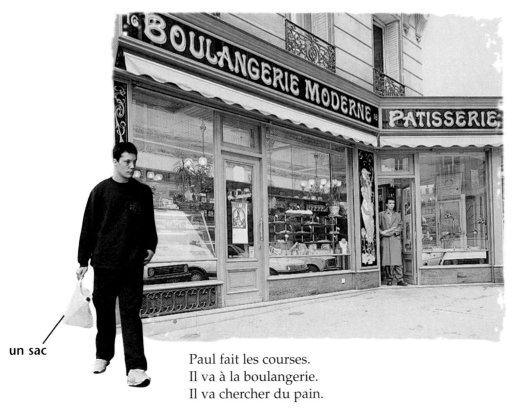

un sac

Paul fait les courses.
Il va à la boulangerie.
Il va chercher du pain.

Je voudrais une baguette, s'il vous plaît.

Ah, je regrette, il n'y a plus de baguettes.

Paul est à la boulangerie.
Il veut acheter une baguette.
Il n'y a plus de baguettes.

Bon, alors un pain complet.

Et avec ça?

C'est tout, merci.

Il ne peut pas acheter de baguette.
Il achète un pain complet.

# Quel est le mot?

**1** **Historiette** **À la crémerie** Inventez une histoire. *(Make up a story.)*

1. Madame Cadet va chercher du beurre. Elle va à la crémerie ou à la boucherie?
2. Elle veut acheter aussi du lait. Elle va à la crémerie?
3. Elle veut des œufs aussi?
4. Elle peut acheter du fromage à la crémerie?
5. Elle va acheter des yaourts pour le dessert?

**2** **Historiette** **On fait les courses.** Répondez d'après les indications. *(Answer according to the cues.)*

1. Qui fait les courses? (Élodie)
2. Elle fait les courses quand? (le samedi matin)
3. Elle a un sac? (oui)
4. Elle va au supermarché? (non)
5. Elle va où? (à la boulangerie)
6. Qu'est-ce qu'elle va acheter à la boulangerie? (du pain)
7. Elle veut une baguette? (oui)
8. Il n'y a plus de baguettes? (non)
9. Alors, qu'est-ce qu'elle achète? (un pain complet)

Une crémerie, Montgeron, France

**3** **À l'épicerie** Complétez d'après la photo. *(Complete according to the photo.)*

On va acheter du ___1___, des ___2___, de la ___3___, du ___4___, de l' ___5___, du ___6___ et du ___7___.

**4** **On va où?** Complétez. *(Complete.)*

1. Pour acheter un poulet, du bœuf, du porc et de l'agneau, on va _____.
2. Pour acheter du lait, on va _____.
3. Pour acheter des croissants et un gâteau, on va _____.
4. Pour acheter de la viande, on va _____.
5. Pour acheter du saucisson et du jambon, on va _____.
6. Pour acheter de la crème et des œufs, on va _____.
7. Pour acheter du poisson et des crevettes, on va _____.
8. Pour acheter des yaourts, on va _____.
9. Pour acheter une tarte aux pommes, on va _____.
10. Pour acheter des crabes, on va _____.

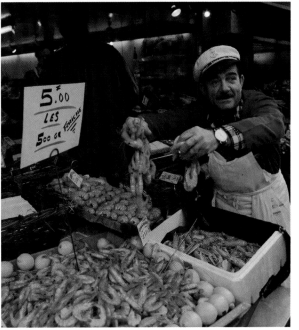

Une poissonnerie, Paris

**5** **Les courses** You're living in Arles with a French family. You offered to do the grocery shopping. Your host gives you this list. Find out from your French brother or sister (your partner) where you go for each item.

des crevettes et des crabes
du saucisson
4 tartes aux pommes
2 baguettes
un poulet
du fromage (du Camembert)
du lait
un gâteau au chocolat

*For more practice using words from* **Mots 1**, *do Activity 16 on page H17 at the end of this book.*

## Mots 2

### Au marché

Il est bon, mon melon!

la marchande

Elle est bonne, ma salade!

une salade

une pomme de terre

des haricots verts

le marchand

une poire

une pomme

des fraises

C'est combien, les carottes?

Un euro le kilo.

Alors, un kilo, s'il vous plaît.

Vous voulez autre chose?

Oui, une livre de tomates et c'est tout.

Alors ça fait deux euros cinquante.

Ariane est au marché.
Elle veut acheter des légumes.
Elle va chez la marchande de fruits et légumes.

un kilo = 1 000 (mille) grammes
une livre = 500 (cinq cents) grammes

Julien et son frère sont au supermarché.
Julien veut acheter de l'eau minérale et du lait.
Il achète une bouteille d'eau minérale et un litre de lait.

*Note* 🎧
Many words for foods in French are cognates.

**un fruit**  **une carotte**
**une banane**  **une tomate**
**une orange**  **un oignon**

**un paquet de légumes surgelés**

**un pot de moutarde**

**un litre de lait**

**250 grammes de beurre**

**une boîte de petits pois**
**une boîte de conserve**

**une tranche de jambon**

**une bouteille d'eau minérale**

**un pot de confiture**

**une douzaine d'œufs**

# Quel est le mot?

**6** **Fruit(s) ou légume(s)?** Identifiez d'après le modèle.
*(Identify according to the model.)*

 **C'est une pomme. C'est un fruit.**

1.   2.   3.   4.

5.   6.   7.   8.

**7** **Historiette** **Mathilde va au marché.** Complétez. *(Complete.)*

Mathilde veut préparer une grande salade. Elle va au marché. Elle va chez la __1__. Elle achète une __2__, des __3__ et des __4__. La marchande demande: «Vous voulez autre chose?» Mathilde répond: «Non, merci, __5__.» Elle donne de l'argent à la __6__.

**8** **Historiette** **Martin va au supermarché.** Complétez. *(Complete.)*

Martin veut acheter de la moutarde, de l'eau minérale, une boîte de petits pois et un paquet de légumes surgelés. Pour acheter tout ça, il va au supermarché. Au supermarché, il prend un chariot. Il achète deux __1__ d'eau minérale, un __2__ de carottes surgelées et trois __3__ de sardines. Et autre chose aussi—un __4__ de moutarde. Martin va à la caisse. Ça __5__ combien, les bouteilles d'eau minérale, le paquet de carottes surgelées, les __6__ de sardines et le __7__ de moutarde? Ça fait onze euros cinquante.

**9**  **C'est combien, s'il vous plaît?** Conversez d'après le modèle.
(*Make up a conversation according to the model.*)

—**C'est combien, la boîte de petits pois?**
—**Un euro quatorze.**

**1.**

**2.**

**3.**

**4.**

**5.**

**6.**

**10**  **Pourquoi pas?** Conversez d'après le modèle.
(*Make up a conversation according to the model.*)

**Tu veux des épinards?** **Des épinards? Non.**

**Pourquoi?** **Parce que je n'aime pas ça.**

1. Tu veux du saucisson?
2. Tu veux des fraises?
3. Tu veux des haricots verts?
4. Tu veux des petits pois?
5. Tu veux de la confiture de fraises?
6. Tu veux du poisson?

**11** **À l'épicerie** You're in a grocery store in Paris. You want to buy the items on the list. Tell the clerk (your partner) how much you want of each item and find out how much it costs.

Carnet

eau minérale
jambon
fraises
œufs
lait
beurre
frites surgelées

**ENCORE PLUS** *For more practice using words from Mots 2, do Activity 17 on page H18 at the end of this book.*

# Structure

## Le verbe faire au présent
### Telling and finding out what people do

**1.** The verb **faire** *(to do, to make)* is an irregular verb. Study the following forms.

| FAIRE | | | |
|---|---|---|---|
| je | fais | nous | faisons |
| tu | fais | vous | faites |
| il/elle/on | fait | ils/elles | font |

**2.** You will use the verb **faire** a great deal in French. **Faire** is used in many expressions that take a different verb in English. Such expressions that cannot be translated directly from one language to another are called "idiomatic expressions." **Faire les courses** *(to go grocery shopping)* and **faire ses devoirs** *(to do homework)* are examples of idiomatic expressions. The following are some others.

> **Maman prépare un bon dîner. Elle aime beaucoup faire la cuisine.**
> **Les copains vont faire un pique-nique.**
> **Moi, je fais de l'allemand et ma sœur fait de l'espagnol.**

## Comment dit-on?

**12**  **On fait les courses.**
Répétez la conversation.
*(Repeat the conversation.)*

**Éric:** Salut, Anne! Ça va?
**Anne:** Ça va. Qu'est-ce que tu fais?
**Éric:** Je fais les courses.
**Anne:** Ben, moi aussi. Je vais au marché de la rue Dejean. On fait nos courses ensemble?
**Éric:** Merci, mais j'ai beaucoup de choses différentes à acheter. Je vais aller au supermarché.
**Anne:** Ben, je vais avec toi. C'est dans la même direction.
**Éric:** D'accord.

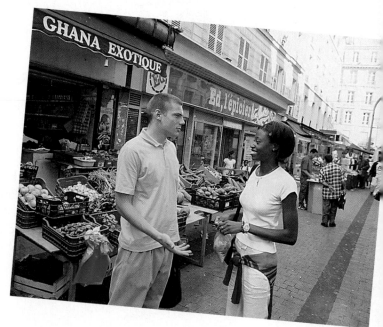

Rue Dejean, Paris

**13** **Qu'est-ce qu'ils font?** Complétez et répondez d'après la conversation. *(Complete and answer according to the conversation.)*

1. Qu'est-ce qu'il ____, Éric?
2. Qu'est-ce qu'elle ____, Anne?
3. Qu'est-ce qu'ils ____, Anne et Éric?
4. Est-ce qu'ils ____ les courses ensemble?

**14** **Et toi?** Donnez des réponses personnelles. *(Give your own answers.)*

1. Tu fais quelquefois la cuisine chez toi?
2. Tu fais tes études dans un lycée français ou dans une école secondaire américaine?
3. Tu fais tes devoirs devant la télévision?
4. Tu fais du français?

**15** **À chacun son travail** Suivez le modèle. *(Follow the model.)*

> Moi, je fais le dîner. Et vous deux, qu'est-ce que vous faites?

> Nous aussi, on fait le dîner.

1. Moi, je fais les courses.
2. Moi, je fais la cuisine.
3. Moi, je fais le déjeuner.
4. Moi, je fais les sandwichs.
5. Moi, je fais le gâteau.

**16** **Historiette** **Mon copain Hugo** Complétez. *(Complete.)*

Hugo et moi, on est copains. Il est très intelligent. Hugo __1__ du russe. Moi aussi, je __2__ du russe. Nous __3__ du russe ensemble. Hugo et moi, nous __4__ quelquefois nos devoirs ensemble.

Hugo et son amie Marie __5__ de l'histoire avec Madame Delcourt. Qu'est-ce qu'ils __6__ au cours d'histoire? Ils apprennent beaucoup de nouvelles choses. Vous __7__ du français, n'est-ce pas? Vous __8__ du français avec qui?

**17** **Nous sommes gentils.** Get together with a classmate. Discuss the things you do to help around the house. Decide who is the most helpful.

*For more practice using the verb **faire**, do Activity 18 on page H19 at the end of this book.*

# Le partitif et l'article défini
## Talking about all or some

1. In French, you use the definite article **(le, la, l', les)** when talking about something in a general sense.

|  |  |
|---|---|
| **Les enfants aiment le lait.** | *Children like milk.* |
| **Je déteste les œufs.** | *I hate eggs.* |
| **Je n'aime pas la salade.** | *I don't like lettuce.* |

2. The partitive expresses an unspecified amount. English uses "some," "any," or no word at all to express the partitive.

> *Do you have (any) toast?*
> *Yes, I do. Would you like (some) jam with your toast?*

3. In French, you use **de** + the definite article to express the partitive. Remember that **de** contracts with **le** and **les** to form one word, **du** and **des**.

| | |
|---|---|
| de + le  = du | Tu as du lait et du beurre? |
| de + les = des | Je vais acheter des fruits et des légumes. |
| de + la  = de la | Je voudrais de la crème. |
| de + l'  = de l' | Je voudrais de l'eau. |

4. Study the following chart. It contrasts the use of a noun in the general sense with the partitive.

| General Sense | Partitive |
|---|---|
| J'aime le poulet. | Je voudrais du poulet. |
| J'aime la viande. | Je voudrais de la viande. |
| J'aime l'eau minérale. | Je voudrais de l'eau minérale. |
| J'aime les pommes. | Je voudrais des pommes. |

Note that verbs indicating likes and dislikes are followed by the definite article. All other verbs are followed by the partitive.

| | |
|---|---|
| **Il déteste la viande.** | **Elle va acheter de la viande.** |
| **J'adore le fromage.** | **Tu prends du fromage?** |

# Comment dit-on?

**18** **Qu'est-ce que je vais acheter?** Répondez d'après le modèle.
*(Answer according to the model.)*

Tu veux des fruits?

Oui, je vais acheter des fruits. J'aime les fruits.

1. Tu veux du pain?
2. Tu veux du fromage?
3. Tu veux des bananes?
4. Tu veux de la glace?

**19** **J'aime tout!** Conversez d'après le modèle.
*(Make up a conversation according to the model.)*

la crème ⟶
—J'aime beaucoup la crème.
—D'accord. Je vais chercher de la crème.

1. le saucisson
2. le lait
3. l'eau minérale
4. la limonade
5. le jambon
6. les pommes

**20** **Historiette** **Des provisions** Complétez. *(Complete.)*

Au marché, Jean-Marc achète __1__ pain, __2__ jambon, __3__ fromage, __4__ fraises et __5__ crème. Il va préparer __6__ sandwichs au jambon et au fromage. Pour le dessert, il va préparer __7__ fraises avec __8__ crème.

**21** **Historiette** **Des différences**
Complétez. *(Complete.)*

Isabelle Marquet a une sœur, Sophie. Quand les deux sœurs vont au restaurant, Isabelle commande toujours __1__ poisson. Elle aime bien __2__ poisson. Mais Sophie n'aime pas du tout __3__ poisson. Elle aime __4__ viande et elle commande toujours __5__ viande. Elle commande toujours __6__ bœuf. Et elle aime son bœuf à point, pas bien cuit!

# Le partitif au négatif
## Expressing what people don't have

**1.** All forms of the partitive, **du, de la, de l',** and **des,** change to **de (d')** after a negative.

| Affirmatif | | Négatif | |
|---|---|---|---|
| Je veux | du pain. | Je ne veux pas | de pain. |
| | de la crème. | | de crème. |
| | de l'eau. | | d'eau. |
| | des carottes. | | de carottes. |

Note that the same is true after **ne… plus.**

**Je ne mange plus de viande.**

**2.** Remember that the definite article does not change in the negative.

**J'aime les carottes. Je n'aime pas les carottes.**

# Comment dit-on?

**22** **Non, merci.** Conversez d'après le modèle.
*(Make up a conversation according to the model.)*

de l'eau ⟶
—**Vous voulez de l'eau?**
—**Non, merci. Pas d'eau pour moi.**

| | | |
|---|---|---|
| **1.** du pain | **3.** du porc | **5.** du lait |
| **2.** de l'agneau | **4.** des crevettes | **6.** de la limonade |

**23** **Qu'est-ce que tu as?** Conversez d'après le modèle.
*(Make up a conversation according to the model.)*

des livres ⟶
—**Tu as des livres?**
—**Non, je n'ai pas de livres. / Oui, j'ai des livres.**

| | | |
|---|---|---|
| **1.** un ami | **3.** un chat | **5.** des frères |
| **2.** une amie | **4.** des cousines | **6.** des sœurs |

**24** **Je voudrais...** Conversez d'après le modèle. *(Make up a conversation according to the model.)*

> Je voudrais du jambon, s'il vous plaît.

> Je regrette, mais il n'y a plus de jambon.

1. Je voudrais de l'eau minérale, s'il vous plaît.
2. Je voudrais de la glace à la vanille, s'il vous plaît.
3. Je voudrais des croissants, s'il vous plaît.
4. Je voudrais des fraises, s'il vous plaît.
5. Je voudrais du fromage, s'il vous plaît.

**25** **Juliette fait les courses.** Répondez d'après le modèle. *(Answer according to the model.)*

—**Elle va acheter du poisson à la boucherie?**

—**Non, elle ne va pas acheter de poisson à la boucherie. Elle va acheter de la viande.**

1. Elle va acheter du pain à la boucherie?
2. Elle va acheter du fromage à la boulangerie?
3. Elle va acheter des légumes à la charcuterie?
4. Elle va acheter de la viande à la crémerie?
5. Elle va acheter des œufs chez le marchand de fruits et légumes?

Une charcuterie, Conques, France

**26** **Je n'aime pas ça!**
Répondez d'après le modèle.
*(Answer according to the model.)*

—**Tu as de la confiture?**

—**Non, je n'ai pas de confiture. Je n'aime pas la confiture.**

1. Tu as du saucisson?
2. Tu as du fromage?
3. Tu as du café?
4. Tu as de la limonade?
5. Tu as des épinards?
6. Tu as des sardines?

**27 Historiette** **Au supermarché** Complétez. (*Complete.*)

Quand je vais au supermarché, je n'achète pas __1__ fruits. Je n'aime pas __2__ fruits du supermarché. J'achète __3__ fruits au marché, chez le marchand de fruits et légumes. Je n'achète pas __4__ café au supermarché. Je n'achète pas __5__ viande. Je n'achète pas __6__ légumes, pas __7__ oignons. Qu'est-ce que j'achète au supermarché? J'achète seulement __8__ boîtes de conserve, __9__ bouteilles d'eau minérale, __10__ sel, __11__ poivre, __12__ vinaigre et __13__ huile.

**28 Dans le frigidaire** Work with a classmate. Ask him or her for something you'd like to eat or drink. Your partner will check to see whether or not it's in the refrigerator. Use the model as a guide.

—**Tu as de la glace au chocolat? J'adore la glace au chocolat.**
—**Je regrette, il n'y a plus de glace au chocolat.**

**29 Un sandwich extraordinaire** Work with a classmate. Discuss what would be a great sandwich. You may (or may not) want to use some of the following ingredients.

du beurre de cacahouète

de la mayonnaise

du chocolat

de la gelée de raisin

des cornichons

des sardines

### Attention!

Pay special attention to the spelling and pronunciation of the following adjectives that double the consonant in the feminine.

| FÉMININ | MASCULIN |
|---------|----------|
| bonne(s) | bon(s) |
| canadienne(s) | canadien(s) |
| gentille(s) | gentil(s) |
| quelle(s) | quel(s) |

Complétez. *(Complete.)*

1. Tu fais de la _____ cuisine? (bon)
2. Tu fais de _____ sandwichs? (bon)
3. Tu as des amis _____ et _____? (canadien, vietnamien)
4. Tu as des amies _____? (tunisien)
5. Tu aimes les filles qui sont _____? (gentil)
6. Tu aimes _____ profs? (quel)

## Les verbes pouvoir et vouloir
### Telling what one can do or wants to do

**1.** Study the forms of the verbs **pouvoir** *(to be able to)* and **vouloir** *(to want)*.

| POUVOIR | | VOULOIR | |
|---------|------|---------|--------|
| je | peux | je | veux |
| tu | peux | tu | veux |
| il/elle/on | peut | il/elle/on | veut |
| nous | pouvons | nous | voulons |
| vous | pouvez | vous | voulez |
| ils/elles | peuvent | ils/elles | veulent |

**Savez-vous que... ?**

**Je voudrais** is a polite form of **je veux.** It means "I would like."

**Je voudrais une livre de haricots verts, s'il vous plaît.**

Michel ne peut pas aller au marché à pied.
Il veut acheter des légumes et des fruits.
Vous voulez manger maintenant?
Vous pouvez si vous voulez.

**2.** In the negative, you put **ne... pas** around the verbs **pouvoir** and **vouloir**.

Je **ne** veux **pas** manger de frites.
Ils **ne** peuvent **pas** aller au restaurant ce soir.

# Comment dit-on?

**30** **Je veux bien, mais je ne peux pas.** Conversez d'après le modèle. (*Make up a conversation according to the model.*)

—**Tu veux aller au restaurant?**

—**Je veux bien, mais je ne peux pas.**

1. Tu veux aller au café?
2. Tu veux dîner avec Caroline?
3. Tu veux travailler après l'école?
4. Ta sœur veut faire les courses?

5. Elle veut aller au marché?
6. Elle veut préparer le dîner?
7. Elle veut inviter des amis?

Un marché, Saint-Rémy-de-Provence, France

**31** **Si vous voulez, vous pouvez.** Conversez d'après le modèle. (*Make up a conversation according to the model.*)

Nous voulons travailler.

Si vous voulez travailler, vous pouvez travailler.

1. Nous voulons manger maintenant.
2. Nous voulons inviter des amis.
3. Nous voulons aller au restaurant.
4. Nous voulons commander de la pizza.
5. Nous voulons regarder le film.
6. Nous voulons écouter nos CD.

**32** **Historiette** **Pas assez d'argent** Complétez avec **pouvoir** ou **vouloir**. (*Complete with* pouvoir *or* vouloir.)

Pierre et son frère ont faim. Ils __1__ aller dans un restaurant où ils __2__ dîner rapidement. Ils __3__ commander deux hamburgers chacun, mais ils ne __4__ pas. Pierre insiste, mais son frère ne __5__ pas: «Pas question! On n'a pas assez d'argent! Tu __6__ commander seulement un hamburger aujourd'hui.»

**33** **Qui peut préparer le dîner?** Complétez. (*Complete.*)

**Marie:** Je voudrais bien faire le dîner ce soir, mais vraiment, je ne __1__ (pouvoir) pas.
**Julien:** Tu ne __2__ (pouvoir) pas? Pourquoi?
**Marie:** Je __3__ (être) très fatiguée! Je __4__ (être) vraiment crevée.
**Julien:** On __5__ (pouvoir) aller au restaurant, si tu __6__ (vouloir).
**Marie:** Oh, je ne __7__ (vouloir) pas aller au restaurant ce soir.
**Julien:** On __8__ (pouvoir) faire des sandwichs.
**Marie:** Oui, ou… toi, tu __9__ (pouvoir) faire le dîner.
**Julien:** Je __10__ (vouloir) bien, mais ce n'__11__ (être) pas une très bonne idée.
**Marie:** Pourquoi?
**Julien:** Parce que je __12__ (faire) très mal la cuisine!

**34**  **Pourquoi pas?** Work with a classmate. Tell each other some things you or you and your friends want to do but can't. When possible, give reasons.

 *For more practice using the verbs **pouvoir** and **vouloir**, do Activity 19 on page H20 at the end of this book.*

*Vous êtes sur le bon chemin. Allez-y!*

# Conversation

## Au marché

**Marchand:** Et maintenant, je suis à vous, madame. Comment allez-vous ce matin?

**Mme Brun:** Très bien, merci. Et vous?

**Marchand:** Oh, comme ci, comme ça! Enfin… Qu'est-ce que vous désirez aujourd'hui?

**Mme Brun:** Je voudrais des haricots verts et des carottes. C'est combien, les haricots verts?

**Marchand:** Quatre euros le kilo. Et ils sont bons!

**Mme Brun:** Alors, un kilo, s'il vous plaît, et une livre de carottes.

**Marchand:** Et avec ça, madame?

**Mme Brun:** C'est tout, merci. Ça fait combien?

**Marchand:** Alors, un kilo de haricots verts, une livre de carottes… Ça fait quatre euros cinquante.

**Mme Brun:** Voilà, monsieur.

**Marchand:** Merci, madame. Et à samedi prochain.

## Vous avez compris?

Répondez. (*Answer.*)

1. Mme Brun fait ses courses?
2. Le marchand va bien?
3. Mme Brun fait ses courses au supermarché?
4. Elle parle au marchand de légumes?
5. Qu'est-ce qu'elle veut acheter?
6. Elle veut des haricots verts?
7. Ça fait combien, les haricots verts et les carottes?

# Parlons un peu plus

**Qu'est-ce qu'on va manger?**
Work with a classmate. Prepare a menu in French for tomorrow's meals—**le petit déjeuner, le déjeuner et le dîner.** Based on your menus, prepare a shopping list. Be sure to include the quantities you need.

Une poissonnerie, Abidjan, Côte d'Ivoire

## Prononciation

### Les sons /œ́/ et /œ̀/

1. Listen to the difference in the vowel sounds in **peut** and **peuvent**. The sound /œ́/ in **peut** is a closed vowel sound and the sound /œ̀/ in **peuvent** is an open vowel sound. Repeat the following words with the sound /œ́/.

   **il peut**    **il veut**    **des œufs**    **deux**

2. Repeat the following words with the sound /œ̀/.

   **ils peuvent**    **ils veulent**    **un œuf**
   **leur sœur**    **du beurre**

3. Now repeat the following pairs of words. Be sure to distinguish between the two vowel sounds.

   **il peut / ils peuvent**
   **il veut / ils veulent**

4. Now repeat the following sentences.

   **Elle veut faire les courses, mais ils ne veulent pas.**
   **Elle veut du beurre et des œufs.**
   **Leur sœur est sérieuse.**

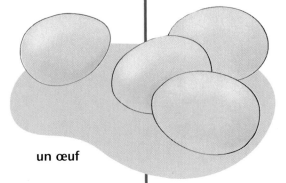

**un œuf**

**des œufs**

# Lectures culturelles

## Les courses

C'est aujourd'hui mardi. À dix heures du matin, comme tous les matins, excepté le lundi quand les magasins sont fermés[1], Mme Lelong quitte son appartement. Elle a son sac et elle va faire les courses. Elle fait les courses dans différents petits magasins. Elle achète du pain tous les jours. Elle va à la boulangerie où elle achète une baguette. Si elle veut de la viande, elle va à la boucherie. Si elle veut du poisson, elle peut aller à la poissonnerie, mais elle est très loin. Pour un pot de confiture ou une bouteille d'eau minérale, l'épicerie n'est pas loin.

Après le déjeuner, si elle n'a pas assez de pain pour le soir, elle peut acheter une autre baguette. Mais pas avant 16 heures. Les petits magasins sont fermés tous les jours de 13 heures à 16 heures, et bien sûr le dimanche!

[1] fermés *closed*

Une boulangerie-pâtisserie, Paris

Un marchand de fruits, Paris

Haïti

La Martinique

Une boucherie, Domme, France

Une boulangerie, Paris

Les Français aiment bien aller chez les petits commerçants du quartier—l'épicier, le boucher, le boulanger, etc. Leurs prix sont un peu plus chers[2] qu'au supermarché, mais la qualité de leurs produits est très bonne. Il y a aussi le côté humain[3]. Les Français aiment bavarder (converser) un peu avec le marchand ou la marchande. On trouve ça sympa.

[2] Leurs prix sont un peu plus chers *Their prices are a little more expensive*
[3] côté humain *human dimension*

## Vous avez compris?

**A Madame Lelong** Répondez. *(Answer.)*
1. Mme Lelong quitte son appartement à quelle heure?
2. Qu'est-ce qu'elle prend pour faire ses courses?
3. Elle fait ses courses où?
4. Elle va où pour acheter du pain?
5. Si elle veut de la viande, elle va où?
6. Si elle veut du poisson, elle peut aller où?
7. Qu'est-ce qu'elle achète à l'épicerie?
8. Quand est-ce que les petits magasins sont fermés?

**B Stratégie de lecture** Reread the Reading Strategy on page 206. You don't know the meaning of the word **commerçants.** Using the suggestion given in the Reading Strategy, can you figure out the meaning of this word?

**C Les petits commerçants** Expliquez. *(Explain.)*
1. Qui sont les petits commerçants du quartier?
2. Comment est la qualité de leurs produits?
3. En général, comment sont leurs prix?
4. Qu'est-ce que les Français aiment faire avec les commerçants?

La Suisse

La Belgique

La Tunisie

Le Maroc

Le Mali

Le Sénégal

# Les grandes surfaces

Beaucoup de Français font leurs courses dans les petits magasins de leur quartier. Mais beaucoup d'autres Français—surtout les gens[1] qui travaillent ou qui n'habitent pas en ville—font leurs courses dans les grandes surfaces.

Les grandes surfaces sont de grands supermarchés ou hypermarchés. Ils sont généralement situés à la périphérie des villes. Il y a toujours un grand parking parce que les clients y vont en voiture.

Dans un hypermarché on peut tout acheter: de la nourriture, mais aussi des vêtements[2], des bicyclettes, des livres, des disques et même des ordinateurs[3]. Les clients prennent des chariots pour transporter leurs achats[4]. Les grandes chaînes ont pour nom Leclerc et Carrefour.

[1] gens *people*
[2] vêtements *clothes*
[3] ordinateurs *computers*
[4] achats *purchases*

Un hypermarché, Nantes

L'intérieur d'un hypermarché

## Vous avez compris?

**Les courses** Vrai ou faux? *(True or false?)*
1. Les supermarchés et les hypermarchés sont des grandes surfaces.
2. Les grandes surfaces sont situées surtout au centre des villes.
3. Les clients vont presque toujours à pied dans les grandes surfaces.
4. Dans un hypermarché on peut acheter toutes sortes de marchandises.

# Les marchés

Dans les villes et les villages de France, il y a toujours un marché. Dans les grandes villes, il y a des marchés permanents et temporaires. Les marchés temporaires ont lieu[1] en général deux fois par semaine, le mercredi ou le jeudi et le samedi. Ils ont lieu dans la rue ou sur une place.

Les marchés existent dans les autres pays francophones. Voici un très joli marché à Dakar. Et voici un marché à Fort-de-France. Les fruits et les légumes ont l'air[2] très bons, n'est-ce pas? Ils sont délicieux!

[1] ont lieu *take place*      [2] ont l'air *look*

Sarlat-la-Canéda, Dordogne

Dakar, Sénégal

Fort-de-France, Martinique

## Vous avez compris?

**Les marchés** Complétez. (*Complete.*)
1. Dans les villes et les villages de France, il y a toujours un _____.
2. Les marchés peuvent être temporaires ou _____.
3. Ils peuvent avoir lieu dans _____ ou _____.
4. Ils ont lieu le _____ ou le _____ et le _____.
5. Il y a aussi des marchés dans _____.

# CONNEXIONS

## Les mathématiques

### Les conversions

When you travel in many of the French-speaking countries, or almost anywhere in Europe, you need to make many mathematical conversions. The metric system, rather than the English system, is used for distance, weights, and measures.

## soupe d'été

Je trouve sympa de présenter la soupe avec tous ces petits morceaux de légumes. Parfois, je la sers accompagnée de croûtons de pain à l'ail et de gruyère coupé en dés. On se régale tous. Au menu, j'ai prévu une salade crue (pour la vitamine C) avec un œuf dur (pour les éléments bâtisseurs: les protéines). 1 œuf, cela peut remplacer 50 g de viande ou de poisson.

**LES USTENSILES**
- 1 planche à découper
- 1 cocotte
- 1 couteau de cuisine en acier inoxydable
- 1 cuillère à soupe
- 1 cuillère en bois

**LES INGREDIENTS POUR 4 PERSONNES**
- Pommes de terre : 250 g — 3 moyennes
- Courgettes : 250 g — 2 moyennes
- Tomates : 3 moyennes
- Oignons : 2
- Huile : 1 cuillerée à soupe
- Eau : 1 litre

### Le système métrique

Le système métrique est un système décimal: il a pour base 10. Les mesures ont pour base le mètre et les poids ont pour base le gramme. Pour les liquides, la base est le litre. Les unités supérieures et inférieures sont formées avec les préfixes suivants:

| | |
|---|---|
| kilo = × 1 000 | un kilogramme = 1 000 grammes |
| hecto = × 100 | un  hectomètre = 100 mètres |
| déca = × 10 | un décalitre = 10 litres |
| déci = ÷ 10 | un décimètre = 1 mètre ÷ 10 |
| centi = ÷ 100 | un centilitre = 1 litre ÷ 100 |
| milli = ÷ 1 000 | un milligramme = 1 gramme ÷ 1 000 |

Un kilogramme (un kilo) est équivalent à environ[1] deux livres[2]. Une livre est équivalente à un peu moins[3] d'un demi-kilo. Un mile américain est équivalent à environ un kilomètre et demi. Un litre est équivalent à environ un quart américain.

[1] environ  *about*
[2] livres  *pounds*
[3] un peu moins  *a little less*

## Vous avez compris?

### Poids et mesures

Vrai ou faux? *(True or false?)*

1. Le système anglais de poids et mesures a pour base 10.
2. Les poids ont comme unité de base le litre.
3. Il y a 1 000 grammes dans un kilo.
4. Un kilo est l'équivalent d'environ deux livres anglaises.
5. Une livre américaine est l'équivalent de 500 grammes.
6. On mesure les liquides en quarts en France.
7. En France, on mesure les liquides en litres.

# C'est à vous

## Use what you have learned

**PARLER 1**

### Au marché
✔ *Buy food from a vendor at the market*

Work with a classmate. You are spending a semester studying in Belgium. You are going to prepare a dinner for your Belgian family. Decide what you need to buy at the market and in what quantities. Then have a conversation with your classmate, who will be the vendor at the market.

**PARLER 2**

### Je veux bien, mais je ne peux pas parce que...
✔ *Talk about what you want to do but can't*

Work in groups of three or four. Tell some things you want to do but can't do because you are going to do something else. Tell what you are going to do.

**PARLER ÉCRIRE 3**

### Jeu Une compétition
✔ *Express quantities*

Compete with a classmate. You each have two minutes. See which one of you can make up the most phrases using the following words.

un kilo de    une livre de    un litre de    une bouteille de

une boîte de    six tranches de    un paquet de

## 4 Une publicité
✔ *Write an advertisement for a supermarket*

Using these French supermarket ads as a guide, write similar food advertisements in French for your local supermarket. Choose any four foods you like to advertise.

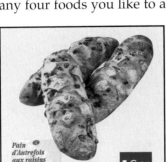

Pain d'Autrefois aux raisins Fabriqué en France, 500 g

1 €01

Jambon LE FUMAY Origine France, le kg

6 €08

Lait 1/2 écrémé AUCHAN Origine France, bouteille de 1 L

0 €53

EAU MINÉRALE NATURELLE

c'est un produit cora

Le lot

€ 1,52

EAU MINÉRALE NATURELLE "CORA" Le lot de 6 bouteilles de 1,5 litre

---

### Writing Strategy

**Ordering ideas** You can order ideas in a variety of ways when writing. Therefore, you must be aware of the purpose of your writing in order to choose the best way to organize your material. When describing an event, it is logical to put the events in the order in which they happen. Using a sensible and logical approach helps readers develop a picture in their minds.

## 5 On fait les courses.

Your class is planning a French meal. Describe the trip you take with your class to the local market or supermarket to buy the ingredients. Tell what you buy, whom you buy it from, and how much everything costs.

Un supermarché, Dakar, Sénégal

# Assessment

## Vocabulaire

**1 Identifiez.** *(Identify each item.)*

To review **Mots 1,** turn to pages 186–187.

1.

2.

3.

4.

**2 Choisissez.** *(Choose.)*

To review **Mots 2,** turn to pages 190–191.

5. Une pomme et une poire sont des _____.
   **a.** fraises      **b.** légumes      **c.** fruits
6. C'est _____, un kilo de carottes?
   **a.** comment      **b.** combien      **c.** un marchand
7. Il va acheter _____ de moutarde.
   **a.** un paquet      **b.** une boîte      **c.** un pot
8. Je voudrais six _____ de jambon, s'il vous plaît.
   **a.** bouteilles      **b.** tranches      **c.** litres

## Structure

To review the verb **faire,** turn to page 194.

**3 Complétez avec «faire».** *(Complete with faire.)*

9. Je _____ les courses le matin.
10. Mon frère _____ du latin.
11. Vous _____ vos devoirs?
12. Les élèves ne _____ pas la cuisine.

**4 Choisissez.** *(Choose.)*

13. Moi, j'aime beaucoup ____ lait.
    **a.** le     **b.** du     **c.** de

14. Je voudrais ____ eau.
    **a.** d'     **b.** de l'     **c.** du

15. Il va acheter ____ fruits et ____ légumes.
    **a.** des     **b.** de     **c.** les

*To review the partitive and the definite article, turn to pages 196, 198.*

**5 Récrivez au négatif.** *(Rewrite the sentences in the negative.)*

16. Je vais acheter du pain.
17. Je voudrais de la crème.

**6 Récrivez les phrases.** *(Rewrite the sentences.)*

18. Les carottes sont très bonnes.
    Le poisson ____.
19. Tu veux quel sandwich?
    Tu veux ____ salade?

*To review these special adjectives, turn to page 201.*

**7 Complétez.** *(Complete.)*

20. Je ____ faire le travail. (pouvoir)
21. Vous ____ aller au restaurant? (vouloir)
22. Tu ____ aller au marché. (pouvoir)
23. Ils ____ parler au prof. (vouloir)

*To review the verbs **pouvoir** and **vouloir**, turn to page 201.*

# Culture

**8 Répondez.** *(Answer.)*

24. Beaucoup de magasins sont fermés quel jour en France?
25. On peut aller où pour acheter un pot de confiture ou une bouteille d'eau minérale?

*To review this cultural information, turn to pages 206–207.*

Tell all you can about this illustration.

## Shopping for food

| | | | |
|---|---|---|---|
| faire les courses *(f. pl.)* | une poissonnerie | le/la marchand(e) | |
| une boulangerie | une charcuterie | un sac | |
| une pâtisserie | une épicerie | surgelé(e) | |
| une crémerie | un marché | | |
| une boucherie | un supermarché | | |

## Identifying some food

| | | | |
|---|---|---|---|
| du pain | de la viande | de l'eau minérale | un légume |
| un pain complet | du bœuf | de la moutarde | une salade |
| un croissant | de l'agneau *(m.)* | un fruit | une carotte |
| une baguette | du porc | une banane | une pomme de terre |
| une tarte aux pommes | du jambon | une pomme | des haricots verts |
| de la crème | du saucisson | une orange | des épinards *(m. pl.)* |
| du lait | du poisson | une poire | des petits pois *(m. pl.)* |
| du beurre | une crevette | une fraise | un oignon |
| du fromage | un crabe | un melon | |
| de la confiture | du sel | une tomate | |
| un œuf | du poivre | | |
| un yaourt | de l'huile *(f.)* | | |
| un poulet | du vinaigre | | |

## Identifying quantities

| | |
|---|---|
| un paquet | un litre |
| un pot | une douzaine |
| un gramme | une boîte |
| un kilo(gramme) | une bouteille |
| une livre | une tranche |

How well do you know your vocabulary?

- Choose two foods that you like from the list.
- Tell how you buy each, for example, *une douzaine, une bouteille*, etc.

## Other useful words and expressions

| | | | |
|---|---|---|---|
| aller chercher | C'est combien? | Vous voulez autre chose? | C'est tout. |
| il n'y a plus de | Ça fait combien? | Et avec ça? | Pourquoi? |
| je regrette | bon(ne) | | parce que |

**VIDÉOTOUR**

### Épisode 6

In this video episode, you will join Manu and Vincent as they do their food shopping. See page 531 for more information.

# Les vêtements

## Objectifs

In this chapter you will learn to:

✔ identify and describe articles of clothing

✔ state color and size preferences

✔ shop for clothing

✔ describe people's activities

✔ compare people and things

✔ express opinions and make observations

✔ discuss clothes and clothes shopping in the French-speaking world

ROYAUME DU MAROC
0.15 POSTES

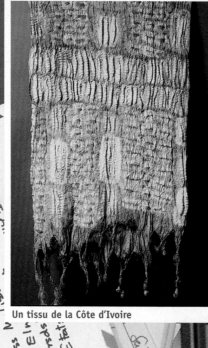

Un tissu de la Côte d'Ivoire

# Vocabulaire

## Les vêtements sport 🎧

un short

un pull

un t-shirt

des sandales

une paire de
chaussures

une casquette

un sweat-shirt

une basket

une chaussette

un anorak

un blouson

un polo
(à manches courtes)

un jean

un survêtement

un manteau

## Les vêtements pour hommes 🎧

- un centre commercial
- une boutique
- une chemise (à manches longues)
- un complet
- une veste
- une cravate
- un pantalon

Marc porte des sandales.
Il voit des chaussures
  dans la vitrine.
Il entre dans la boutique.

plus cher

le prix

35€

20€

moins cher

Les prix sont moins chers
  quand il y a des soldes.

## Les vêtements pour femmes 🎧

Johanne va au grand magasin.
Elle voit beaucoup de chemisiers.
Elle voit des chemisiers au rayon des
  vêtements pour femmes.
Tous les chemisiers sont en solde!

Qu'est-ce que je vais mettre samedi?

- une robe sport
- un chemisier
- un tailleur
- une jupe plissée
- une vendeuse
- une robe habillée

# Quel est le mot?

**1**  **Chloé et Adrien**  Répondez d'après les photos. *(Answer according to the photos.)*

1. Qu'est-ce que Chloé porte?
2. Et Adrien? Qu'est-ce qu'il porte?

**2**  **Qu'est-ce qu'on va mettre?**
Répondez. *(Answer.)*

1. Ce soir M. Ben Azar va aller dans un restaurant chic. Qu'est-ce qu'il va mettre?
2. Qu'est-ce que sa femme va mettre?
3. Qu'est-ce que tu portes à l'école?
4. Qu'est-ce que tu portes à la maison?
5. Qu'est-ce qu'on porte en juillet et en août?
6. Qu'est-ce qu'on porte en décembre et janvier?
7. Qu'est-ce qu'une femme porte quand elle va travailler?
8. Qu'est-ce qu'un homme porte quand il va au travail?

**Chloé**

**Adrien**

La vitrine d'une boutique, Paris

**3**  **Sport ou habillé?**  Identifiez.
*(Tell whether each item is casual or formal.)*

1. des baskets
2. un tailleur
3. un jean
4. un complet
5. un blouson
6. une cravate
7. un polo à manches courtes
8. une chemise à manches longues
9. un survêtement
10. une jupe plissée

**4**  **Historiette** **Au rayon des chemisiers** Inventez une histoire. *(Make up a story.)*

1. Mélanie entre dans un grand magasin ou dans une boutique?
2. La boutique est dans une rue ou dans un centre commercial?
3. Il y a des soldes aujourd'hui?
4. Il y a des chemisiers dans la vitrine?
5. Elle va au rayon des chemisiers?
6. Elle voit beaucoup de chemisiers?
7. Elle parle à la vendeuse?
8. Elle veut un chemisier à manches courtes ou à manches longues?
9. Elle veut un chemisier habillé ou sport?
10. Les chemisiers sont en solde?
11. Les vêtements sont moins chers quand ils sont en solde?

**5**  **C'est qui?** Work with a classmate. One of you describes what someone in the class is wearing and the other has to guess who it is. Take turns.

**6**  **Mon ensemble favori** Work with a classmate. Discuss what you consider an ideal outfit for school. Tell what you like to wear and what you don't like to wear. See if you are on the same wavelength.

Des jeunes habillés sport

 *For more practice using words from* **Mots 1**, *do Activity 20 on page H21 at the end of this book.*

# Vocabulaire

## Mots 2

On fait des courses.

*Il est joli, le pantalon vert. Tu ne trouves pas?*

*Si, j'aime beaucoup!*

le shopping

*Vous faites quelle pointure?*

*Je fais du 38.*

*Ça va, le pantalon?*

une cabine d'essayage

*Non, il est trop grand. Il est trop large. Je voudrais la taille au-dessous.*

*Vous faites quelle taille?*

*Je fais du 38.*

*Non, il est trop petit. Il est trop serré. Je voudrais la taille au-dessus.*

essayer

Julien essaie le pantalon.

De quelle couleur est la jupe?
Elle est verte.

Et les chaussures?
Elles sont marron.

## Note

The following colors are invariable. They do not change to agree with the noun they modify.

**bleu marine**   **marron**   **orange**

# Quel est le mot?

**7** **Historiette** **Olivier fait des courses.** Inventez une histoire.

*(Make up a story.)*

1. Olivier fait des courses?
2. Il veut acheter un blue jean?
3. Il voit un jean qu'il aime dans la vitrine?
4. Il entre dans le grand magasin?
5. Il fait quelle taille?
6. Il va essayer le jean?
7. Il est comment, le pantalon—grand, petit, juste à sa taille?
8. Il veut la taille au-dessus ou la taille au-dessous?
9. Les jeans sont en solde?
10. Ils sont moins chers quand ils sont en solde?
11. Olivier trouve que les jeans sont chers?
12. Olivier va acheter le jean?

Rayon des vêtements pour hommes, Galeries Lafayette, Paris

**8** **Ta couleur favorite** Donnez des réponses personnelles. *(Give your own answers.)*

1. De quelle couleur est ton blouson favori?
2. De quelle couleur est ton jean favori?
3. De quelle couleur est ta chemise favorite ou ton chemisier favori?
4. Qu'est-ce que tu portes aujourd'hui? De quelle couleur sont tes vêtements?

**9** **Mes préférences** Donnez des réponses personnelles. *(Give your own answers.)*

1. Tu aimes mieux les vêtements sport ou habillés?
2. Les baskets ou les chaussures?
3. Les chemises ou les chemisiers à manches longues ou à manches courtes?
4. Les vêtements un peu serrés ou larges?
5. Les couleurs sombres ou les couleurs claires?
6. Les vêtements chers ou pas chers?

**10** **De petits problèmes** Répondez. *(Answer.)*

**1.** Les chaussures sont trop petites ou trop grandes?

**2.** La jupe est trop longue ou trop courte?

**3.** Le pantalon est un peu serré ou un peu large?

**4.** Les manches sont trop longues ou trop courtes?

**5.** Le tailleur est joli ou pas?

**11** **Les couleurs** Complétez d'après la couleur. *(Complete with the color.)*

**1.** Aurélien va acheter un pantalon _____.

**2.** Anne va acheter un chemisier _____.

**3.** Fred va acheter une chemise _____.

**4.** Justine va acheter une robe _____.

**5.** Mélodie va acheter une jupe _____.

**6.** Cyril va acheter des chaussures _____.

**12** **Jeu** **Qui porte une jupe bleue?** Study the clothing of all the students in the next row for several minutes. Then turn your back to that row. One of your classmates will mention an item of clothing and ask you who is wearing it. If you don't remember, your classmates can help you out by giving hints such as: **La personne est blonde. Elle est très amusante.**

*For more practice using words from* **Mots 2,** *do Activity 21 on page H22 at the end of this book.*

# Structure

 ## Le verbe mettre au présent
### Describing people's activities

**1.** Study the forms of the verb **mettre** *(to put, to put on)* in the present tense.

| METTRE | | | |
|---|---|---|---|
| je | mets | nous | mettons |
| tu | mets | vous | mettez |
| il/elle/on | met | ils/elles | mettent |

**FRENCH Online**

For more information about shopping for clothing in the Francophone world, go to the Glencoe French Web site: french.glencoe.com

**2.** Note that **mettre** has various meanings.

> Il **met une chemise** et une cravate pour aller au travail.
> Les serveurs **mettent la table** au restaurant.
> On **met la télévision** pour regarder un film.

# Comment dit-on?

**13** **Qu'est-ce qu'on met?**
Répondez. *(Answer.)*

1. Tu mets un survêtement quand tu fais du jogging?
2. Tu mets la table pour le dîner?
3. Ton père met la télé le matin pendant le petit déjeuner?
4. Ta mère met la radio pour écouter les informations?
5. Tes copains mettent une cravate pour aller à l'école?
6. Tes copines mettent une jupe plissée pour aller à l'école?

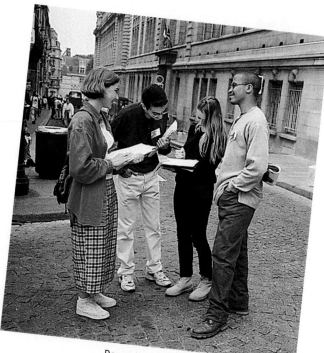

*Des amis devant l'école*

**14** **Dans le sac à dos** Complétez avec **mettre** d'après les dessins. *(Complete with* mettre *according to the illustrations.)*

1. Qu'est-ce qu'ils ____ dans leur sac à dos?
   Ils _____.

2. Qu'est-ce que tu ____ dans ton sac à dos?
   Je _____.

3. Qu'est-ce que vous ____ dans votre sac à dos?
   On _____.

**15** **Qu'est-ce que vous mettez?** Work with a classmate. Compare what you wear on different occasions.

- pour aller à l'école
- quand vous allez dîner chez des amis de vos parents
- pour aller au cinéma le samedi soir
- pour aller à un mariage
- pour aller dans un restaurant chic

## Attention!

Pay particular attention to the spelling and pronunciation of the following adjectives. Note that the final consonant sound is pronounced in the feminine forms but not in the masculine forms.

| FÉMININ | MASCULIN |
|---|---|
| sérieuse(s) | sérieux |
| longue(s) | long(s) |
| favorite(s) | favori(s) |
| blanche(s) | blanc(s) |

Note that all forms of **cher—chère(s)**, **cher(s)**—sound alike.

Complétez et prononcez. *(Complete and pronounce aloud.)*

1. sérieux
   un élève ____ et une élève ____

2. long
   une jupe ____ et un manteau ____

3. favori
   mon pull ____ et ma robe ____

4. blanc
   une chemise ____ et un chemisier ____

5. long
   des pantalons ____ et des manches ____

*For more practice using the verb* **mettre**, *do Activity 22 on page H23 at the end of this book.*

# Le comparatif des adjectifs
## Comparing people and things

**1.** When you compare two or more people or things, you use **plus (+)... que,** **moins (−)... que,** and **aussi (=)... que.** Study the following chart.

> Le jean est plus   cher que le pantalon.
> Le jean est aussi   cher que le pantalon.
> Le jean est moins cher que le pantalon.

**Les sandales sont moins confortables que les baskets.**
**Mais elles sont plus confortables que les chaussures.**

**Attention!**

Note the liaison with **plus** and **moins.**
**plus** $_z$ **intéressant(e)**
**moins** $_z$ **élégant(e)**

**2.** You use the stress pronouns **moi, toi, lui, elle, nous, vous, eux,** and **elles** after **que (qu')** when comparing people.

> Elle est plus   sympa que moi.
> Elle est aussi   sympa que lui.
> Elle est moins sympa que vous.

**Il est aussi intelligent que moi.**
**Mais il est plus intelligent qu'eux.**

# Comment dit-on?

**16**  **À mon avis** Donnez des réponses personnelles. *(Give your own answers.)*

1. Le français, c'est plus difficile ou plus facile que les maths?
2. Le professeur de français est plus strict, moins strict ou aussi strict que les autres professeurs?
3. Le football américain est plus amusant ou moins amusant que le basket-ball?
4. Ton école secondaire est plus grande ou moins grande que ton école primaire?
5. Ta classe de français est aussi grande ou plus petite que ta classe de sciences?

**17**  **Plus ou moins que l'autre** Répondez d'après les dessins. Suivez le modèle. *(Answer according to the illustrations.)*

—**Le blouson bleu est aussi grand que le blouson noir?**
—**Oui, le blouson bleu est aussi grand que le blouson noir.**

1. Le blouson bleu est aussi cher que le blouson noir?
2. Le blouson bleu est moins beau que le blouson noir?
3. La jupe jaune est moins chère que la jupe grise?
4. La jupe grise est plus courte que la jupe jaune?

**18** **Ma famille et mes copains** Donnez des réponses personnelles. *(Give your own answers.)*

1. Ta sœur, elle est plus petite ou plus grande que toi?
   Tu es plus grand(e) ou plus petit(e) qu'elle?
2. Tu es plus patient(e) ou moins patient(e) que ton frère?
   Il est plus patient ou moins patient que toi?
3. Tes grands-parents sont aussi stricts que tes parents?
   Ils sont vraiment moins stricts qu'eux?
4. Tes copains sont plus sociables que toi?
   Tu es plus timide qu'eux?

**19**   **Comparaisons** Work with a classmate. Compare people you know. You may want to use the following words.

grand  petit  sociable  intéressant  dynamique

amusant  beau  sympa  sérieux

# Les verbes voir et croire
## Seeing and believing

Study the forms of the verbs **voir** *(to see)* and **croire** *(to believe)*.

| VOIR | CROIRE |
|------|--------|
| je vois | je crois |
| tu vois | tu crois |
| il/elle/on voit | il/elle/on croit |
| nous voyons | nous croyons |
| vous voyez | vous croyez |
| ils/elles voient | ils/elles croient |

**Savez-vous que... ?**

When **voir** and **croire** are followed by a clause, you must use **que (qu')**.
Je vois que vous êtes content.
Je crois qu'il est content aussi.

# Comment dit-on?

**20** **À votre avis** Répondez que oui. *(Answer yes.)*

1. Vos parents croient que vous êtes intelligents?
2. Votre professeur de français croit que vous travaillez bien?
3. Vos camarades de classe croient que vous êtes sympathiques?
4. Vos grands-parents croient que vous êtes adorables?

**21** **Dans une boutique**
Répondez que oui. *(Answer yes.)*

1. Tu vois des choses que tu aimes dans la vitrine?
2. Tu crois qu'on peut entrer dans la boutique?
3. Tu crois que tu vas acheter le pantalon noir?
4. Tu crois qu'ils vont avoir ta taille?
5. Tu vois le prix?

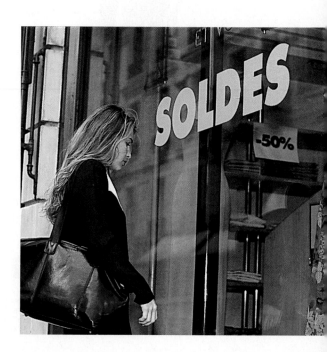

**22** **Vraiment?** Conversez d'après le modèle.
*(Make up a conversation according to the model.)*

—Il va bientôt arriver.
—Vous croyez?

1. Il va bientôt téléphoner.
2. Il va bientôt payer.
3. Il va bientôt rentrer.
4. Il va bientôt acheter une maison.

**23** **Des opinions différentes!** Complétez avec **croire**.
*(Complete with* croire.*)*

1. Il _____ que tout est moins cher pendant les soldes. Et vous, vous _____ ça aussi?

2. Julien _____ que l'examen va être facile, mais nous, on _____ qu'il va être difficile.

3. Tu _____ que les chats sont plus intelligents que les chiens, mais moi, je _____ que les chiens sont plus intelligents que les chats.

4. Alice _____ que Paris est près de Nice, mais nous, nous _____ que c'est loin de Nice.

5. Moi, je _____ que la cousine de Sandra est française, mais mes copains _____ qu'elle est italienne.

**Attention!**

Pay particular attention to the spelling of verbs that end in **–yer.**

| ESSAYER | j'essaie | nous essayons |
|---------|----------|---------------|
| | tu essaies | vous essayez |
| | il essaie | ils essaient |
| PAYER | je paie | nous payons |
| | tu paies | vous payez |
| | il paie | ils paient |

Complétez. *(Complete.)*

1. Vous _____ où? (payer)

2. On _____ à la caisse. (payer)

3. Je _____ parce que j'invite. (payer)

4. Il va _____ la chemise? (essayer)

5. Non, mais il _____ le pantalon. (essayer)

For more practice using the verbs **voir** and **croire**, do Activity 23 on page H24 at the end of this book.

*Vous êtes sur le bon chemin. Allez-y!*

# Conversation

## Dans une petite boutique

**Vendeur:** Bonjour, monsieur. Vous voulez voir quelque chose?

**Fabien:** Bonjour. Oui, je voudrais un jean, s'il vous plaît.

**Vendeur:** Oui, vous faites quelle taille?

**Fabien:** Je fais du 36.

**Vendeur:** Voilà un 36. La cabine d'essayage est juste là.
*(Fabien essaie le jean dans la cabine d'essayage.)*

**Vendeur:** Ça va, la taille?

**Fabien:** Pas vraiment. Je crois que c'est un peu petit.

**Vendeur:** Vous voulez la taille au-dessus?

**Fabien:** Oui, je veux bien.
*(Fabien essaie l'autre jean.)*

**Fabien:** Ah oui, c'est bien.

**Vendeur:** Vous désirez autre chose?

**Fabien:** Oui, un polo bleu marine ou blanc.

**Vendeur:** Vous avez de la chance. Ils sont en solde.

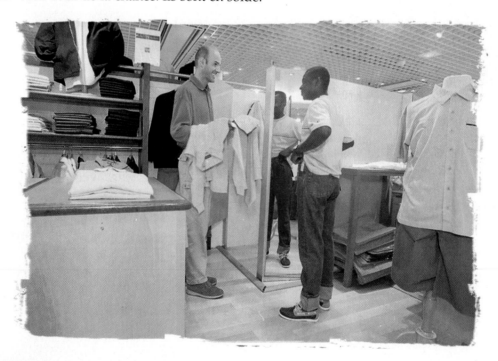

## Vous avez compris?

Répondez. *(Answer.)*

1. À qui parle Fabien?
2. Qu'est-ce qu'il veut voir?
3. Il fait quelle taille?
4. Où est-ce qu'il essaie son jean?
5. Le jean est trop grand ou trop petit?
6. Il veut la taille au-dessus ou la taille au-dessous?
7. Il veut acheter autre chose?

# Parlons un peu plus

**A** **Au magasin** Work with a classmate. Take turns playing the role of the salesperson and the customer in the following situations.

- **Au rayon des vêtements pour hommes** You want to buy a shirt as a gift for your father or a friend. They have his size but not the color you want.

- **Au rayon des chaussures** You are looking for a pair of brown shoes. The ones the salesperson shows you are quite expensive.

**B** **Jeu** **Qu'est-ce qu'il/elle porte?** Have one student leave the room while others choose a classmate to describe. The student who left comes back in and has to guess which classmate the others have chosen by asking questions about his or her clothes.

## Prononciation

### Les sons /sh/ et /zh/ 🎧

It is important to make a distinction between the sounds /sh/ as in **chat** and /zh/ as in **joli.** Put your fingers on your throat. When you say the sound /zh/ as in **joli,** you should feel a vibration, but not when you say /sh/ as in **chat.** Repeat the following words with the sound /sh/.

| | | |
|---|---|---|
| **acheter** | **chaussure** | **chemise** |
| **chemisier** | **achat** | **short** |

Now repeat the following words with the sound /zh/.

| | | |
|---|---|---|
| **large** | **jupe** | **orange** |
| **beige** | **joli** | |

Now repeat the following sentences that combine both sounds.

> **J'achète toujours mes chaussures au marché.**
> **Le t-shirt jaune est joli, mais le short orange est moins cher.**

**chemise orange**

# Lectures culturelles

## On fait des courses où, à Paris?

### Chez les grands couturiers[1]

Les noms des grands couturiers français—Yves Saint-Laurent, Dior, Cardin, Givenchy, Coco Chanel—sont célèbres dans le monde entier. On peut voir les boutiques élégantes des grands couturiers dans l'avenue Montaigne ou dans la rue du Faubourg-Saint-Honoré. C'est là que les gens aisés (riches) vont acheter leurs vêtements et accessoires.

Rue du Faubourg-Saint-Honoré, Paris

Magasin de la Samaritaine, Paris

### Les petites boutiques et les grands magasins

Mais la plupart (la majorité) des Parisiens ne font pas leurs achats chez les grands couturiers. Partout à Paris, il y a de petites boutiques qui sont beaucoup moins chères que les boutiques des grands couturiers. Il y a aussi des grands magasins. À Paris, les grands magasins du Printemps et des Galeries Lafayette sont les plus renommés (célèbres). Il y a aussi des chaînes de magasins bon marché[2] comme le Prisunic.

Dans les grands magasins, on peut aller d'un rayon à un autre. Il y a souvent des articles en promotion[3] et deux fois par an il y a des soldes—début janvier et début juillet.

[1] grands couturiers  *designers*
[2] bon marché  *inexpensive*
[3] en promotion  *on special*

Haïti

La Martinique

## Les marchés aux puces⁴

Les adolescents aiment bien aller aux puces. Ils y vont pendant le week-end parce que les marchés aux puces sont fermés⁵ pendant la semaine.

Les marchés aux puces sont de grands marchés où on trouve de tout—des vêtements, de la nourriture, des tables, des chaises, etc. On peut trouver un vêtement ou un accessoire avec la griffe⁶ d'un grand couturier très bon marché… ou très cher!

⁴ marchés aux puces *flea markets*
⁵ fermés *closed*
⁶ griffe *label*

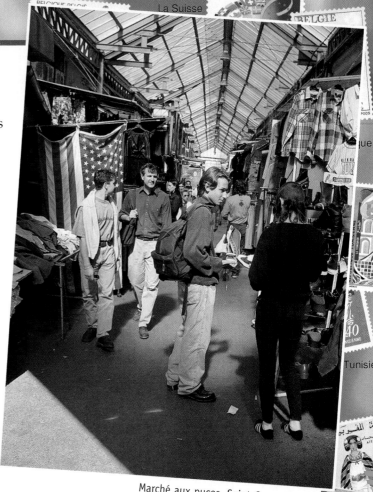

Marché aux puces, Saint-Ouen, Paris

## Vous avez compris?

### A Des informations  Donnez les informations suivantes.
*(Give the following information.)*
1. les noms de quelques grands couturiers français
2. les noms de quelques rues très élégantes à Paris
3. là où la plupart des Parisiens vont faire leurs achats
4. le nom d'un grand magasin parisien assez élégant
5. le nom d'une chaîne de magasins aux prix plus modestes
6. là où les adolescents aiment faire leurs achats

### B Les achats  Vrai ou faux? *(True or false?)*
1. La plupart des Parisiens font leurs achats chez les grands couturiers.
2. Les petites boutiques sont plus chères que les boutiques des grands couturiers.
3. Les Galeries Lafayette, c'est le nom d'un grand magasin à Paris.
4. Les grands magasins n'ont pas de soldes.
5. On va souvent au marché aux puces le lundi.
6. On peut acheter beaucoup de marchandises différentes dans un marché aux puces.

Marché aux puces, Nice

# Les vêtements

### En Afrique du Nord

Dans les pays du Maghreb (le Maroc, l'Algérie et la Tunisie), beaucoup de gens[1] vont dans les souks pour acheter leurs vêtements. Un souk est un grand marché, souvent situé dans la médina, le vieux quartier d'une ville arabe. Dans les pays du Maghreb, beaucoup d'hommes portent un pull et un jean.

Beaucoup de femmes portent une jupe et un chemisier. Mais on voit souvent des vêtements plus traditionnels. On voit des hommes qui portent une djellaba, par exemple. En Tunisie, beaucoup de femmes ont un sifsari. Le sifsari est un type de voile[2]. Le sifsari n'a pas de signification religieuse.

Deux hommes en djellaba, Tunisie

Un souk,
Marrakech, Maroc

### En Afrique Occidentale

Dans les pays d'Afrique Occidentale, les femmes portent souvent un boubou. Un boubou est une longue tunique ample. Les boubous sont très jolis. Les hommes aussi portent un boubou. Ils portent un boubou par-dessus[3] un pantalon et une chemise.

[1] gens *people*
[2] voile *veil*
[3] par-dessus *on top of, over*

Deux femmes en boubou, Sénégal

## Vous avez compris?

**Quel est le mot?** Identifiez le mot.
*(Identify the word.)*
1. un marché arabe
2. le vieux quartier d'une ville arabe
3. un vêtement masculin des pays du Maghreb
4. un type de voile tunisien
5. un vêtement porté par les hommes et les femmes en Afrique Occidentale

# Lecture supplémentaire 2

## Les tailles

En France et dans les autres pays d'Europe, les pointures et les tailles ne sont pas les mêmes qu'aux États-Unis. Voici des tableaux qui indiquent les correspondances.

| FEMMES | | | | | |
|---|---|---|---|---|---|
| **Chaussures** | | | | | |
| États-Unis | 6 | 7 | 8 | 9 | |
| France | 36 | 37 | 38 | 39 | |
| **Robes, Tailleurs, Pulls, Chemisiers** | | | | | |
| États-Unis | 6 | 8 | 10 | 12 | 14 |
| France | 38 | 40 | 42 | 44 | 46 |

| HOMMES | | | | | |
|---|---|---|---|---|---|
| **Chaussures** | | | | | |
| États-Unis | 9 | 10 | 11 | 12 | |
| France | 40 | 41 | 42 | 43 | |
| **Chemises** | | | | | |
| États-Unis | $14\frac{1}{2}$ | 15 | $15\frac{1}{2}$ | 16 | $16\frac{1}{2}$ |
| France | 37 | 38 | 39 | 40 | 41 |

Si vous trouvez des chaussures que vous aimez et que vous voulez acheter, vous allez demander quelle pointure?

Si vous voyez une chemise ou un chemisier que vous voulez acheter, vous allez demander quelle taille?

## Vous avez compris?

**Moi** Donnez des réponses personnelles.
*(Give your own answers.)*
1. Vous êtes en France. Vous voulez des chaussures. Vous faites quelle pointure?
2. Vous voulez une chemise ou un chemisier. Quelle est votre taille?

La Belgique

La Tunisie

Le Maroc

Le Mali

# CONNEXIONS

## *Les lettres*

### La poésie

A poem is a literary piece most often written in verse. The poet uses images, meter, rhythm, and sounds to evoke or suggest ideas, sensations, and emotions in the reader. Many poets say a great deal in very few words. The poem we are about to read by the French poet Apollinaire is an example.

**Apollinaire (1880–1918)**

Guillaume Apollinaire a une vie[1] bohème. Sa poésie reflète sa vie. Il visite beaucoup de pays européens. Les mouvements intellectuels et artistiques de son époque intéressent Apollinaire. C'est une période (avant la guerre[2] de 1914) très riche en idées. Les poètes et les artistes peintres échangent leurs nouvelles idées. Apollinaire discute ses idées avec son bon ami, le peintre Picasso.

Apollinaire est un des premiers grands poètes modernes français. Certains de ses poèmes sont des calligrammes. Le poème a la forme de l'objet que le poète décrit[3]. Le poème «La cravate» est un exemple de calligramme.

[1] vie *life*
[2] guerre *war*
[3] décrit *describes*

Pablo Picasso

Giorgio de Chirico *Guillaume Apollinaire*

LA CRAVATE
DOU
LOU
REUSE°                    douloureuse
                          *painful*
QUE TU
PORTES
ET QUI T'
ORNE Ô CI
VILISÉ
ÔTE-        TU VEUX
LA°         BIEN          ôte-la *take it off*
SI          RESPI
            RER°         respirer *breathe*

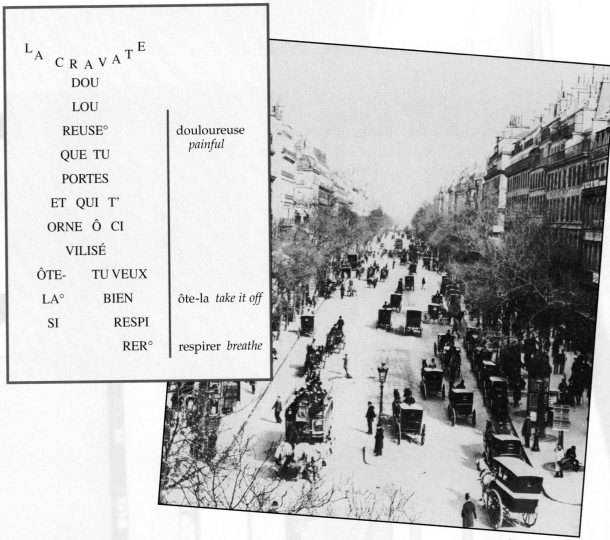

Paris vers 1900

## Vous avez compris?

**A** **Mes idées** Répondez. *(Answer.)*

1. Si tu es un garçon, tu aimes mettre une cravate?
2. Si tu es une fille, tu trouves que c'est une bonne idée
   d'obliger un garçon à porter une cravate?
3. Apollinaire aime les cravates?
4. Il croit qu'on peut bien respirer si on porte une cravate?
5. Il croit que l'homme civilisé porte une cravate?

**B** **Explication du texte** Explain in English
Apollinaire's ideas and tell whether you agree with him.

# C'est à vous

## Use what you have learned

### 1 Une fête
✔ *Identify and describe articles of clothing*

You are talking with a friend after school. You are both invited to a party, but you don't know what to wear. Discuss what kind of a party it is and what would be appropriate.

### 2 Un nouveau look
✔ *State your color and style preferences in clothes*

You and your partner have decided that you are going to change your style of clothes. Discuss what the new "you" is going to look like.

Des amies à Ouagadougou, Burkina Faso

### 3 Des cadeaux
✔ *Shop for clothing*

You have just spent a few weeks in France and want to buy some gifts for family and friends back home. Make a list of what you want to buy. Go to different stores to buy the items you want. With a classmate, take turns being the customer and salesperson at the stores where you are purchasing the items on your list.

**REVUE DE DETAILS**
**NEWS MODE** Repéré aux quatre coins de la mode, tout ce qui nous plaît. De la tête aux pieds.

**Coloris:** noir, beige.
**Tailles:** du 36 au 40 pour la femme; du 40 au 45 pour l'homme.

**modèle femme**
**du 36 au 40** 76,07€

**modèle homme**
**du 40 au 45** 76,07€

**l'une**
15,23€

**Chemise**
77% viscose,
23% polyester.

Coloris assortis.
Du 37/38 au 43/44.

**l'une**
15,23€

**Cravate**
100% soie.
Coloris assortis.

(1) Robe en velours (150€, 5 tailles, 8 coloris).
(2) Veste sur jupe en taffetas de soie (75€, 3 tailles, 5 coloris (veste) et 150€, du 36 au 42, en noir ou bronze (jupe) ).

ÉCRIRE
**4**

## On commande des vêtements.
✔ *Order clothing from a catalogue and give color preferences and size*

You want to order from the catalogue to the right. Write a letter stating which items you want, what color, what size.

ÉCRIRE
**5**

## Le catalogue
✔ *Write descriptions of clothing*

Write five descriptions for an online clothing catalogue. Describe the items, tell the sizes they come in, the colors, the occasions they could be worn for, and the prices.

---

### Writing Strategy

**Clustering** · Most writers brainstorm ideas before they begin to write. The next logical step is to "cluster" these ideas. This is done by writing down your main ideas and drawing a box around each one. Then draw a line indicating which ideas are connected to each other. Once you do this, it is easy to add other details to each cluster of ideas. When beginning to write, sort out your clusters and present each in a logical and organized paragraph.

Quel est leur look?

ÉCRIRE
**6**

## Le look de ton école

Write a note to your French friend describing **le look** at your school. Tell him or her what boys and girls usually wear to school and what types of clothing and colors are "in" (**à la mode).**

# Assessment

## Vocabulaire

To review Mots 1, turn to pages 220–221.

**1 Identifiez.** *(Identify.)*

1.
2.
3.
4.

To review Mots 2, turn to pages 224–225.

**2 Complétez.** *(Complete.)*

5. —_____, le pantalon?
   —Non, il est trop grand.
6. —Vous faites quelle ____?
   —Je fais du 38, pour les chemises.
7. —De quelle ____ est la jupe?
   —Elle est grise.
8. —Le jean est trop petit.
   —Je voudrais la taille ____.

## Structure

To review the verb **mettre**, turn to page 228.

**3 Complétez avec «mettre».** *(Complete with* mettre.*)*

9. Les garçons ne ____ pas de cravate pour aller à l'école.
10. Après le dîner je ____ la télé.
11. Qu'est-ce que vous ____ quand vous faites du jogging?
12. Qu'est-ce que tu ____ dans ton sac à dos?

To review the forms of these adjectives, turn to page 229.

**4 Complétez.** *(Complete.)*

13. C'est ma boutique ____. (favori)
14–15. La chemise est ____ et le pantalon est ____ aussi. (blanc)
16. Elle met une robe ____. (long)

## 5 Complétez. *(Complete.)*

17. —Jean est très sympa.
    —Oui. Mais il n'est pas ____ sympa ____ toi.

18. —Ce jean ne coûte pas cher.
    —Non, il est ____ cher ____ les autres.

19. —Les deux frères sont très intelligents.
    —C'est vrai. Paul est ____ intelligent ____ Loïc.

To review the comparative of adjectives, turn to page 230.

## 6 Récrivez chaque phrase. *(Rewrite each sentence.)*

20. Je crois que oui.
    Vous ____.

21. Elle voit de jolies chaussures dans la vitrine.
    Elles ____.

22. Vous voyez ça?
    Tu ____?

To review the verbs **voir** and **croire**, turn to page 232.

# Culture

## 7 Vrai ou faux? *(True or false?)*

23. Les boutiques des grands couturiers sont très chères.
24. Un grand magasin a beaucoup de rayons différents.
25. On trouve les marchés aux puces dans les quartiers élégants de Paris.

To review this cultural information, turn to pages 236–237.

La boutique d'un grand couturier, Paris

Tell all you can about this illustration.

# Vocabulaire

## Identifying articles of clothing

| | | | |
|---|---|---|---|
| les vêtements (m. pl.) | une veste | un polo | une basket |
| un jean | un pantalon | un manteau | une chaussure |
| un short | un t-shirt | un anorak | une chaussette |
| une casquette | une sandale | un blouson | |
| un pull | un sweat-shirt | un survêtement | |

## Identifying men's clothing

une chemise
une cravate
un complet

## Identifying women's clothing

| | |
|---|---|
| une jupe plissée | une robe |
| un chemisier | un tailleur |

**How well do you know your vocabulary?**

- Choose words that describe an outfit you would like to have.
- Describe your shopping trip to look for the outfit.

## Shopping

| | | | |
|---|---|---|---|
| une boutique | un vendeur | cher (chère) | trouver |
| un centre commercial | une vendeuse | faire des courses | mettre |
| un grand magasin | un rayon | essayer | |
| une vitrine | des soldes (m. pl.) | entrer (dans) | |
| une cabine d'essayage | le prix | porter | |

## Describing clothes

| | | | |
|---|---|---|---|
| large | sport | à manches | la pointure |
| serré(e) | joli(e) | longues | la taille |
| habillé(e) | favori(te) | courtes | au-dessus |
| | | | au-dessous |

## Identifying colors

| | | | |
|---|---|---|---|
| De quelle couleur? | noir(e) | rouge | marron |
| blanc(he) | gris(e) | beige | orange |
| brun(e) | bleu(e) | rose | |
| vert(e) | jaune | bleu marine | |

## Other useful words and expressions

| | | |
|---|---|---|
| Vous faites quelle taille? | en solde | voir |
| Je fais du 40. | à mon avis | croire |

**VIDÉOTOUR**

**Épisode 7**

In this video episode, you will visit a boutique with Chloé and Christine. See page 532 for more information.

## Conversation

### Faire la cuisine!

**Julie:** Tu vas préparer le déjeuner?

**Miéna:** Moi? Préparer le déjeuner? Tu rigoles! Je déteste faire la cuisine.

**Julie:** Tu veux aller au resto, alors?

**Miéna:** Non, je ne peux pas. Je n'ai pas le temps. Je vais manger une tranche de pizza.

**Julie:** Tu n'as pas le temps d'aller au resto? Pourquoi?

**Miéna:** Je veux acheter quelque chose pour samedi. Je vais à une fête chez une amie.

**Julie:** Qu'est-ce que tu vas acheter?

**Miéna:** Je crois que je vais acheter une robe.

**Julie:** Près de chez moi, il y a des soldes dans une petite boutique sympa.

**Miéna:** Merci, mais je vais aller aux Galeries. Je trouve toujours quelque chose là.

Galeries Lafayette, Paris

## Vous avez compris?

Répondez. (*Answer.*)

1. Miéna va préparer le déjeuner?
2. Elle aime faire la cuisine?
3. Elle veut aller déjeuner au restaurant?
4. Elle ne peut pas aller au restaurant?
5. Qu'est-ce qu'elle va manger?
6. Qu'est-ce qu'elle veut acheter?
7. Elle va où samedi?
8. Elle va aller dans quel magasin?

# Structure

## Les verbes irréguliers au présent

**1.** Review the following irregular verbs.

| ALLER | je vais, tu vas, il/elle/on va,<br>nous<sub>z</sub> allons, vous<sub>z</sub> allez, ils/elles vont |
|---|---|
| PRENDRE | je prends, tu prends, il/elle/on prend,<br>nous prenons, vous prenez, ils/elles prennent |
| FAIRE | je fais, tu fais, il/elle/on fait,<br>nous faisons, vous faites, ils/elles font |
| POUVOIR | je peux, tu peux, il/elle/on peut,<br>nous pouvons, vous pouvez, ils/elles peuvent |
| VOULOIR | je veux, tu veux, il/elle/on veut,<br>nous voulons, vous voulez, ils/elles veulent |
| METTRE | je mets, tu mets, il/elle/on met,<br>nous mettons, vous mettez, ils/elles mettent |
| CROIRE | je crois, tu crois, il/elle/on croit,<br>nous croyons, vous croyez, ils/elles croient |
| VOIR | je vois, tu vois, il/elle/on voit,<br>nous voyons, vous voyez, ils/elles voient |

**2.** Note that for all the preceding verbs except **aller,** the three singular forms sound alike. For all these verbs except **faire,** the **nous** and **vous** stems are the same.

**1**  **Historiette On fait des courses.** Répondez d'après les indications. *(Answer according to the cues.)*

1. Tu vas aller où? (aux Galeries Lafayette)
2. Qu'est-ce que tu vas faire? (acheter un cadeau)
3. Qu'est-ce que tu veux acheter? (une chemise blanche)
4. C'est pour qui, la chemise? (mon père)
5. Il fait quelle taille? (du 39)
6. Tu vois un chemisier pour ta mère? (oui)
7. Qui met le chemisier dans un sac? (le vendeur)

**2** **Historiette À l'école** Mettez au pluriel. *(Make the sentences plural.)*

1. Je vais à l'école.
2. Je prends le car pour aller à l'école.
3. Je veux poser une question.
4. L'élève peut poser des questions.
5. Sandrine croit qu'elle a la bonne réponse.
6. Elle prend ses cahiers.

Galeries Lafayette, Paris

Des pâtisseries

## Les contractions au et du

The prepositions **à** and **de** contract with **le** to form **au** and **du**, and with **les** to form **aux** and **des**.

| | |
|---|---|
| à + le = **au** | Il va **au** collège. |
| à + les = **aux** | Le prof parle **aux** élèves. |
| de + le = **du** | Il rentre **du** collège. |
| de + les = **des** | Il parle **des** élèves. |

**3**  **Où?** Répondez d'après les indications. *(Answer according to the cues.)*

1. On achète des tartes où? (pâtisserie)
2. Et du saucisson? (charcuterie)
3. Et de l'eau minérale? (épicerie)
4. Et du poisson? (marché)
5. On parle à qui au marché? (marchands)

**4** **D'où?** Complétez en utilisant **de** + un article défini. *(Answer with* de + *a definite article.)*

1. Mon frère rentre _____ lycée.
2. Mon autre frère rentre _____ collège.
3. Ma sœur rentre _____ école.
4. Mon autre sœur rentre _____ cantine.
5. Nous parlons tous _____ professeurs.

# Le partitif

1. Remember that the partitive, "some," "any," is expressed in French by **de** + the definite article. **De** contracts with **le** to form **du** and with **les** to form **des.** In the negative, **du, de la, de l',** and **des** all become **de** or **d'.**

   | | |
   |---|---|
   | **Je veux de l'argent.** | **Je ne veux pas d'argent.** |
   | **J'ai des croissants.** | **Je n'ai pas de croissants.** |

2. Remember that **un** and **une** also become **de** or **d'** after a negative expression.

   | | |
   |---|---|
   | **Tu veux un couteau?** | **Tu ne veux pas de couteau?** |
   | **J'ai une serviette.** | **Je n'ai pas de serviette.** |

**5**  **Dans le chariot** Dites ce qu'il y a dans le chariot. *(Tell what is in the cart.)*

**6**  **Pas dans le chariot** Dites ce qu'il n'y a pas dans le chariot de l'Activité 5. *(Tell what is not in the cart in Activity 5.)*

**Révision**

**7** **J'ai faim** Répondez d'après le modèle.
*(Answer according to the model.)*

—**Tu veux du poisson?**

—**Non, je ne veux pas de poisson. Je n'aime pas le poisson!**

1. Tu veux du bœuf?
2. Tu veux des œufs?
3. Tu veux des carottes à la crème?
4. Tu veux du poulet?
5. Tu veux de la salade?
6. Tu veux du gâteau au chocolat?

## Le comparatif

1. You use the comparative to compare two people or two items.

   **Aurélie est plus (aussi, moins) sportive que son frère.**
   **Le pantalon est plus (aussi, moins) cher que le jean.**

2. You use the stress pronouns **moi, toi, lui, elle, nous, vous, eux,** and **elles** after **que (qu')** when comparing people.

   **Il est moins sympa qu'elle (que toi, qu'eux).**

Marie est plus fatiguée que sa sœur.

**8** **Cyril et moi** Répondez d'après le modèle.
*(Answer according to the model.)*

**Cyril est très sérieux.** →

—**Il est plus sérieux que moi?**

—**Non, il est aussi sérieux que toi.**

1. Cyril est très timide.
2. Cyril est très grand.
3. Cyril est très amusant.
4. Cyril est très patient.
5. Cyril est très beau.
6. Cyril est très sympathique.

**9**   **Christelle et moi**  Remplacez Cyril par Christelle dans l'Activité 8. *(Replace* Cyril *with* Christelle *in Activity 8.)*

**10** **Au restaurant**  With a classmate, make up a conversation between a waiter or a waitress and a customer.

Un restaurant, Paris

**11**  **Qu'est-ce que tu fais?**  Work with a classmate. Ask each other questions about the things you do or want to do. Use the following words in the conversation.

prendre    vouloir    pouvoir    croire    faire    aller

**12**  **Des courses**  Work with a classmate. Each of you will make up a grocery list. Exchange lists. Then tell each other where you are going to go and what you are going to do.

 **LITERARY COMPANION**  *You may wish to read the poem «Dors mon enfant», by Elolongué Epanya Yondo, who was born in Cameroun and studied in Paris. This poem is found on page 510.*

1. Maisons du pays Dogon au Mali
2. Masque sénoufo de la Côte d'Ivoire
3. Danse rituelle et tambourinaires du Burundi
4. Une petite fille du Mali
5. Dakar, la capitale du Sénégal
6. Youssou N'Dour, le célèbre chanteur pop du Sénégal
7. Un griot raconte aux jeunes du village l'histoire de leurs ancêtres

NATIONAL
GEOGRAPHIC

# REFLETS
## de l'Afrique

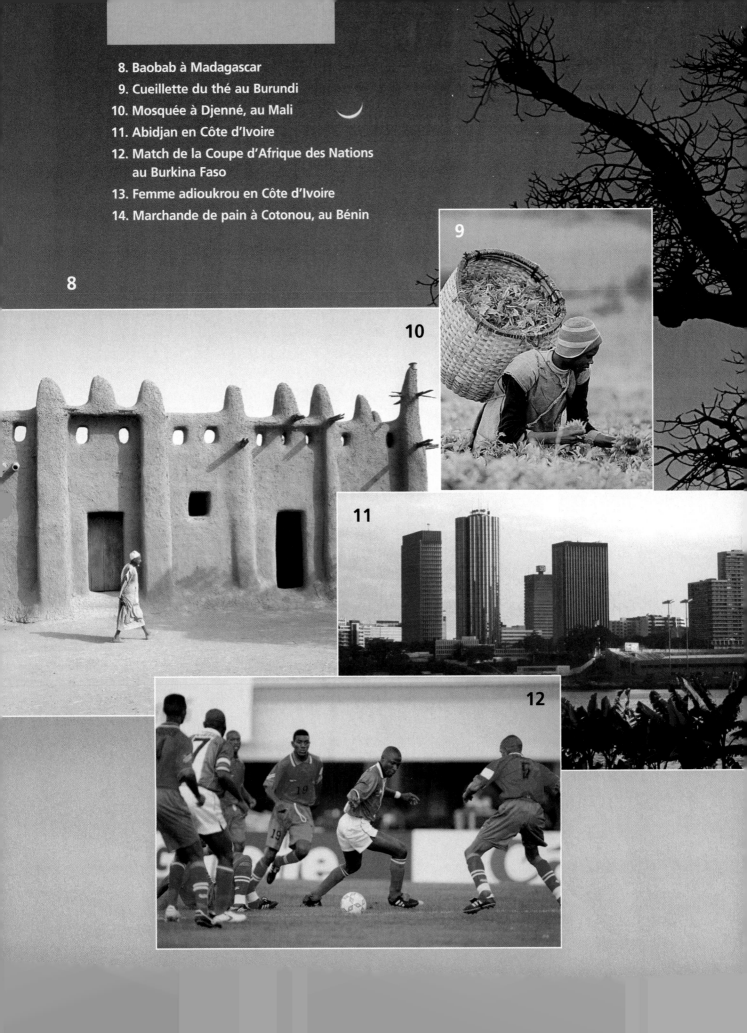

8

9

10

11

12

NATIONAL
GEOGRAPHIC

# REFLETS
## de l'Afrique

# 14

# Literary Companion

*These literary selections develop reading and cultural skills and introduce students to French literature.*

# Littérature 1

## *La petite Fadette* George Sand

### Vocabulaire

des frères jumeaux · · · les yeux

forts

Les jumeaux sont semblables.
Ils ont les yeux bleus.
Ils sont forts.

Il y a deux autres garçons dans la famille.
L'aîné a cinq ans.
Le cadet a deux ans.

pleurer · · ·

Il est triste. Il pleure.

Le petit garçon a peur.

un paysan

un champ

Les paysans travaillent dans les champs.
La petite fille est très pauvre.

Elle est (tombe) malade.

## Activités

**A** **Historiette** **Les jumeaux**
Répondez.

1. Les deux frères sont jumeaux?
2. Ils sont très semblables?
3. Ils ont les yeux bleus?
4. Ils sont forts ou faibles?
5. Le cadet a cinq ans ou deux ans?
6. Et l'aîné, il a quel âge?

**B** **Quel est le mot?** Complétez.

1. Des _____ sont des frères qui ont le même âge.
2. Le petit garçon est triste. Il _____.
3. Il pleure aussi quand il a _____.
4. Les jumeaux sont blonds et ils ont les yeux bleus. Ils sont très _____.
5. M. et Mme Gaillard ont deux enfants. L'_____ a quinze ans et le
   _____ a huit ans.
6. M. et Mme Gaillard _____ dans les champs. M. et Mme Gaillard
   sont des _____.
7. La petite fille n'est pas riche. Elle est _____.
8. La petite fille est _____. Elle a la grippe.

Le Berry, France

**INTRODUCTION** Le vrai nom de George Sand (1804–1876) est Aurore Dupin. Elle est née[1] à Paris, mais elle passe son enfance à Nohant, dans le Berry. Le Berry est une région rurale.

George Sand a un mariage malheureux. Séparée de son mari, elle rentre à Paris avec ses deux enfants. Ses romans les plus connus[2] sont des romans champêtres[3]. Dans ses romans, elle montre un grand intérêt pour les paysans du Berry. *La petite Fadette* est un roman champêtre publié en 1849.

[1] née *born*
[2] romans les plus connus *best-known novels*
[3] champêtres *pastoral*

# La petite Fadette

Le père Barbeau habite à la Cosse. Le père Barbeau est un homme important. Il a deux champs. Il cultive ses deux champs pour nourrir° sa famille. Il a aussi une maison avec un jardin. C'est un homme courageux et bon. Il aime beaucoup sa famille—sa femme, la mère Barbeau, et ses trois enfants.

C'est alors que le père Barbeau et la mère Barbeau ont deux garçons à la fois°: deux beaux jumeaux. Il est impossible de distinguer les jumeaux l'un de l'autre parce qu'ils° sont très semblables. Sylvinet est l'aîné et Landry est le cadet.

**2**

Les deux garçons grandissent° sans problème. Ils sont blonds avec de grands yeux bleus. Ils parlent avec la même voix°. Ils sont très amis. Ils sont toujours ensemble.

Les enfants ont maintenant 14 ans. Le père Barbeau dit qu'ils ont l'âge de travailler. Mais il n'y a pas assez de travail pour les deux garçons chez les Barbeau. Le père décide d'envoyer° un des garçons chez un voisin, le père Caillaud. Le père Caillaud habite à la Priche.

nourrir *to feed*

à la fois *at the same time*
parce qu'ils *because they*

grandissent *grow up*
voix *voice*

envoyer *to send*

Les jumeaux sont très tristes. Être séparés, c'est horrible. Sylvinet commence à pleurer et Landry pleure aussi.

—Mais, le père Caillaud n'habite pas très loin, dit Landry.

—C'est vrai. Je vais chez le père Caillaud…

—Non, Sylvinet. Pas toi, moi! Je vais chez le père Caillaud!

Donc Landry quitte la maison de son père… Maintenant, il travaille chez le père Caillaud. Le père Caillaud est content que Landry travaille pour lui. Landry est très fort.

Le père Caillaud aime beaucoup Landry. Il traite Landry comme un de ses enfants. Landry aussi aime beaucoup le père Caillaud. Il est content de travailler à la Priche. Mais Sylvinet n'est pas content. Il est jaloux de Landry.

Françoise Fadet est une petite fille très pauvre. Elle habite avec sa grand-mère et son petit frère handicapé. Ils habitent près de la rivière°, pas très loin de la Priche. On appelle Françoise «la petite Fadette». La petite Fadette est très solitaire. Elle n'est pas comme les autres enfants. Elle est assez différente des autres. Les autres enfants ont peur de la petite Fadette. Certains détestent la petite fille.

rivière *river*

Un jour, Landry rentre à la Priche et rencontre° la petite Fadette qui pleure.

—Pourquoi° tu pleures comme ça?

—Parce qu'on me déteste.

—C'est un peu ta faute°, Fadette.

—Ma faute? Pourquoi?

—Parce que tu es toujours très sale° et désagréable avec les autres.

rencontre *meets*
Pourquoi *Why*

faute *fault*

sale *dirty*

Émile Lambinet *Écouen, près de Paris*

Landry, lui, ne trouve° pas la petite Fadette désagréable. Il trouve même qu'elle est intelligente et intéressante. La petite Fadette trouve Landry très beau. Elle aime Landry. Landry et la petite Fadette sont souvent ensemble et Landry change la personnalité de la petite Fadette.

Le jumeau de Landry, Sylvinet, est très jaloux de Landry et la petite Fadette. Il tombe très malade. Sa famille est désespérée. Mais qui sauve Sylvinet? La petite Fadette, l'amie de son frère Landry. Maintenant, tout° est possible, même le mariage de Landry et de la petite Fadette.

trouve *finds*

tout *everything*

William Bouguereau *Jeune fille au panier de fruits*

## Vous avez compris?

**A** **Les enfants Barbeau** Répondez.

1. M. et Mme Barbeau ont combien d'enfants?
2. Ils ont des jumeaux?
3. L'aîné, c'est Sylvinet ou Landry?
4. Et le cadet?
5. Comment sont les jumeaux?
6. Ils sont bruns ou blonds?
7. Ils ont les yeux de quelle couleur?
8. Ils ont la même voix?

**B** **Le père Barbeau** Décrivez le père Barbeau.

**C** **Les jumeaux** Décrivez les jumeaux Barbeau.

**D** **Séparation** Complétez.

1. Quand les enfants ont _____ ans, le père Barbeau dit qu'ils ont l'âge de _____.
2. Le père Barbeau décide d'envoyer un enfant chez un _____, le père Caillaud.
3. Le père Caillaud _____ à la Priche.
4. Les jumeaux sont très _____ parce qu'ils vont être séparés.
5. Ils sont très tristes et ils _____.
6. _____ travaille chez le père Caillaud.
7. Le père Caillaud _____ beaucoup Landry. Il _____ Landry comme un de ses enfants.

**E** **La petite Fadette** Répondez.

1. Avec qui habite la petite Fadette?
2. Elle habite où?
3. Comment est la petite Fadette?
4. Qui a peur de la petite Fadette?
5. La petite Fadette pleure. Pourquoi?
6. Elle parle à qui?
7. Landry trouve la petite Fadette comment?
8. Qui change la personnalité de la petite Fadette?
9. Qui tombe malade?
10. Qui sauve Sylvinet?

# «Dors mon enfant» Elolongué Epanya Yondo

## Vocabulaire

un écrivain

un oranger fleuri

**une revue** un magazine
**l'avenir** le futur

## Activité

**Un oranger** Répondez.

1. Un oranger, c'est un fruit ou un arbre?
2. L'orange, c'est le fruit de l'oranger?
3. Tu aimes les oranges?
4. Tu aimes le jus d'orange?
5. Il y a des orangers dans les régions tropicales?
6. C'est beau un oranger fleuri?

Gerard Sekoto *Jeune fille à l'orange*

**INTRODUCTION** La poésie africaine francophone est la poésie écrite par des Africains de langue française. La poésie africaine francophone est riche et variée. Deux écrivains de langue française célèbres sont Léopold Sédar Senghor et Aimé Césaire. Ces deux écrivains créent dans les années 30 le mouvement de «la négritude». La négritude, c'est «l'ensemble des valeurs culturelles de l'Afrique noire.»

En 1947, Alioune Diop fonde à Paris la revue *Présence Africaine.* La revue publie les œuvres[1] d'écrivains africains francophones et diffuse le concept de la négritude.

[1] œuvres *works*

Aujourd'hui, *Présence Africaine* est une maison d'édition[2] qui publie les œuvres d'écrivains africains.

«Dors mon enfant» est tiré de[3] *Kamérun! Kamérun!* du poète Elolongué Epanya Yondo. Elolongué Epanya Yondo est né au Cameroun en 1930. Il va étudier à Paris où il habite chez Alioune Diop. Elolongué Epanya Yondo veut inspirer un esprit de solidarité chez ses compatriotes pour établir un avenir[4] solide sans oublier[5] les traditions passées.

[2] maison d'édition *publishing house*
[3] tiré de *taken from*
[4] avenir *future*
[5] sans oublier *without forgetting*

### «Dors mon enfant»

Dors° mon enfant dors      Dors
Quand tu dors              *Sleep*
Tu es beau
Comme un oranger fleuri…
Dors mon enfant dors
Tu es si° beau             si *so*
Quand tu dors…
Mon beau bébé noir dors

Elizabeth Barakah Hodges *Madone noire*

## Vous avez compris?

**Dors mon enfant** Répondez.

1. Qui parle dans le poème?
2. La mère trouve son enfant beau?
3. Elle compare son enfant à quel arbre?
4. Un oranger est un bel arbre?
5. Un oranger est beau surtout quand il fleurit?
6. La mère compare son enfant à un bel oranger fleuri?
7. Le petit enfant est de quelle race?
8. C'est un bébé ou un petit garçon?

# Video Companion

## Using video in the classroom

The use of video in the classroom can be a wonderful asset to the World Languages teacher and a most beneficial learning tool for the language student. Video enables students to experience whatever it is they are learning in their textbook in a real-life setting. With each lesson, they are able to take a vicarious field trip. They see people interacting at home, at school, at the market, etc., in an authentic milieu. Students sitting in a classroom can see real people going about their real life in real places. They may experience the target culture in many countries. The cultural benefits are limitless.

**Developing listening and viewing skills** In addition to its tremendous cultural value, video, when properly used, gives students much needed practice in developing good listening and viewing skills. Video allows students to look for numerous clues that are evident in a tone of voice, facial expressions, and gestures. Through video students can see and hear the diversity of the target culture and, as discerning viewers and listeners, compare and contrast the French-speaking cultures to each other and to their own culture. Video introduces a dimension into classroom instruction that no other medium — teachers, overhead, text, Audio CDs—can provide.

**Reinforcing learned language** Video that is properly developed for classroom use has speakers reincorporate the language students have learned in a given lesson. In keeping with reality, however, speakers introduce some new words, expressions, and structures because students

functioning in a real-life situation would not know every word native speakers use with them in a live conversation. The lively and interactive nature of video allows students to use their listening and viewing skills to comprehend new language in addition to seeing and hearing the language they have learned come to life.

**Getting the most out of video** The intrinsic benefit of video is often lost when students are allowed to read the scripted material before viewing. In many cases, students will have come to understand language used by the speakers in the video by means of reading comprehension, thus negating the inherent benefits of video as a tool to develop listening and viewing skills. Because today's students are so accustomed to the medium of video as a tool for entertainment and learning, a well-written and well-produced video program will help them develop real-life language skills and confidence in those skills in an enjoyable way.

# On Location!

Je suis Christine. Je suis de Fort-de-France, à la Martinique.

Je suis Vincent. Je suis de Paris.

Je suis Chloé. Je suis de Lyon, en France.

Je suis Manu. Je suis algérien.

Je suis Amadou. Je suis malien.

# Vidéotour

## Bon voyage!

## Épisode 1: Une amie et un ami

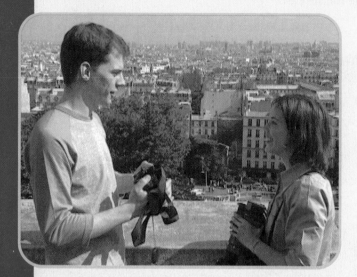

Vincent et Chloé à Montmartre

Une vue splendide sur Paris

## Avant de regarder

Can you spot the following?

1. un garçon brun
2. une fille brune
3. une vue splendide sur Paris
4. une caméra
5. une fille enthousiaste

## Après avoir regardé

**Expansion** You will be taking a video tour of Paris. As you watch, look for similarities you notice between Paris and the city or town where you live. What differences do you notice? Choose several places in Paris that you would like to visit. Do some research to find out more about Paris. Why do you find it interesting?

# Vidéotour

## Bon voyage!

## Épisode 2: Les cours et les profs

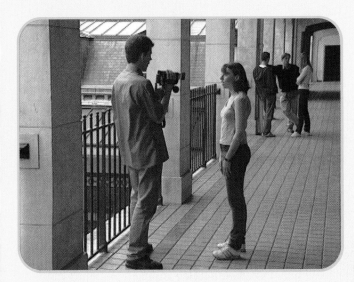

Vincent et une amie, Élodie, au lycée Louis-le-Grand

Manu et Vincent en cours de chimie

## Avant de regarder

Make an educated guess!

1. In the first photograph, what do you think Vincent is doing?

2. In the second photo, does Manu look as if he knows what he is doing?

3. How does Vincent look as he watches Manu?

4. Do you think the experiment is going to be successful?

## Après avoir regardé

**Expansion**   As you watch the video, think about whether there are any similarities between the school you see in the video and the one you attend. Do you notice any differences? Which might you prefer? Why? Do some research about schedules in French schools. Are the schedules for French students like yours?

# Vidéotour

## Bon voyage!

## Épisode 3: Pendant et après les cours

Amadou et Christine dans la rue après les cours

Amadou et Christine dans la papeterie

## Avant de regarder

Can you spot the following?

1. une papeterie
2. une calculatrice
3. une rue
4. des fournitures scolaires
5. deux amis

## Après avoir regardé

**Expansion**   You will see something in the video that Christine enjoys doing after school. Compare her likes to some of those that you may have. See whether or not you have anything in common with your new French friends. Think about the other people in the video. Knowing what you know about them, what might they enjoy doing after school?

# Vidéotour

## Bon voyage!

## Épisode 4: La famille et la maison

Christine a une surprise pour Mme Séguin.

Christine et Mme Séguin dans la cuisine de la maison de Monet

## Avant de regarder

Can you spot the following? If so, give an adjective to describe each.

1. un jardin
2. un immeuble
3. une cuisine
4. une fleur
5. une voiture

## Après avoir regardé

**Expansion**   Giverny, a charming village northwest of Paris, is a beautiful spot. Can you think of any place near where you live that could compare to Giverny? Do some research to find out more about this famous place where Monet lived and write a paragraph about it or discuss with a friend what you found out that is of interest to you.

# Vidéotour

## Bon voyage!

## Épisode 5: Au café et au restaurant

Chloé et Christine vont dans un café.

Elles commandent une boisson.

## Avant de regarder

Invent the following.

1. le nom du café
2. ce que Chloé commande
3. ce que Christine commande
4. ce que dit le serveur

## Après avoir regardé

**Expansion**   As you can imagine from what you saw in the video, café life is an important part of French culture. Do you have any cafés near where you live? If you do, do you and your friends go there often? If not, do you think you might enjoy them based on what you viewed in the video?

# Vidéotour

## Bon voyage!

## Épisode 6: La nourriture et les courses

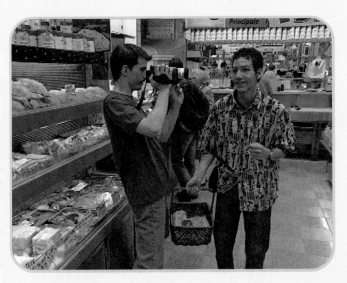

Vincent et Manu font les courses.

Manu «prépare» un repas fabuleux.

## Avant de regarder

Answer the questions.

1. Où sont Vincent et Manu?
2. Qu'est-ce qu'ils font?
3. Qu'est-ce qu'ils achètent, d'après vous?
4. Qui va payer, d'après vous?
5. Qu'est-ce qu'ils vont manger?

## Après avoir regardé

**Expansion**  What foods that you saw in the French supermarket are similar to those found in your supermarket? Do some research on the Internet to find a French recipe that you and your family might enjoy. Then make a list of all the ingredients you need from the supermarket to prepare this recipe.

# Vidéotour

## Bon voyage!

## Épisode 7: Les vêtements

Christine et Chloé veulent acheter une robe.

Chloé essaie une robe.

## Avant de regarder

Describe the following.

1. ce que porte Christine
2. ce que porte Chloé
3. ce que porte la vendeuse
4. la robe que Christine essaie

## Après avoir regardé

**Expansion** The world of fashion is significant in Paris and in other parts of the French-speaking world. Do some research on a famous French designer. Tell whether or not you might enjoy wearing his or her clothing. If you are artistic, draw a fashion that your designer might design.

# Vidéotour

## Bon voyage!

## Épisode 8: L'aéroport et l'avion

Où est Christine en réalité?

Manu est à l'aéroport avec Christine?

## Avant de regarder

Can you spot the following? How many of each do you see?

1. une valise
2. un passager
3. une carte d'embarquement
4. un comptoir
5. un bagage à main

## Après avoir regardé

**Expansion**  You have been exposed to many parts of the French-speaking world. Choose a place that you would most like to visit. Do some research on the Internet to plan your itinerary. Include the places you would like to visit in the city or town of your choice and explain how you would get there.

# Vidéotour

## Bon voyage!

## Épisode 9: La gare et le train

Amadou et Chloé partent pour Lille. Ils prennent leurs billets.

Leur train part d'où?

## Avant de regarder

Answer the questions.

1. Où sont Amadou et Chloé?
2. Qu'est-ce qu'ils font?
3. D'après vous, qui est l'homme avec eux?
4. D'après vous, qu'est-ce que nos amis demandent à cet homme?

## Après avoir regardé

**Expansion**   What is your favorite means of transportation for long trips. Why? Do you think most Americans would make the same choice? Survey your friends to find out their preferences.

# Vidéotour

## Bon voyage!

## Épisode 10: Les sports

Manu joue bien au basket.

Manu est fana de basket-ball. C'est son sport favori.

## Avant de regarder

Make an educated guess!

1. Où est Manu?
2. Qui joue au basket-ball?
3. Ce sont des amies de Manu?
4. Quel est le score?
5. Que fait Manu à la fin du match?

## Après avoir regardé

**Expansion** Think of some famous French athletes and do some research to find out about them. Choose one you think is particularly good and research his or her career.

# Vidéotour
## Bon voyage!

## Épisode 11: L'été et l'hiver

Christine «apprend» à faire du ski.

Manu est un très bon moniteur.

## Avant de regarder

Can you spot the following? If so, describe each one.

1. une montagne
2. un skieur
3. une piste
4. un sommet
5. un anorak

## Après avoir regardé

**Expansion**   What fun activity do you do in the winter? And in the summer? Are video games a big part of your life?

# Vidéotour

## Bon voyage!

## Épisode 12: La routine quotidienne

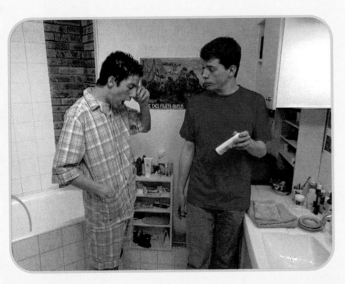

Manu se réveille.

Manu prend son petit déjeuner.

## Avant de regarder

Answer the questions.

1. Que fait Manu?
2. Que lui donne Vincent dans la salle de bains?
3. Que va faire Manu avec ça?
4. Qu'est-ce que Vincent donne à Manu dans sa chambre?
5. Qu'est-ce que Manu va faire?

## Après avoir regardé

**Expansion** Is it easy for you to get up in the morning or not? Do you go to bed early or late? Do you sleep well at night? Compare Manu's day with a typical day in your life.

# Vidéotour

## Bon voyage!

## Épisode 13: Les loisirs culturels

Chloé visite le musée d'Orsay. Elle trouve les tableaux fabuleux.

Chloé et Vincent sur la place Igor Stravinsky

## Avant de regarder

Can you spot the following?

1. une exposition
2. une danseuse
3. un tableau
4. une peinture
5. une statue

## Après avoir regardé

**Expansion** Are you aware of your cultural heritage? Can you name some famous American painters, musicians, architects? Do some research on the Internet about the musée d'Orsay. Who are some of the artists whose art is shown there? Can you find out what special exhibitions there are currently?

# Épisode 14: La santé et la médecine

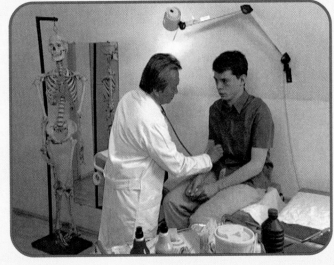

Le docteur Nguyen est très sympa.

Vincent n'est pas en bonne santé.

## Avant de regarder

Answer the questions.

1. Où est Vincent?

2. Pourquoi, d'après vous?

3. Vincent a un mouchoir dans la main. Pourquoi?

4. D'après vous, Vincent est très malade?

5. Que lui dit le médecin?

## Après avoir regardé

**Expansion** Do you go to the doctor's every time something is wrong with you? Why or why not? Does your doctor make house calls? Do some research online about medical achievements and famous doctors in France. You may want to begin with an online visit to **l'Institut Pasteur**.

# Activity 1

**Élève A** Ask your partner the following questions. Correct answers are in parentheses.

1. Comment est Sophie, petite ou grande?
   *(Sophie est petite.)*

2. Comment est Sylvie?
   *(Elle est grande.)*

3. Il est d'où, Olivier?
   *(Il est de Nice.)*

4. Luc est américain ou français?
   *(Il est français.)*

5. Comment est Olivier, brun ou blond?
   *(Il est brun.)*

6. Qui est de Montréal?
   *(Sylvie est de Montréal.)*

**Élève A** Answer your partner's questions based on the pictures below.

Sophie / Paris

Olivier / Nice

Sylvie / Montréal

Luc / Lyon

---

**Élève B** Answer your partner's questions based on the pictures below.

Sophie / Paris

Sylvie / Montréal

Olivier / Nice

Luc / Lyon

**Élève B** Ask your partner the following questions. Correct answers are in parentheses.

1. **Comment est Olivier, petit ou grand?**
   *(Olivier est petit.)*

2. **Comment est Luc?**
   *(Luc est grand.)*

3. **Elle est d'où, Sophie?**
   *(Elle est de Paris.)*

4. **Qui est de Lyon?**
   *(Luc est de Lyon.)*

5. **Sophie est française ou américaine?**
   *(Elle est française.)*

6. **Comment est Luc, brun ou blond?**
   *(Il est blond.)*

# Activity 2

**Élève A** Ask your partner the following questions. Correct answers are in parentheses.

1. Qui est Luc?
   (*Luc est le frère de Nathalie.*)

2. Qui est Philippe?
   (*Philippe est l'ami de Nathalie.*)

3. Carol est élève dans une école américaine?
   (*Oui, Carol est élève dans une école américaine.*)

4. Bruno est élève dans un collège français?
   (*Oui, Bruno est élève dans un collège français.*)

**Élève A** Answer your partner's questions based on the pictures below.

Nathalie et
Luc Simonet

Nathalie Simonet et
Philippe Latour

Carol Smith

Bruno Lapierre

---

**Élève B** Answer your partner's questions based on the pictures below.

Nathalie et
Luc Simonet

Nathalie Simonet et
Philippe Latour

Carol Smith

Bruno Lapierre

**Élève B** Ask your partner the following questions. Correct answers are in parentheses.

1. Qui est Nathalie?
   (*Nathalie est la sœur de Luc.*)

2. Nathalie est sympathique?
   (*Oui, Nathalie est très sympathique.*)

3. Carol est américaine?
   (*Oui, Carol est américaine.*)

4. Bruno est français?
   (*Oui, Bruno est français.*)

# Activity 3

*CHAPITRE 1, Structure, pages 26–33*

**Élève A** Correct your partner's statements based on the pictures below.

Napoléon Bonaparte

Oprah Winfrey

Charles de Gaulle

Meg Ryan

**Élève A** Read your partner the following false statements. Correct answers are in parentheses.

1. Meg Ryan est brune.
*(Non, elle n'est pas brune. Elle est blonde.)*

2. Charles de Gaulle est américain.
*(Non, il n'est pas américain. Il est français.)*

3. Oprah Winfrey est timide.
*(Non, elle n'est pas timide. Elle est sociable.)*

4. Napoléon est très grand.
*(Non, il n'est pas très grand. Il est assez petit.)*

---

**Élève B** Correct your partner's statements based on the pictures below.

Meg Ryan

Charles de Gaulle

Oprah Winfrey

Napoléon Bonaparte

**Élève B** Read your partner the following false statements. Correct answers are in parentheses.

1. Meg Ryan est timide.
*(Non, elle n'est pas timide. Elle est dynamique.)*

2. Charles de Gaulle est petit.
*(Non, il n'est pas petit. Il est grand.)*

3. Oprah Winfrey est française.
*(Non, elle n'est pas française. Elle est américaine.)*

4. Napoléon est américain.
*(Non, il n'est pas américain. Il est français.)*

# Activity 4

**Élève A** Answer your partner's questions based on the picture below.

**Élève A** Ask your partner the following questions. Correct answers are in parentheses.

1. Le cours de français est facile?
   *(Oui, le cours de français est facile.)*
2. Le prof est très sympathique?
   *(Oui, le prof est très sympathique.)*
3. Les élèves sont françaises ou américaines?
   *(Les élèves sont françaises.)*
4. Les élèves sont amies?
   *(Oui, les élèves sont amies.)*

**Élève B** Answer your partner's questions based on the picture below.

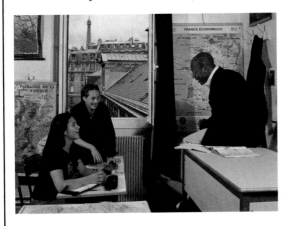

**Élève B** Ask your partner the following questions. Correct answers are in parentheses.

1. Les élèves sont dans le même lycée?
   *(Oui, les élèves sont dans le même lycée.)*
2. Les élèves sont dans la salle de classe?
   *(Oui, les élèves sont dans la salle de classe.)*
3. Les élèves sont sympathiques?
   *(Oui, les élèves sont sympathiques.)*
4. Le cours de français est difficile?
   *(Non, le cours de français n'est pas difficile.)* or
   *(Non, le cours de français est facile.)*

# Activity 5

**Élève A** Ask your partner the following questions. Correct answers are in parentheses.

1. Guy est fort en mathématiques?
   (*Oui, il est fort en mathématiques.*)

2. Guy est très fort en sciences naturelles?
   (*Non, il n'est pas fort en sciences naturelles.*)
   or (*Non, il est mauvais en sciences naturelles.*)

3. Il est mauvais en géométrie?
   (*Non, il n'est pas mauvais en géométrie.*)
   or (*Non, il est fort en géométrie.*)

4. L'économie est une science naturelle?
   (*Non, l'économie n'est pas une science naturelle.*) or (*Non, l'économie est une science sociale.*)

**Élève A** Answer your partner's questions based on the report card below.

Marie Dauphin

| Les langues: | |
| --- | --- |
| Le français | A– |
| L'anglais | B+ |
| **Les sciences sociales:** | |
| L'histoire | D |
| La géographie | C+ |
| **D'autres matières:** | |
| La musique | A |

---

**Élève B** Answer your partner's questions based on the report card below.

Guy Laurent

| Les sciences naturelles: | |
| --- | --- |
| La biologie | C– |
| La chimie | D |
| **Les mathématiques:** | |
| La géométrie | A |
| Le calcul | B+ |
| **Les sciences sociales:** | |
| L'économie | B |

**Élève B** Ask your partner the following questions. Correct answers are in parentheses.

1. Marie est très forte en sciences sociales?
   (*Non, elle est mauvaise en sciences sociales.*) or
   (*Elle n'est pas forte en sciences sociales.*)

2. Le cours de français est très difficile?
   (*Non, le cours de français est très facile.*)
   or (*Non, le cours de français n'est pas difficile.*)

3. Marie est mauvaise en histoire?
   (*Oui, Marie est mauvaise en histoire.*)

4. L'anglais est une science sociale?
   (*Non, l'anglais est une langue.*) or
   (*Non, l'anglais n'est pas une science sociale.*)

# Activity 6

**Élève A** Answer your partner's questions in complete sentences, using either **Oui** or **Non.**

**Élève A** Ask your partner the following questions. Correct answers are in parentheses.

1. La salle de classe est petite?
   *(Oui, la salle de classe est petite.)* or *(Non, la salle de classe n'est pas petite.)*

2. Les élèves sont intelligents?
   *(Oui, les élèves sont intelligents.)* or *(Non, les élèves ne sont pas intelligents.)*

3. Le lycée est grand?
   *(Oui, le lycée est grand.)* or *(Non, le lycée n'est pas grand.)*

4. Vous deux, vous êtes élèves dans un lycée français?
   *(Oui, nous sommes élèves dans un lycée français.)* or *(Non, nous ne sommes pas élèves dans un lycée français.)*

5. Tu es fort(e) en maths?
   *(Oui, je suis fort[e] en maths.)* or *(Non, je ne suis pas fort[e] en maths.)*

---

**Élève B** Answer your partner's questions in complete sentences, using either **Oui** or **Non.**

**Élève B** Ask your partner the following questions. Correct answers are in parentheses.

1. La prof est patiente?
   *(Oui, la prof est patiente.)* or *(Non, la prof n'est pas patiente.)*

2. Les élèves sont sympas?
   *(Oui, les élèves sont sympas.)* or *(Non, les élèves ne sont pas sympas.)*

3. Le prof est intéressant?
   *(Oui, le prof est intéressant.)* or *(Non, le prof n'est pas intéressant.)*

4. Vous êtes copains?
   *(Oui, nous sommes copains.)* or *(Non, nous ne sommes pas copains.)*

5. Tu es fort(e) en histoire?
   *(Oui, je suis fort[e] en histoire.)* or *(Non, je ne suis pas fort[e] en histoire.)*

# Activity 7

**Élève A** Ask your partner the following questions. Correct answers are in parentheses.

1. Les élèves sont où?
   *(Les élèves sont dans la cour.)*

2. Ils parlent entre les cours?
   *(Oui, ils parlent entre les cours.)*

3. Ils étudient dans la cour?
   *(Non, ils n'étudient pas dans la cour.)*

4. Les copains rigolent?
   *(Oui, ils rigolent.)*

**Élève A** Answer your partner's questions based on the picture below.

---

**Élève B** Ask your partner the following questions. Correct answers are in parentheses.

1. Les élèves passent la journée à l'école?
   *(Oui, ils passent la journée à l'école.)*

2. Ils regardent la prof?
   *(Oui, ils regardent la prof.)*

3. Un élève pose une question?
   *(Oui, il pose une question.)*

4. Les élèves déjeunent pendant le cours?
   *(Non, ils ne déjeunent pas pendant le cours.)*

**Élève B** Answer your partner's questions based on the picture below.

# Activity 8

**Élève A** Answer your partner's questions based on the picture below.

Sophie   Marc

**Élève A** Ask your partner the following questions. Correct answers are in parentheses.

1. Camille est à la papeterie?
   *(Oui, elle est à la papeterie.)*

2. Elle achète des fournitures scolaires?
   *(Oui, elle achète des fournitures scolaires.)*

3. Elle achète un classeur et une calculatrice?
   *(Oui, elle achète un classeur et une calculatrice.)*

4. Elle paie où?
   *(Elle paie à la caisse.)*

---

**Élève B** Answer your partner's questions based on the picture below.

Camille

**Élève B** Ask your partner the following questions. Correct answers are in parentheses.

1. Sophie travaille après les cours?
   *(Oui, elle travaille après les cours.)*

2. Elle travaille où?
   *(Elle travaille dans une papeterie.)*

3. Marc achète un sac à dos?
   *(Oui, il achète un sac à dos.)*

4. Il achète un classeur?
   *(Oui, il achète un classeur.)*

# Activity 9

**Élève A** Answer your partner's questions using the correct form of the verb below.

1. arriver
2. poser
3. rigoler
4. parler
5. travailler

**Élève A** Ask your partner the following questions. Possible responses are in parentheses.

1. Tu quittes la maison à quelle heure le matin?
   *(Je quitte la maison à sept heures et demie.)*

2. Qui écoute quand le prof parle?
   *(Les élèves écoutent quand le prof parle.)*

3. On parle français en Belgique?
   *(Oui, on parle français en Belgique.)*

4. Vous étudiez quelle langue?
   *(Nous étudions le français.)*

5. Vous détestez les examens?
   *(Oui, nous détestons les examens.)* or
   *(Non, nous ne détestons pas les examens.)*

---

**Élève B** Answer your partner's questions using the correct form of the verb below.

1. quitter
2. écouter
3. parler
4. étudier
5. détester

**Élève B** Ask your partner the following questions. Possible responses are in parentheses.

1. On arrive à l'école à quelle heure?
   *(On arrive à l'école à huit heures.)*

2. Qui pose des questions?
   *(Les élèves posent des questions.)* or
   *(Le prof pose des questions.)*

3. Vous rigolez dans la cour?
   *(Oui, nous rigolons dans la cour.)* or
   *(Non, nous ne rigolons pas dans la cour.)*

4. Tu parles beaucoup au téléphone?
   *(Oui, je parle beaucoup au téléphone.)* or
   *(Non, je ne parle pas beaucoup au téléphone.)*

5. Tu travailles après les cours?
   *(Oui, je travaille après les cours.)* or
   *(Non, je ne travaille pas après les cours.)*

**Élève A** Read your partner the following statements. He or she will fill in the blank. Correct answers are in parentheses.

1. Le frère de mon père est mon ———.
   *(oncle)*

2. La mère de mon cousin est ma ———.
   *(tante)*

3. Le mari de ma mère est mon ———.
   *(père)*

4. La mère de mon père est ma ———.
   *(grand-mère)*

5. Le fils de ma tante est mon ———.
   *(cousin)*

**Élève A** Complete your partner's statements with the name of the relative.

---

**Élève B** Complete your partner's statements with the name of the relative.

**Élève B** Read your partner the following statements. He or she will fill in the blank. Correct answers are in parentheses.

1. La sœur de ma mère est ma ———.
   *(tante)*

2. La femme de mon père est ma ———.
   *(mère)*

3. La fille de mes parents est ma ———.
   *(sœur)*

4. Les parents de ma mère sont mes ———.
   *(grands-parents)*

5. Les enfants de mon oncle sont mes ———.
   *(cousins)*

**Élève A** Ask your partner the following questions. Correct answers are in parentheses.

**Élève A** Now answer your partner's questions.

1. On regarde la télé dans la salle de bains ou la salle de séjour?
   (On regarde la télé dans la salle de séjour.)

2. On dîne dans la chambre à coucher ou la salle à manger?
   (On dîne dans la salle à manger.)

3. Le balcon donne sur la cour ou sur la cuisine?
   (Le balcon donne sur la cour.)

4. On habite au troisième étage d'un immeuble ou d'une maison?
   (On habite au troisième étage d'un immeuble.)

5. La voiture est dans la cuisine ou le garage?
   (La voiture est dans le garage.)

**Élève B** Answer your partner's questions.

**Élève B** Ask your partner the following questions. Correct answers are in parentheses.

1. On parle avec les voisins dans la cour ou la salle de bains?
   (On parle avec les voisins dans la cour.)

2. On prépare le dîner dans l'ascenseur ou la cuisine?
   (On prépare le dîner dans la cuisine.)

3. On monte à l'appartement dans le métro ou l'ascenseur?
   (On monte à l'appartement dans l'ascenseur.)

4. Les toilettes sont dans l'appartement ou dans la cour?
   (Les toilettes sont dans l'appartement.)

5. On habite dans un quartier ou dans une entrée?
   (On habite dans un quartier.)

# Activity 12

**Élève A** Ask your partner the following questions. Correct answers are in parentheses.

1. Marc a quel âge?
   (*Il a quinze ans.*)

2. Tes grands-parents ont une maison?
   (*Non, ils ont un joli appartement.*)

3. Tu as quel âge, toi?
   (*J'ai —— ans.*)

4. Qui a deux chiens?
   (*La prof de maths a deux chiens.*)

5. Quel âge ont tes grands-parents?
   (*Ils ont quatre-vingts ans.*)

**Élève A** Use the chart below to answer your partner's questions. Reminder: **toi** is you.

| Paul | 15 ans | Une sœur |
| --- | --- | --- |
| Tes grands-parents | 75 ans | Un chien |
| Toi | ? | Des profs intéressants |
| Tes cousines | 16 ans | Deux chats |
| Marie | 14 | Une petite famille |

---

**Élève B** Use the chart below to answer your partner's questions. Reminder: **toi** is you.

| Marc | 15 ans | Une sœur |
| --- | --- | --- |
| Tes grands-parents | 80 ans | Un joli appartement |
| Toi | ? | Des profs intéressants |
| La prof de maths | 35 | Deux chiens |
| Sophie | 14 | Une petite famille |

**Élève B** Ask your partner the following questions. Correct answers are in parentheses.

1. Qui a des profs intéressants?
   (*Moi, j'ai des profs intéressants.*)

2. Tes cousines ont combien de chats?
   (*Mes cousines ont deux chats.*)

3. Tes grands-parents ont quel âge?
   (*Mes grands-parents ont soixante-quinze ans.*)

4. Qui a une petite famille?
   (*Marie a une petite famille.*)

5. Paul a un frère ou une sœur?
   (*Paul a une sœur.*)

## Activity 13

**Élève A** Now your partner is the server.
Use the following picture menu to give
your order.

**Élève A** You are the server in a French café.
Ask your partner what he or she wants to
order. Correct answers are in parentheses.

1. Vous désirez?
   *(Un citron pressé, s'il vous plaît.)*

2. Vous désirez?
   *(Un croissant, s'il vous plaît.)*

3. Vous désirez?
   *(Une salade verte, s'il vous plaît.)*

4. Vous désirez?
   *(Un café, s'il vous plaît.)* or *(Un express, s'il vous plaît.)*

5. Vous désirez?
   *(Une tartine de pain beurré, s'il vous plaît.)*

---

**Élève B** Your partner is the server in a
French café. Use the following picture menu
to give your order.

**Élève B** Now you are the server. Ask your
partner what he or she wants to order. Correct
answers are in parentheses.

1. Vous désirez?
   *(Un jus d'orange, s'il vous plaît.)*

2. Vous désirez?
   *(Une saucisse de Francfort, s'il vous plaît.)* or
   *(Un hot-dog, s'il vous plaît.)*

3. Vous désirez?
   *(Un croque-monsieur, s'il vous plaît.)*

4. Vous désirez?
   *(Une soupe à l'oignon, s'il vous plaît.)*

5. Vous désirez?
   *(Une omelette nature, s'il vous plaît.)*

# Activity 14

**Élève A** Use the pictures below to answer your partner's questions.

**Élève A** Ask your partner the following questions. Correct answers are in parentheses.

1. Un couteau, c'est pour la soupe?
   *(Non, une cuillère, c'est pour la soupe.)*

2. Un verre, c'est pour le café?
   *(Non, une tasse, c'est pour le café.)*

3. Une soupe à l'oignon, c'est pour le dessert?
   *(Non, une glace au chocolat, c'est pour le dessert.)*

4. Un couteau, c'est pour le steak?
   *(Oui, un couteau, c'est pour le steak.)*

5. Un verre, c'est pour la limonade?
   *(Oui, un verre, c'est pour la limonade.)*

**Élève B** Use the pictures below to answer your partner's questions.

1.

2.

3.

4.

5.

**Élève B** Now ask your partner the following questions. Correct answers are in parentheses.

1. On prend un croissant pour le dîner?
   *(Non, on prend une omelette pour le dîner.)*

2. On prend une crêpe pour le déjeuner?
   *(Non, on prend un sandwich au jambon pour le déjeuner.)*

3. C'est un pourboire ou une fourchette?
   *(C'est un pourboire.)*

4. C'est un steak saignant ou bien cuit?
   *(C'est un steak bien cuit.)*

5. C'est une assiette ou une serviette?
   *(C'est une serviette.)*

## Activity 15

**Élève A** Ask your partner the following questions. Correct answers are in parentheses.

1. Les copains vont où?
   *(Ils vont à l'école.)*

2. Ils y vont comment?
   *(Ils y vont en voiture.)*

3. Tu vas où?
   *(Je vais à la papéterie.)*

4. Tu y vas à pied?
   *(Non, j'y vais en bus.)*

**Élève A** Answer your partner's questions based on the cues below.

1. l'école
2. à pied
3. le café
4. le métro

**Élève B** Answer your partner's questions based on the cues below.

1. l'école

2. en voiture

3. la papeterie

4. en bus

**Élève B** Ask your partner the following questions. Correct answers are in parentheses.

1. Vous allez où?
   *(Nous allons à l'école.)*

2. Vous y allez comment?
   *(Nous y allons à pied.)*

3. Tu vas où?
   *(Je vais au café.)*

4. Tu prends le bus pour aller au café?
   *(Non, je prends le métro.)*

# Activity 16

**Élève A** Ask your partner the following questions. Correct answers are in parentheses.

1. Pour acheter du pain, on va où?
   *(On va à la boulangerie-pâtisserie.)*

2. Pour acheter du lait, on va où?
   *(On va à la crémerie.)*

3. Pour acheter une tarte aux pommes, on va où?
   *(On va à la boulangerie-pâtisserie.)*

4. Pour acheter du jambon, on va où?
   *(On va à la charcuterie.)*

5. Pour acheter de la crème, on va où?
   *(On va à la crémerie.)*

**Élève A** Use the following pictures to answer your partner's questions.

---

**Élève B** Answer your partner's questions based on the pictures below.

**Élève B** Ask your partner the following questions. Correct answers are in parentheses.

1. Pour acheter de la viande, on va où?
   *(On va à la boucherie.)*

2. Pour acheter du poisson, on va où?
   *(On va à la poissonnerie.)*

3. Pour acheter du poivre, on va où?
   *(On va à l'épicerie.)*

4. Pour acheter du porc, on va où?
   *(On va à la boucherie.)*

5. Pour acheter des crevettes, on va où?
   *(On va à la poissonnerie.)*

# Activity 17

**Élève A** You play the part of the vendor. Ask your partner the following questions. Correct answers are in parentheses.

1. Vous voulez de la confiture?
   *(Oui, je voudrais un pot de confiture, s'il vous plaît.)*

2. Vous voulez des légumes surgelés?
   *(Oui, je voudrais un paquet de légumes surgelés, s'il vous plaît.)*

3. Vous voulez des petits pois?
   *(Oui, je voudrais une boîte de petits pois, s'il vous plaît.)*

4. Vous voulez du lait?
   *(Oui, je voudrais un litre de lait, s'il vous plaît.)*

5. Vous voulez du jambon?
   *(Oui, je voudrais une tranche de jambon, s'il vous plaît.)*

**Élève A** Answer your partner's questions based on the information below.

une bouteille

une douzaine

une boîte

250 grammes

un pot

---

**Élève B** Answer your partner's questions based on the information below.

un pot

un paquet

un pot     un paquet

une boîte     un litre

une tranche

**Élève B** Now you are the vendor. Ask your partner the following questions. Correct answers are in parentheses.

1. Vous voulez de la moutarde?
   *(Oui, je voudrais un pot de moutarde, s'il vous plaît.)*

2. Vous voulez du beurre?
   *(Oui, je voudrais deux cent cinquante grammes de beurre, s'il vous plaît.)*

3. Vous voulez des œufs?
   *(Oui, je voudrais une douzaine d'œufs, s'il vous plaît.)*

4. Vous voulez des petits pois?
   *(Oui, je voudrais une boîte de petits pois, s'il vous plaît.)*

5. Vous voulez de l'eau minérale?
   *(Oui, je voudrais une bouteille d'eau minérale, s'il vous plaît.)*

# Activity 18

**Élève A** Ask your partner the following questions. Correct answers are in parentheses.

1. Qui fait le déjeuner?
   *(Moi, je fais le déjeuner.)*

2. Qui fait du français?
   *(Nous faisons du français.)*

3. Qui fait des études?
   *(Tu fais des études.)*

4. Qui fait les exercices?
   *(Alain et Eric font les exercices.)*

5. Qui fait le gâteau?
   *(Vous faites le gâteau.)*

**Élève A** Use the information in the chart below to answer your partner's questions.

| Qui? | Activité |
|---|---|
| Moi, je | (faire) les courses |
| Hugo et Marie | (faire) un pique-nique |
| Nous | (faire) de l'allemand |
| Vous | (faire) la cuisine |
| Tu | (faire) les devoirs |

---

**Élève B** Use the information in the chart below to answer your partner's questions.

| Qui? | Activité |
|---|---|
| Moi, je | (faire) le déjeuner |
| Nous | (faire) du français |
| Tu | (faire) des études |
| Alain et Eric | (faire) les exercices |
| Vous | (faire) le gâteau |

**Élève B** Ask your partner the following questions. Correct answers are in parentheses.

1. Qui fait les courses?
   *(Moi, je fais les courses.)*

2. Qui fait un pique-nique?
   *(Hugo et Marie font un pique-nique.)*

3. Qui fait de l'allemand?
   *(Nous faisons de l'allemand.)*

4. Qui fait la cuisine?
   *(Vous faites la cuisine.)*

5. Qui fait les devoirs?
   *(Tu fais les devoirs.)*

**Élève A** Ask your partner the following questions. Correct answers are in parentheses.

1. Qui veut aller au restaurant?
   *(Moi, je veux aller au restaurant.)*

2. Qui peut travailler après l'école?
   *(Il peut travailler après l'école.)*

3. Qui veut inviter des amis?
   *(Tu veux inviter des amis.)*

4. Qui veut manger maintenant?
   *(Nous voulons manger maintenant.)*

5. Qui peut regarder le film?
   *(Vous pouvez regarder le film.)*

6. Qui veut aller au marché?
   *(Pierre veut aller au marché.)*

7. Qui veut écouter des CD?
   *(Eric et Michel veulent écouter des CD.)*

**Élève A** Use the information in the chart below to answer your partner's questions.

| Qui? | Activité |
|------|----------|
| Moi, je | (pouvoir) regarder le film |
| Elle | (vouloir) aller au restaurant |
| Nous | (pouvoir) faire des sandwichs |
| Ils | (vouloir) écouter des CD |
| Tu | (pouvoir) manger maintenant |
| Alain | (pouvoir) aller au marché |
| Hugo et Marie | (pouvoir) inviter des amis |

---

**Élève B** Use the information in the chart below to answer your partner's questions.

| Qui? | Activité |
|------|----------|
| Moi, je | (vouloir) aller au restaurant |
| Il | (pouvoir) travailler après l'école |
| Tu | (vouloir) inviter des amis |
| Nous | (vouloir) manger maintenant |
| Vous | (pouvoir) regarder le film |
| Pierre | (vouloir) aller au marché |
| Eric et Michel | (vouloir) écouter des CD |

**Élève B** Ask your partner the following questions. Correct answers are in parentheses.

1. Qui peut regarder le film?
   *(Moi, je peux regarder le film.)*

2. Qui veut aller au restaurant?
   *(Elle veut aller au restaurant.)*

3. Qui peut faire des sandwichs?
   *(Nous pouvons faire des sandwichs.)*

4. Qui veut écouter des CD?
   *(Ils veulent écouter des CD.)*

5. Qui peut manger maintenant?
   *(Tu peux manger maintenant.)*

6. Qui peut aller au marché?
   *(Alain peut aller au marché.)*

7. Qui peut inviter des amis?
   *(Hugo et Marie peuvent inviter des amis.)*

# Activity 20

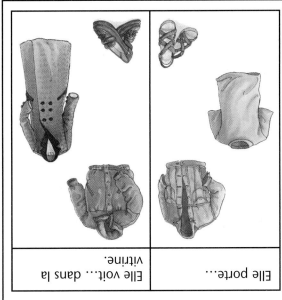

**Élève A** Ask your partner the following questions. Correct answers are in parentheses.

1. Marc porte un anorak?
   *(Oui, il porte un anorak.)*

2. Marc porte un blouson?
   *(Non, il voit un blouson dans la vitrine.)*

3. Marc porte un pull?
   *(Oui, il porte un pull.)*

4. Marc porte un t-shirt?
   *(Non, il voit un t-shirt dans la vitrine.)*

5. Marc porte une paire de chaussures?
   *(Oui, il porte une paire de chaussures.)*

6. Marc porte un survêtement?
   *(Non, il voit un survêtement dans la vitrine.)*

**Élève A** Use the information in the chart below to answer your partner's questions.

| Elle porte… | Elle voit… dans la vitrine. |
|---|---|

---

**Élève B** Use the information in the chart below to answer your partner's questions.

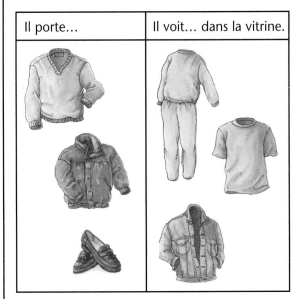

| Il porte… | Il voit… dans la vitrine. |
|---|---|

**Élève B** Ask your partner the following questions. Correct answers are in parentheses.

1. Chloé porte des sandales?
   *(Oui, elle porte des sandales.)*

2. Chloé porte un anorak?
   *(Non, elle voit un anorak dans la vitrine.)*

3. Chloé porte un blouson?
   *(Oui, elle porte un blouson.)*

4. Chloé porte une paire de chaussures?
   *(Non, elle voit une paire de chaussures dans la vitrine.)*

5. Chloé porte un t-shirt?
   *(Oui, elle porte un t-shirt.)*

6. Chloé porte un manteau?
   *(Non, elle voit un manteau dans la vitrine.)*

# Activity 21

**Élève A**  Use the information below to answer your partner's questions.

Oui, c'est ma couleur favorite.

un peu large

trop chères

trop petit

trop grand

**Élève A**  Find out your partner's opinion of different clothing items. Correct answers are in parentheses.

1. Il est joli, le pull bleu. Tu ne trouves pas?
   *(Non, il est trop serré.)*

2. Il est joli, le manteau gris. Tu ne trouves pas?
   *(Non, il est trop long.)*

3. Il est joli, l'anorak rouge. Tu ne trouves pas?
   *(Non, il est trop cher.)*

4. Elle est jolie, la jupe verte. Tu ne trouves pas?
   *(Non, elle est un peu courte.)*

5. Elles sont jolies, les chaussures marron. Tu ne trouves pas?
   *(Oui, c'est ma couleur favorite.)*

---

**Élève B**  Use the information below to answer your partner's questions.

trop serré

trop long

trop cher

un peu courte

Oui, c'est ma couleur favorite.

**Élève B**  Find out your partner's opinion of different clothing items. Correct answers are in parentheses.

1. Il est joli, le short vert. Tu ne trouves pas?
   *(Non, il est trop grand.)*

2. Il est joli, le t-shirt orange. Tu ne trouves pas?
   *(Non, il est trop petit.)*

3. Elles sont jolies, les sandales bleues. Tu ne trouves pas?
   *(Non, elles sont trop chères.)*

4. Il est joli, le survêtement jaune. Tu ne trouves pas?
   *(Non, il est un peu large.)*

5. Il est joli, le blouson bleu. Tu ne trouves pas?
   *(Oui, c'est ma couleur favorite.)*

# Activity 22

**Élève A** Use the information in the chart below to answer your partner's questions.

| Qui? | Activité |
|---|---|
| Moi, je | (mettre) la télé le matin |
| Les serveurs | (mettre) la table au restaurant |
| Ma mère | (mettre) une jupe pour aller au marché |
| Nous | (mettre) des chaussettes rouges |
| Tu | (mettre) des baskets pour faire du jogging |
| Vous | (mettre) un pantalon pour aller à l'école |

**Élève A** Ask your partner the following questions. Correct answers are in parentheses.

1. Qui met un short?
   (*Moi, je mets un short pour faire du jogging.*)

2. Qui met la radio le matin?
   (*Mes copains mettent la radio le matin.*)

3. Qui met une cravate?
   (*Mon père met une cravate pour aller au travail.*)

4. Qui met la table?
   (*Vous mettez la table pour le dîner.*)

5. Qui met un jean?
   (*Tu mets un jean pour aller au cinéma.*)

6. Qui met un complet?
   (*Nous mettons un complet pour aller à un mariage.*)

---

**Élève B** Use the information in the chart below to answer your partner's questions.

| Qui? | Activité |
|---|---|
| Moi, je | (mettre) un short pour faire du jogging |
| Mes copains | (mettre) la radio le matin |
| Mon père | (mettre) une cravate pour aller au travail |
| Vous | (mettre) la table pour le dîner |
| Tu | (mettre) un jean pour aller au cinéma |
| Nous | (mettre) un complet pour aller à un mariage |

**Élève B** Ask your partner the following questions. Correct answers are in parentheses.

1. Qui met la télé?
   (*Moi, je mets la télé le matin.*)

2. Qui met la table?
   (*Les serveurs mettent la table au restaurant.*)

3. Qui met une jupe?
   (*Ma mère met une jupe pour aller au marché.*)

4. Qui met des chaussettes rouges?
   (*Nous mettons des chaussettes rouges.*)

5. Qui met des baskets?
   (*Tu mets des baskets pour faire du jogging.*)

6. Qui met un pantalon?
   (*Vous mettez un pantalon pour aller à l'école.*)

# Activity 23

**Élève A** Read the statements about clothing to your partner. Your partner does not agree with what you believe to be true. Correct answers are in parentheses.

1. Moi, je crois que le polo est plus grand que le t-shirt.
(Non, je vois que le t-shirt est plus grand que le polo.) or (Non, je vois que le polo est plus petit que le t-shirt.)

2. Moi, je crois que la chemise est plus grande que le polo.
(Non, je vois que la chemise est aussi grande que le polo.)

3. Moi, je crois que la jupe plissée est moins élégante que le chemisier.
(Non, je vois que la jupe plissée est aussi élégante que le chemisier.)

**Élève A** Your partner tells you what he or she thinks about articles of clothing. Use the chart below to give your partner the correct information. Begin your response with **Non, je vois que…**

| | l'anorak | le blouson | le manteau |
|---|---|---|---|
| **cher** | $ $ $ | $ | $ $ $ $ $ $ |
| **confortables** | les baskets + + | | les chaussures + + |

---

**Élève B** Your partner tells you what he or she thinks about articles of clothing. Use the chart below to give your partner the correct information. Begin your response with **Non, je vois que…**

| | | | |
|---|---|---|---|
| **grand(e)** | le t-shirt + + + + + | la chemise + + + | le polo + + + |
| **élégant(e)** | la jupe plissée + + | | le chemisier + + |

**Élève B** Read the statements about clothing to your partner. Your partner does not agree with what you believe to be true. Correct answers are in parentheses.

1. Moi, je crois que les chaussures sont moins confortables que les baskets.
(Non, je vois que les chaussures sont aussi confortables que les baskets.)

2. Moi, je crois que le blouson est aussi cher que l'anorak.
(Non, je vois que le blouson est moins cher que l'anorak.) or (Non, je vois que l'anorak est plus cher que le blouson.)

3. Moi, je crois que l'anorak est plus cher que le manteau.
(Non, je vois que le manteau est plus cher que l'anorak.) or (Non, je vois que l'anorak est moins cher que le manteau.)

# For students and parents/guardians

*This guide is designed to help you as students achieve success as you embark on the adventure of learning another language and to enable your parents or guardians to help you on this exciting journey. There are many ways to learn new information. You may find some of these suggestions more useful than others, depending upon which style of learning works best for you. Before you begin, it is important to understand how we acquire language.*

## Receptive Skills

Each day of your life you receive a great deal of information through the use of language. In order to obtain (get, receive) this information, it is necessary to understand the language being used. It is necessary to understand the language in two different ways. First you must be able to understand what people are saying when they speak to you. This is referred to as oral or listening comprehension. Oral comprehension or listening comprehension is the ability to understand the spoken language.

You must also be able to understand what you read. This is referred to as reading comprehension. Reading comprehension is the ability to understand the written language.

Listening comprehension and reading comprehension are called the *receptive skills.* They are receptive skills because as you listen to what someone else says or read what someone else has written you receive information without having to produce any language yourself.

It is usually very easy to understand your native language. It is a bit more problematic to understand a second language that is new to you. As a beginner, you are still learning the sounds of the new language, and you recognize only a few words. Throughout **Bon voyage!** we will give you hints or suggestions to help you understand when people are speaking to you in French or when you are reading in French. Following are some general hints to keep in mind.

### HINTS FOR LISTENING COMPREHENSION

When you are listening to a person speaking French, don't try to understand every word. It is not necessary to understand everything to get the idea of what someone is saying. Listen for the general message. If some details escape you, it doesn't matter. Also, never try to translate what people are saying in French into English. It takes a great deal of experience and expertise to be a translator. Trying to translate will hinder your ability to understand.

### HINTS FOR READING COMPREHENSION

Just as you will not always understand every word you hear in a conversation, you will not necessarily understand every word you encounter in a reading selection, either. In **Bon voyage!,** we have used only words you know or can easily figure out in the reading selections. This will make reading comprehension much easier for you. However, if at some time you wish to read a newspaper or magazine article in French, you will most certainly come across some unfamiliar words. Do not stop reading. Continue to read to get the "gist" of the selection. Try to guess the meanings of words you do not know.

## Productive Skills

There are two productive skills in language. These two skills are speaking and writing. They are called productive skills because it is you who has to produce the language when you say or write something. When you speak or write, you have control over the language and which words you use. If you don't know how to say something, you don't have to say it. With the receptive skills, on the other hand, someone else produces the language that you listen to or read, and you have no control over the words they use.

There's no doubt that you can easily speak your native language. You can write, too, even though you may sometimes make errors in spelling or punctuation. In French, there's not a lot you can say or write as a beginner. You can only talk or write about those topics you have learned in French class.

HINTS FOR SPEAKING  Try to be as accurate as possible when speaking. Try not to make mistakes. However, if you do, it's not the end of the world. French people will understand you. You're not expected to speak a language perfectly after a limited time. You have probably spoken with people from other countries who do not speak English perfectly, but you can understand them. Remember:

* Keep talking! Don't become inhibited for fear of making a mistake.
* Say what you know how to say. Don't try to branch out in the early stages and attempt to talk about topics or situations you have not yet learned in French.

HINTS FOR WRITING  There are many activities in each lesson of **Bon voyage!** that will help you speak and write in French. When you have to write something on your own, however, without the guidance or assistance of an activity in your book, be sure to choose a topic for which you know the vocabulary in French. Never attempt to write about a topic you have not yet studied in French. Write down the topic you are going to write about. Then think of the words you know that are related to the topic. Be sure to include some action words (verbs) that you will need.

From your list of words, write as many sentences as you can. Read them and organize them into a logical order. Fill in any gaps. Then proof your paragraph(s) to see if you made any errors. Correct any that you find.

When writing on your own, be careful not to rely heavily, if at all, on a bilingual dictionary. It's not that bilingual dictionaries are bad, but when you look up a word you will very often find that there are several translations for the same word. As a beginning language student, you do not know which translation to choose; the chances are great that you will pick the wrong one.

As a final hint, never prepare your paragraph(s) in English and attempt to translate word for word. Always write from scratch in French.

*In each chapter of **Bon voyage!**, you will learn how to say and write new words. In Chapter 1, you learn how to describe a person. It won't be long before you'll be able to talk about many things in French. **Bon voyage!***

## CHAPITRE 1

### Vocabulaire

**Mots 1 & 2**

1. Repeat each new word in the **Mots** section as many times as possible. The more you use a word, the more apt you are to remember it and keep it as part of your active vocabulary.

2. Read the words as you look at the illustrations.

3. If you're the type who has to write something down in order to remember it, copy each word once or twice.

4. Do these activities diligently. They provide you with the opportunity to use your new words many times.

5. This may sound strange, but it's a good idea to read these exercises aloud at home or when using the CD-ROM.

6. When doing the vocabulary activities by yourself or for homework, try to do each item orally before writing the answer.

7. After doing any activity that says **Historiette,** read all the answers aloud. Each time you do this, you will be telling a story in French. It's an excellent way to keep using the material you are learning.

**CLASSROOM SUGGESTION** Listen to what your classmates say when they respond in class. Do not tune them out. Paying attention to them allows you additional opportunities to hear your new words. The more you hear them, the more likely you are to learn and retain them.

### Structure

**L'accord des adjectifs** (pages 28–30)
Pay particular attention to the final sound of many of the descriptive words you are learning. Remind yourself that you hear the final consonant sound of many descriptive words when you are describing a girl. You do not hear the sound when describing a boy.

**HINT FOR SPELLING** What letter do you delete from the feminine form? Remember that you delete the **e** that follows the consonant when referring to a male.

**Le verbe être au singulier** (pages 30–32)
1. **Être** is the first verb you are learning in French. Throughout your study of French, you will continue to learn many more verbs. Verbs are extremely important in French. At this point, you know three verb forms:

    **je suis** when talking about yourself

    **tu es** when talking to someone

    **il/elle est** when talking about someone

Get off to a good start! Learn these three simple forms and remember them.

2. As you do the activities, don't try to use words you don't know in French. For example, you may want to talk about someone who is very outgoing, but you don't know a French equivalent for "outgoing." Give the message using what you do know. For example, you can say: **Jean n'est pas timide, pas du tout.** You can also say: **Marie, elle est timide? Non, pas du tout. Marie n'est pas timide.** Using **ne… pas** with a word you know, you can convey the meaning you wish even though you do not know the precise word.

**CLASSROOM SUGGESTION** Listen to your classmates as they respond to the structure activities. Remember, the more you hear a form, the more readily you will be able to use it.

3. After doing any activity that says **Historiette,** read all the answers aloud. Each time you do this, you will be telling a story in French. It's an excellent way to keep using the material you are learning.

## Lecture culturelle
### *Un garçon et une fille* (pages 36–37)

1. Always read the Reading Strategy at the beginning of the **Lecture culturelle.** Practice these strategies and try applying them to other selections you read in French. The Reading Strategy on page 36 talks about cognates and how they help you guess the meanings of words you do not know. For example, you read: **Jean est un garçon français. Il est très intelligent, très capable.** You have probably never seen or used the word **capable** in French. However, you can guess its meaning because it is a cognate of the English word *capable.*

   In addition, it is used in apposition to **intelligent.** When you see a word or expression followed by a comma and then another word (in apposition), the word in apposition almost always clarifies the precise word and has the same or similar meaning.

2. Let's look at another way to guess meaning: **Jean est intelligent et il est aussi très sage. Il est prudent.** You don't know the word **sage,** but its meaning is clarified by **prudent.** Which of the following do you think **sage** means? *Talented? Wise, smart? Nice?* Hopefully you chose *wise, smart.* Think about how and why you arrived at this correct answer.

**HINTS FOR WRITING** As you complete your first chapter in French, you are able to write a description of a person. At this point, you cannot tell what the person does because you don't have the necessary vocabulary. So avoid this. However, you are able to tell what he or she is like. Write down the words you know in order to write your description. Do not think of words in English. Try to think only of the words you know in French. Begin to write your description. Remember what you learned about **e** if your description is of a female.

## VOCABULAIRE *(page 47)*
As you complete the chapter, look at the reference vocabulary list. If there are several words you don't remember, go back to the **Mots 1** and **Mots 2** sections and review. If there are only one or two, you can choose to look them up in the dictionaries beginning on page H72 at the end of this book.

## CHAPITRE 2
Get off to a good start! Do your French homework diligently and study for a short period of time each day. Do not skip some days and then try to cram. It doesn't work when studying a foreign language.

   In each lesson of **Bon voyage!** you will learn a very manageable amount of new material. Since French is a romance language, much of the new material will involve word endings. Study each small set of new endings on a daily basis, and you'll have no problem. Don't wait until you have lots of them and try to cram them in all at once.

## Vocabulaire
### *Mots 1 & 2* (pages 50–57)

1. In Chapter 1, you learned that adjectives describing something feminine end in **e.** The final consonant is pronounced. The **e** is dropped and the consonant is not pronounced when describing something masculine. In Chapter 2, you have four new words that reinforce the same concept: **fort, mauvais, strict,** and **intéressant.**

   **Elle est forte en maths.**
   **Il est fort en maths.**
   **La classe est intéressante.**
   **Le cours est intéressant.**

**HINT FOR PRONOUNCING NEW WORDS**
Imitate the pronunciation of your teacher or the CDs to the best of your ability. Try to acquire the best pronunciation possible.

However, don't be worried if you have a slight American accent. There are three levels of pronunciation.

* **Near-native** Try to pronounce like a native. Strive for a near-native pronunciation.
* **Accented but comprehensible** Many people have an accent when they speak a foreign language. You can tell they are not native speakers, but in spite of their accent, you can understand them. If you have such an accent, don't be concerned.
* **Very accented and incomprehensible** Some people have such a strong accent that it's impossible to understand what they're saying. If you have such a strong accent, it will be necessary to repeat and imitate more carefully.

Always remember to listen carefully, repeating as accurately as possible, and you'll succeed in acquiring acceptable pronunciation.

HINT FOR SPEAKING Listen to your teacher pronounce new words or phrases and then repeat them several times. Once you know how to pronounce the words, read the words in your book. If you try to read a word in French before ever having pronounced it, the spelling will most probably interfere with your pronunciation. Always try to listen, repeat, and then read.

2. The vocabulary in **Mots 2** should be very easy to recognize and learn because many words are cognates. A cognate is a word that looks alike in both English and French and has the same meaning in both languages. In the early lessons of **Bon voyage!** we have used many cognates to help you acquire a substantial vocabulary quickly and easily. However, be careful with the pronunciation of cognates. Even though they look alike and mean the same thing in both languages, they can be pronounced very differently.

## Structure
### Le pluriel: articles, noms et adjectifs
*(pages 58–60)*
When listening, you will not hear the **s** ending for the plural of a descriptive word. When speaking, you will not pronounce the **s.** However, when writing, you have to remember to write the **s** for plural words.

**Les garçons intelligents**
**Les filles intelligentes**

### Le verbe être au pluriel *(pages 60–63)*
In this lesson, you learn three new verb forms:

**nous sommes** when talking about yourself and someone else

**vous êtes** when talking to two or more people

**ils/elles sont** when talking about two or more people or things

Go over these three forms until you feel confident that you know them.

## Conversation
*(page 66)*
When you listen to people speak, you will notice that they often use little words or expressions that you will never see in written form. *Yeah* and *ya' know* are examples in English. You can often guess the meaning of these expressions by the speaker's tone of voice. In this conversation, listen to the tone of voice when the young woman says **Ben oui.** Do you think **Ben oui** means *No* or *Yeah?*

## Lecture culturelle
### Le français aux États-Unis *(pages 68–69)*
1. Read the Reading Strategy at the beginning of the **Lecture culturelle.** Look at the title of the reading on page 68. It lets you know immediately the general topic you'll be reading about.
2. Read the three subtitles or heads in the passage. They give you a more specific idea of what you'll be reading. Without having read the reading selection, you now have some

understanding of what the reading is about. This will make comprehension much easier.

3. After looking at the title and subtitles, you may very quickly skim the reading. Rather than trying to remember all the information, look at the comprehension questions that follow it. Then go back to the reading and look for the specific factual information called for.

# CHAPITRE 3
## Vocabulaire

**Mots 1 & 2** *(pages 82–89)*

1. Look at each photo or illustration carefully.
2. Read the labels. What does each word refer to?
3. Each word is then used in a meaningful context in a complete sentence. Repeat the individual words and then the sentences.
4. Note that in Activity 4 on page 85, the answer to the question word **qu'est-ce que (qu')** is always a thing. Therefore you should be able to guess the meaning of this question word. Does it mean *who* or *what?*
5. On page 86, after you have practiced your new words, cover up the words as you look at the drawing or photo of each classroom item. See how many you remember. If you don't remember many, you'll have to practice the words some more.

**HINT** Always pay careful attention to both the pronunciation and the spelling of your new words. You have now seen more than one form of certain verbs. For example: **Ils jouent. Il joue. Ils regardent. Il regarde.** Have you noticed that there is no difference in pronunciation between **regardent** and **regarde** even though they are written differently?

**HINT FOR SPEAKING** Whenever possible, read all the answers aloud to any activity labeled **Historiette.** Every time you do, you'll be telling a story on your own with the guidance of the activity in the text. This is an easy and useful way to get yourself speaking lots of French.

## Structure
### Les verbes réguliers en -er au présent
*(pages 90–93)*

1. Now that you know the word **on,** which almost always replaces **nous,** you will see that you really only have to pronounce two forms of a regular **-er** verb. When speaking, whether the subject of the sentence is **je, tu, il, on, elle, ils,** or **elles,** the verb sounds the same. Only the **vous** form has a different pronunciation. This makes spoken French quite easy.

| 1 | 2 |
|---|---|
| je parle | |
| tu parles | vous parlez |
| il/elle/on parle | |
| ils/elles parlent | |

2. However, when you write, remember that there are spelling changes.
   je parle
   tu parles
   il/elle/on parle
   ils/elles parlent

**HINT** Note that the structure activities in your book build from easy to more complex. In the beginning activities, you very often have to use only one verb form. For example, in Activity 13 on page 91, you only use the **il** form. However, in Activity 20 on page 93, you have to use all forms of the verb.

3. When doing Activity 21 on page 93, remember to use only French that you know. Refer to the list of words given here. This list will prevent you from thinking about things you cannot yet say in French.

### La négation des articles indéfinis *(page 94)*
Try to condense a grammatical rule into one easy sentence that you can remember easily: **Un, une,** and **des** all become **de** after **ne... pas.**

### Verbe + infinitif *(page 95)*
Note that the infinitive form of the verb used

after a verb is pronounced the same as the **vous**
form:     **Vous travaillez.**
          **J'aime travailler.**
**Travaillez** and **travailler** are pronounced the
same. When writing, remember the difference
in spelling:
          **Vous travaillez? Moi, j'aime travailler.**
          **Vous rigolez? Moi, j'aime rigoler.**

## Conversation
*(page 96)*

1. This conversation should be very easy for
   you. You have already learned all the French
   that is used in the conversation. When
   practicing this conversation with a classmate,
   feel free to make as many changes as you
   want, as long as they make sense.
2. In the conversation, you hear Carol say, **C'est
   pas vrai.** In spoken French, **ne** is often
   dropped from the expression **ne… pas.**
3. Note also that Cedric says **Si, c'est vrai.** When
   someone tells you **no** in French and you want
   to contradict, you say **si** rather than **oui.**

## Lecture culturelle
### *Une journée avec Jacqueline* *(pages 98–99)*

1. Look at the photos on pages 98–99. These
   photos let you know the reading is about:
   **a.** shopping for clothes
   **b.** going to school
   **c.** making a meal
2. Skim the reading selection and look for the
   important information such as:
   ✤ Who's the story about?
   ✤ Where does she live and go to school?
   ✤ What are her school hours?
3. Factual recall is an important reading skill.
   First, find the facts in the reading and then
   commit them to memory. Activity B tells you
   what factual information to look for.

#### VOCABULAIRE *(page 109)*
As you complete the chapter, look at the
reference vocabulary list. If there are several
words you don't remember, go back to the
**Mots 1** and **Mots 2** sections and review. If there

are only one or two, you can choose to look
them up in the dictionaries beginning on page
H72 at the end of this book.

## CHAPITRE 4
### Vocabulaire
**Mots 1 & 2** *(pages 112–119)*

1. In **Mots 1**, remember to listen to the words
   and repeat orally before reading them. Many
   names for family members are cognates. Be
   careful to repeat them correctly.

**HINT** If you're the type of learner who has to
write something before you can remember, copy
the words in the **Mots** section once or twice.
Use the following learning sequence: *listen,
repeat, read, write.*

2. Activity 2 on page 114 helps you review
   several important question words. The answer
   in parentheses tells you the meaning of the
   question word for that sentence. Look at the
   following question words and answers:
   | Quand? | aujourd'hui |
   | Qu'est-ce que? | une fête, des cadeaux |
   | Qui? | ses cousins, ses cousines |

Decide which question words mean *who, what,*
and *when.*

3. Activity 4 on page 115 helps you with
   productive skills. Remember that when you
   speak or write about yourself, you must
   always use the masculine form if you are a
   male and the feminine form if you are a female.
4. After you have learned the new words in
   **Mots 2,** look at each illustration, cover up the
   sentences, and say as much as you can about
   the illustration. If you can describe the
   illustration, you know your vocabulary. If
   you cannot describe it, you have to study
   some more.

**HINT** Read or say aloud all the answers to the
**Historiette** activities to give you practice in
telling coherent stories in French.

## Structure

*Le verbe* **avoir** *au présent* (*pages 120–122*)
So far, you have learned one irregular verb in French, the verb **être**. All forms of **être** are different. You will now learn your second irregular verb, **avoir**. All forms of **avoir** are also different.

1. Familiarize yourself with the forms of **avoir** as you go over the explanation in class.
2. Do the activities diligently. They give you the opportunity to use and learn the new verb forms without having to memorize them one by one.
3. Do the activities orally and in writing.
4. After doing the activities, reread the grammar explanation. See if you can give the forms of **avoir** on your own without reading them.

**REVIEW** You know that **un, une,** and **des** all change to **de** after **ne... pas.** The activities on pages 120–122 will help you review this point as you talk about your own home and family.

## Conversation

(*page 128*)
Pay careful attention when you listen to the conversation on the CD-ROM or when other students are repeating it in class. The more you hear spoken French, the easier it will be for you to understand.

## Lecture culturelle

*Où habitent les Français?* (*pages 130–131*)

1. Read the title. When you finish this reading, what will you be able to tell?
   a. where France is
   b. who the French are
   c. where the French people live
2. As you read each paragraph, draw a mental picture of what you're reading. To help you draw your mental picture, look at the photographs, too.

## C'est à vous

(*pages 136–137*)
In Activity 5 on page 137, you are going to write about your house or a house of your dreams.

1. Picture the house.
2. In French, think of or write a list of words you can use to identify parts of the house.
3. In French, think about or write a list of words you can use to describe a house or rooms of a house.
4. Organize your story. Divide the house into parts, such as living area, sleeping area, first floor, second floor. You may even want to make a drawing of your house. Write a few sentences about each area.
5. Put the sentences in a logical order.
6. Add a few sentences to describe the area around your house.

## CHAPITRE 5

## Vocabulaire

**Mots 1 & 2** (*pages 154–161*)

1. It can be fun to study with a classmate. You can do the following.
   * Ask one another questions in French about the illustrations.
   * Have a contest. See who can give more French words describing the illustrations in a three-minute period.
   * Tell your friend which of the items you would order if you were at a café.
2. Activity 1 on page 156 helps you reinforce the meaning of the important question words:

   | où | au café |
   |---|---|
   | qui | Chantal, le serveur |
   | qu'est-ce que | une table libre, une boisson |
   | quand | après les cours |

3. Act out Activity 4 on page 157 with a classmate. The more you practice speaking French together, the better you'll be able to communicate.

## Structure

### Le verbe aller au présent (pages 162–164)

You will now learn your third irregular verb. Make an association with another irregular verb you have already learned. Repeat the following aloud.

je vais ➝ j'ai
tu vas ➝ tu as
il va ➝ il a
ils vont ➝ ils ont

The forms of **aller** almost sound like the forms of **avoir** with a **v** sound.

HINT The more you practice speaking French, the better. When doing your homework, go over all the activities aloud. Don't just do your French homework silently.

### Aller + infinitif (page 165)

1. The concept of an infinitive after a verb is not new to you. You already know how to express what you like to do:

   **J'aime manger.**
   **J'aime aller au restaurant.**

2. Now, using the same type of construction, you will be able to tell what you are going to do.

   **J'aime manger et je vais manger quelque chose.**
   **J'aime aller au restaurant et je vais aller au restaurant vendredi.**

## Conversation

(page 170)

Listen carefully to the conversation. You can listen to your teacher or use the CD-ROM. Listen more than once. Each time listen for a different bit of information.

✤ Where are Claire and Loïc?
✤ What do they order?
✤ Why is there a possible disagreement?

## Lecture culturelle

### Au restaurant? Vraiment? (pages 172–173)

1. Making comparisons while reading is an important reading comprehension skill. In this reading, you learned about a cultural difference that's quite interesting. What is it? You may want to share this information with family or friends who don't know any French.

2. Finding the main idea is another important reading comprehension skill. As you read, look for the main idea in the second paragraph. What is it? What is the main idea in the third paragraph?

## C'est à vous

(pages 178–179)

In Activity 4 on page 179, you're going to write about a restaurant in French.

1. Get a mental picture of the restaurant.
2. Write words you know in French to describe a restaurant and restaurant activities.
3. List items that people may order.
4. Put these words into sentences. Your first paragraph will describe the restaurant. Your second paragraph will tell what your "characters" order and how they pay.

## CHAPITRE 6

## Vocabulaire

### Mots 1 & 2 (pages 186–193)

1. Try to use your French as often as possible. When you see a food item at home or in a store that is labeled in French, say the French word to yourself. You'll learn to identify many more food items as you continue with your study of French.

2. As you complete the activities, answer each question orally before you write the answers for homework. Try reading your written responses aloud for Activities 2 and 3 on page 188. Activity 2 reviews the question words **qui, qu'est-ce que, quand, où.**

3. On your own, review the foods you have learned by putting them with an appropriate package or container. For example:

   **un paquet de fromage**
   **un paquet de six tranches de jambon**
   **un pot de confiture**
   **un paquet de légumes surgelés**

**HINTS** Note that Activity 10 on page 193 points out that in spoken French, you can omit the **ne** in the expression **ne… pas.**

Be sure you understand the meaning of **pourquoi** and **parce que** when you finish this activity.

## Structure

### *Le verbe* faire *au présent* (pages 194–195)

1. Look at the forms of the verb **faire.** Repeat them aloud, then copy them.
2. When you complete homework activities, go back to the verb chart. Cover the verb forms and see if you can say the forms without looking at them.

### *Le partitif et l'article défini* (pages 196–197)

1. Always try to make what you are learning as simple as possible. If you're talking about something in general, you use **le, la, les.** If you're talking about "some" or "any," you use **du, de la, des.**
2. When doing Activities 18 and 19 on page 197, pay particular attention to the contrast between the general sense and the partitive. You want to buy some (partitive) of the things you like (in general).

### *Le partitif au négatif* (pages 198–200)

This concept of **de** is not new. Just remember **du, de la, de l',** and **des** all change to **de** after **ne… pas.** It's really simple, but you have to keep reminding yourself.

**HINT** Pay close attention as you and your classmates participate in each of these activities. The more you hear **j'ai du** (or **de la, des**) versus **je n'ai pas de,** the easier it will be for you to use the partitive.

### HINTS FOR SPEAKING AND WRITING

Listen carefully for the difference in pronunciation between **bonne, bon,** and **gentille, gentil** as explained on page 201. Repeat the words carefully. Repeat the model sentences aloud, then copy them. Pay particular attention to the doubling of the consonant.

### *Les verbes* pouvoir *et* vouloir
*(pages 201–203)*

Pay attention to the similarity between the forms of **pouvoir** and **vouloir.**

**REVIEW** Using the infinitive after a helping verb is not new. Remember:

> **J'aime dîner au restaurant.**
> **Je vais dîner au restaurant.**

## Conversation
*(page 204)*

1. Intonation is the melody of a language. Intonation is produced by the rise and fall of the voice. Each language has its own intonation patterns. English intonation is very different from French intonation. Pay special attention to the rise and fall of the speakers' voices as you listen to the conversations on the CD or CD-ROM.
2. Try to imitate the native speakers' intonation as accurately as possible. If you do, you'll sound much more French. Don't be inhibited. Pretend you are acting while you imitate the intonation.

## Lecture culturelle

### *Les courses* (pages 206–207)

You may not know the meaning of a certain word you come across in a reading selection. However, you can often guess the meaning of the word by the way it is used in the context of the sentence. A new word in this reading is **les commerçants.** Guess what it means by the context of these sentences:

> **Les Français aiment bien aller chez les petits commerçants du quartier—l'épicier, le boucher, le boulanger, etc.**

The fact that the word **commerçants** is followed by the words **l'épicier, le boucher, le boulanger** helps you figure out the meaning of **commerçants.** What do you think the word **commerçants** means in this context?

   **a.** office workers
   **b.** shopkeepers
   **c.** commercials

# CHAPITRE 7

## Vocabulaire

**Mots 1 & 2** *(pages 220–227)*

1. Look at the illustrations in **Mots 1** and repeat each word aloud.
2. Write each word for additional reinforcement.
3. When you have finished studying the vocabulary, determine how much you remember. Say to yourself or aloud all the items you know for boy's clothing, girl's clothing, and unisex clothing. When you get dressed in the morning for school, notice how many words you know in French for those items you are wearing.
4. Before you write the answers to the vocabulary activities, work with a friend. Go over each exercise together orally. Then, each of you can write your answers. If you wish, you can check each other's work.
5. After studying the vocabulary in **Mots 2,** make a list of the things that you would most probably want to say in French to a salesperson when shopping for clothes.

**REVIEW** These vocabulary activities contain many adjectives, or descriptive words. Remember that many adjectives have an **e** when used with a feminine noun. They drop the **e** when used with a masculine noun.

| La jupe est | verte. | Le blouson est | vert. |
|---|---|---|---|
| | grise. | | gris. |
| | petite. | | petit. |
| | grande. | | grand. |
| | bleue. | | bleu. |
| | jolie. | | joli. |

## Structure

### Le verbe **mettre** *au présent* *(pages 228–229)*

1. Remember that you hear and pronounce the **t** in the plural forms of **mettre.** You do not hear or pronounce the **t** in the singular forms.
2. Do the **Attention** activity on page 229 aloud at least twice. As you do, pay very careful attention to pronunciation as well as spelling.

### Le comparatif des adjectifs *(pages 230–231)*

1. Remember to make the association that **plus** (**+**) is more, **moins** (**−**) is less, and **aussi** (**=**) is the same. All three words are followed by **que.**
2. As you do these activities, pay particular attention to each adjective.

### Les verbes **voir** et **croire** *(pages 232–233)*

1. Note that many forms of **voir** and **croire** are pronounced the same.

| je crois | tu crois | il croit | ils croient |
|---|---|---|---|
| je vois | tu vois | il voit | ils voient |

## Conversation
*(page 234)*

This conversation should be very easy for you. You have already learned all the French that is used in the conversation. When practicing this conversation with a classmate, feel free to make as many changes as you want, as long as they make sense.

## Lecture culturelle
### On fait des courses où, a Paris?
*(pages 236–237)*

1. Look at the photos on pages 236–237. These photos let you know what the reading is about.
2. Look at the titles. They will give you an idea of what you'll be reading about.
3. Quickly scan the reading to get a general idea of what it's all about.
4. Activity A on page 237 will help you practice factual recall. To recall certain facts, it is often necessary to go back over the reading selection and look for details.
5. Drawing conclusions from a reading selection is another important reading comprehension skill. Based on what you read, draw a personal conclusion. Where would you shop in Paris? Why?

### VOCABULAIRE *(page 247)*
As you complete the chapter, look at the reference vocabulary list. If there are quite a few words you don't know, go back to the **Mots 1** and **Mots 2** sections and review.

# Verb Charts

| VERBES RÉGULIERS | | | |
|---|---|---|---|
| **INFINITIF** | **parler** *to speak* | **finir** *to finish* | **répondre** *to answer* |
| **PRÉSENT** | je parle<br>tu parles<br>il parle<br>nous parlons<br>vous parlez<br>ils parlent | je finis<br>tu finis<br>il finit<br>nous finissons<br>vous finissez<br>ils finissent | je réponds<br>tu réponds<br>il répond<br>nous répondons<br>vous répondez<br>ils répondent |

| VERBES AVEC CHANGEMENTS D'ORTHOGRAPHE | | | |
|---|---|---|---|
| **INFINITIF** | **acheter** *to buy* | **appeler** *to call* | **commencer** *to begin* |
| **PRÉSENT** | j'achète<br>tu achètes<br>il achète<br>nous achetons<br>vous achetez<br>ils achètent | j'appelle<br>tu appelles<br>il appelle<br>nous appelons<br>vous appelez<br>ils appellent | je commence<br>tu commences<br>il commence<br>nous commençons<br>vous commencez<br>ils commencent |
| **INFINITIF** | **manger** *to eat* | **payer** *to pay* | **préférer** *to prefer* |
| **PRÉSENT** | je mange<br>tu manges<br>il mange<br>nous mangeons<br>vous mangez<br>ils mangent | je paie<br>tu paies<br>il paie<br>nous payons<br>vous payez<br>ils paient | je préfère<br>tu préfères<br>il préfère<br>nous préférons<br>vous préférez<br>ils préfèrent |

## VERBES IRRÉGULIERS

| INFINITIF | **aller**<br>*to go* | **avoir**<br>*to have* | **croire**<br>*to believe* |
|---|---|---|---|
| **PRÉSENT** | je vais<br>tu vas<br>il va<br>nous allons<br>vous allez<br>ils vont | j'ai<br>tu as<br>il a<br>nous avons<br>vous avez<br>ils ont | je crois<br>tu crois<br>il croit<br>nous croyons<br>vous croyez<br>ils croient |
| INFINITIF | **être**<br>*to be* | **faire**<br>*to do, to make* | **mettre**<br>*to put* |
| **PRÉSENT** | je suis<br>tu es<br>il est<br>nous sommes<br>vous êtes<br>ils sont | je fais<br>tu fais<br>il fait<br>nous faisons<br>vous faites<br>ils font | je mets<br>tu mets<br>il met<br>nous mettons<br>vous mettez<br>ils mettent |
| INFINITIF | **pouvoir**<br>*to be able to* | **prendre**[1]<br>*to take* | |
| **PRÉSENT** | je peux<br>tu peux<br>il peut<br>nous pouvons<br>vous pouvez<br>ils peuvent | je prends<br>tu prends<br>il prend<br>nous prenons<br>vous prenez<br>ils prennent | |
| INFINITIF | **voir**<br>*to see* | **vouloir**<br>*to want* | |
| **PRÉSENT** | je vois<br>tu vois<br>il voit<br>nous voyons<br>vous voyez<br>ils voient | je veux<br>tu veux<br>il veut<br>nous voulons<br>vous voulez<br>ils veulent | |

---

[1] *Verbes similaires:* **apprendre, comprendre**

*This French-English Dictionary contains all productive and receptive vocabulary from the text. The numbers following each productive entry indicate the chapter and vocabulary section in which the word is introduced. For example, **2.2** means that the word first appeared in **Chapitre 2, Mots 2. BV** refers to the introductory **Bienvenue** lessons. **L** refers to the optional literary readings. If there is no number or letter following an entry, this means that the word or expression is there for receptive purposes only.*

## A

**à** at, in, to, **3.1**
  **À bientôt!** See you soon!, **BV**
  **À demain.** See you tomorrow., **BV**
  **à mon (ton, son, etc.) avis** in my (your, his, etc.) opinion, **7.2**
  **à pied** on foot, **4.2**
  **à point** medium-rare *(meat)*, **5.2**
  **À tout à l'heure.** See you later., **BV**
**accessible** accessible
l' **accessoire** *(m.)* accessory
**accompagner** to accompany, to go with
l' **achat** *(m.)* purchase
  **faire des achats** to shop
**acheter** to buy, **3.2**
l' **addition** *(f.)* check, bill *(restaurant)*, **5.2**
**additionner** to add
l' **adolescent(e)** adolescent, teenager
**adorable** adorable, **4.1**
**adorer** to love
l' **adresse** *(f.)* address
l' **adulte** *(m. et f.)* adult
l' **affiche** *(f.)* poster
**africain(e)** African
l' **Afrique** *(f.)* Africa
l' **âge** *(m.)* age, **4.1**
  **Tu as quel âge?** How old are you?, **4.1**
l' **agneau** *(m.)* lamb, **6.1**

l' **aide** *(f.)* aid, help
  **à l'aide de** with the help of
**aimer** to like, love, **3.1**
  **aimer mieux** to prefer, **7.2**
l' **aîné(e)** older, **L1**
l' **air** *(m.):* **avoir l'air** to look
  **aisé(e)** well-to-do
l' **album** *(m.)* album
l' **algèbre** *(f.)* algebra, **2.2**
l' **Algérie** *(f.)* Algeria
  **algérien(ne)** Algerian
l' **aliment** *(m.)* food
l' **Allemagne** *(f.)* Germany
l' **allemand** *(m.)* German *(language)*, **2.2**
**aller** to go, **5.1**
  **aller chercher** to go (and) get, **6.1**
**alors** so, then, well then, **BV**
  **américain(e)** American, **1.1**
l' **ami(e)** friend, **1.2**
  **ample** large, full
  **amusant(e)** funny; fun, **1.1**
l' **an** *(m.)* year, **4.1**
  **avoir... ans** to be . . . years old, **4.1**
l' **analyse** *(f.)* analysis
  **analyser** to analyse
  **analytique** analytical
l' **anatomie** *(f.)* anatomy
l' **anglais** *(m.)* English *(language)*, **2.2**
  **anglais(e)** English

l' **animal** *(m.)* animal
l' **année** *(f.)* year
l' **anniversaire** *(m.)* birthday, **4.1**
**annoncer** to announce
l' **anorak** *(m.)* ski jacket, **7.1**
  **Antilles: la mer des Antilles** Caribbean Sea
l' **appartement** *(m.)* apartment, **4.2**
**appeler** to call
**apprécier** to appreciate
**apprendre (à)** to learn (to), **5**; to teach
**après** after, **3.2**
l' **après-midi** *(m.)* afternoon, **3.2**
**arabe** Arab
l' **arabe** *(m.)* Arabic *(language)*
l' **arbre** *(m.)* tree
l' **argent** *(m.)* money, **5.2**
**arriver** to arrive, **3.1**; to happen
l' **arrondissement** *(m.)* district (in Paris)
l' **article** *(m.)* article
l' **artiste** *(m. et f.)* artiste
  **l'artiste peintre** *(m. et f.)* painter
  **artistique** artistic
l' **ascenseur** *(m.)* elevator, **4.2**
  **asiatique** Asian
  **assez** fairly, quite; enough, **1.1**
l' **assiette** *(f.)* plate, **5.2**
l' **attention** *(f.)* attention

**Attention!** Careful! Watch out!, **4.2**
**au revoir** good-bye, **BV**
**au-dessous (de)** below
  **la taille au-dessous** the next smaller size, **7.2**
**au-dessus (de)** above
  **la taille au-dessus** the next larger size, **7.2**
**aujourd'hui** today, **BV**
**auprès de** with
**aussi** also, too, **1.1;** as (*comparisons*), **7;** so
l' **auteur** (*m.*) author (*m. and f.*)
**autour de** around, **4.2**
**autre** other, **L1**
  **autre chose** something else
  **Autre chose?** Anything else? (*shopping*), **6.2**
  **d'autres** some other, **2.2**
  **l'un… l'autre** one . . . the other
**avant** before
**avec** with, **3.2**
  **Avec ça?** What else? (*shopping*), **6.1**
l' **avenir** (*m.*) future, **L2**
l' **avenue** (*f.*) avenue
l' **avis** (*m.*) opinion, **7.2**
  **à mon avis** in my opinion, **7.2**
**avoir** to have, **4.1**
  **avoir l'air** to look
  **avoir… ans** to be . . . years old, **4.1**
  **avoir de la chance** to be lucky, to be in luck
  **avoir faim** to be hungry, **5.1**
  **avoir une faim de loup** to be very hungry
  **avoir lieu** to take place
  **avoir peur** to be afraid, **L1**
  **avoir soif** to be thirsty, **5.1**

le **baccalauréat** French high school exam

la **bactérie** bacterium
  **bactérien(ne)** bacterial, **14.1**
la **baguette** loaf of French bread, **6.1**
le **bain: la salle de bains** bathroom, **4.2**
le **balcon** balcony, **4.2**
la **banane** banana, **6.2**
la **banlieue** suburbs
la **base** base; basis
  **à base de** based on
la **basket** sneaker; running shoe, **7.1**
le **basket(-ball)** basketball, **10.2**
  **bavarder** to chat
  **beau (bel), belle** beautiful, handsome, **4.2**
  **beaucoup** a lot, **3.1**
    **beaucoup de** a lot of, many, **3.2**
le **beau-père** stepfather, **4.1**
le **bébé** baby
  **beige** (*inv.*) beige, **7.2**
  **belge** Belgian
la **Belgique** Belgium
la **belle-mère** stepmother, **4.1**
  **ben** (*slang*) well
  **ben oui** yeah
le **beurre** butter, **6.1**
la **bicyclette** bicycle, **10.2**
  **bien** fine, well, **BV**
    **bien cuit(e)** well-done (*meat*), **5.2**
    **bien élevé(e)** well-behaved; well-mannered
    **bien sûr** of course
    **eh bien** well
  **bientôt** soon
    **À bientôt!** See you soon! **BV**
le/la **bienvenu(e)** welcome
la **biologie** biology, **2.2**
  **biologique** biological
le/la **biologiste** biologist
  **blanc, blanche** white, **7.2**
  **bleu(e)** blue, **7.2**
    **bleu marine** (*inv.*) navy blue, **7.2**

le **bloc-notes** notepad, **3.2**
  **blond(e)** blond, **1.1**
le **blouson** (waist-length) jacket, **7.1**
le **blue-jean** (pair of) jeans
le **bœuf** beef, **6.1**
  **bohème** bohemian
  **boire** to drink, **10.2**
    **quelque chose à boire** something to drink
le **bois** wood
la **boisson** beverage, drink, **5.1**
la **boîte: la boîte de conserve** can of food, **6.2**
  **boiteux, boiteuse** lame
le **bol** bowl
  **bon(ne)** correct; good, **6.2**
    **Bon!** Okay!, Right!, **6.1**
  **bon marché** (*inv.*) inexpensive
  **bonjour** hello, **BV**
la **botanique** botany
le **boubou** boubou (*long, flowing garment*)
le **boucher, la bouchère** butcher
la **boucherie** butcher shop, **6.1**
la **bougie** candle, **4.1**
la **boulangerie-pâtisserie** bakery, **6.1**
la **bouteille** bottle, **6.2**
la **boutique** shop, boutique, **7.1**
la **Bretagne** Brittany
  **breton(ne)** Breton, from Brittany
le/la **Breton(ne)** Breton (*person*)
la **brousse** bush (*wilderness*)
  **brun(e)** brunette; dark-haired, **1.1**
le **bungalow** bungalow
le **bus** bus, **5.2**

**ça** that, **BV**
  **Ça fait… euros.** It's (That's) . . . euros., **6.2**
  **Ça va.** Fine., Okay., **BV**

**Ça va?** How's it going?,
How are you? (inform.),
**BV;** How does it look?,
**7.2**

le **cabaret** cabaret

la **cabine d'essayage** fitting
room

le **cadeau** gift, present, **4.1**

le **cadet, la cadette**
younger person, **L1**

le **café** café, **BV;** coffee, **5.1**

la **cafétéria** cafeteria

le **cahier** notebook, **3.2**

la **caisse** cash register,
checkout counter, **3.2**

le **calcul** arithmetic, **2.2**

le **calcul différentiel**
differential calculus

le **calcul intégral**
integral calculus

la **calculatrice** calculator,
**3.2**

le **calligramme** picture-poem

**calme** quiet, calm

le **camembert** Camembert
cheese

**canadien(ne)** Canadian, **6**

la **cantine** school dining hall,
**3.1**

**capable** able

la **capitale** capital

la **caractéristique**
characteristic

**Caraïbes: la mer des
Caraïbes** Caribbean Sea

la **carotte** carrot, **6.2**

la **carte** menu, **5.1;** map; card

la **casquette** cap, baseball
cap, **7.1**

**casse-pieds** pain in the
neck (slang)

la **cassette** cassette, tape **3.1**

le **catalogue** catalog

la **catégorie** category

le **CD** CD, **3.1**

le **CD-ROM** CD-ROM

**ce (cet), cette** this, that, **9**

**ce soir** tonight

**célèbre** famous

**celte** Celtic

**celtique** Celtic

**cent** hundred, **2.2**

**pourcent** percent

le **centilitre** centiliter

le **centre** center

le **centre commercial**
shopping center, mall,
**7.1**

le **centre-ville** downtown

le **cercle** circle

les **céréales** (f. pl.) cereal,
grains

**certains** some

**c'est** it is, it's, **BV**

**C'est combien?** How
much is it?, **3.2**

**C'est quel jour?** What
day is it?, **BV**

**C'est tout.** That's all., **6.1**

**c'est-à-dire** that is

**chacun(e)** each (one), **5.2**

la **chaîne** chain; TV channel,
**12.2**

la **chaise** chair

la **chambre à coucher**
bedroom, **4.2**

le **champ** field, **L1**

**champêtre** pastoral

la **chance** luck

**avoir de la chance** to be
lucky, to be in luck

la **chanson** song

la **charcuterie** deli(catessen),
**6.1**

le **chariot** shopping cart, **6.2**

le **charme** charm

le **charpentier** carpenter

le **chat** cat, **4.1**

le **château** castle, mansion

la **chaussette** sock, **7.1**

la **chaussure** shoe, **7.1**

le **chemin** route; road; path

la **chemise** shirt, **7.1**

le **chemisier** blouse, **7.1**

**cher, chère** dear;
expensive, **7.1**

**chercher** to look for, seek

**aller chercher** to go
(and) get, **6.1**

**chez** at (to) the home
(business) of, **3.2**

le **chien** dog, **4.1**

la **chimie** chemistry, **2.2**

le/la **chimiste** chemist

**chinois(e)** Chinese

la **chose** thing

**ciao** good-bye
(inform.), **BV**

le **cirque** circus

**citer** to cite, mention

le **citron pressé** lemonade,
**5.1**

le/la **civilisé(e)** civilized person

**clair(e)** light (color)

la **classe** class, **2.1**

**la salle de classe**
classroom, **2.1**

le **classeur** loose-leaf binder,
**3.2**

le **clavier** keyboard

le/la **client(e)** customer

le **clown** clown

le **coca** cola, **5.1**

le **code** code, **4.2**

le **coin: du coin**
neighborhood (adj.)

la **collection** collection

le **collège** junior high,
middle school, **1.2**

le/la **collégien(ne)** middle
school/junior high
student

**combien (de)** how much,
how many, **3.2**

**C'est combien?** How
much is it (that)?, **3.2**

**commander** to order, **5.1**

**comme** like, as; for; since

**comme ci, comme ça**
so-so

**commencer** to begin

**comment** how, what, **1.1**

**Comment ça?** How is
that?

le/la **commerçant(e)** shopkeeper

la **comparaison** comparison

**comparer** to compare

le/la **compatriote** compatriot

la **compétition** contest

le **complet** suit (man's), **7.1**

**complet, complète** full,
complete

**le pain complet** whole-
wheat bread

**complètement** completely,
totally

**compléter** to complete

le **compositeur, la**

**compositrice** composer

la **composition** composition

**comprendre** to understand, **5**

**compris(e)** included, **5.2**
   **Le service est compris.** The tip is included., **5.2**

**compter** to count

le **concept** concept

le **concert** concert

le **concert-bal** concert and ball

la **confiture** jam, **6.2**

**confortable** comfortable

**connecter** to connect

**connu(e)** well-known; famous, **13.1**
   **le (la) plus connu(e)** best-known

la **conserve: la boîte de conserve** can of food, **6.2**

la **consommation** drink, beverage, **5.1**
   **content(e)** happy, glad

le **continent** continent

**continuer** to continue

la **conversation** conversation

**converser** to converse

le **copain** friend, pal (m.), **2.1**

la **copine** friend, pal (f.), **2.1**

la **cornemuse** bagpipes

le **corps** body

la **correspondance** correspondence, x

**corriger** to correct

**cosmopolite** cosmopolitan

la **Côte d'Azur** French Riviera

la **Côte d'Ivoire** Ivory Coast

le **côté** side

la **couleur** color, **7.2**

la **cour** courtyard, **3.2**; court
   **courageux, courageuse** courageous, brave

le **cours** course, class, **2.1**
   **en cours de (français, etc.)** in (French, etc.) class

les **courses** (f. pl.): **faire des courses** to go shopping, **6.1**

**court(e)** short, **7.2**

le **couscous** couscous

le/la **cousin(e)** cousin, **4.1**

le **couteau** knife, **5.2**

**coûter** to cost, **3.2**
   **Ça coûte combien?** How much does this cost?, **3.1**

le **couturier** designer (of clothes)

le **couvert** table setting; silverware, **5.2**

le **crabe** crab, **6.1**

la **cravate** tie, **7.1**

le **crayon** pencil, **3.2**
   **créer** to create

le **crème** coffee with cream (in a café), **5.1**

la **crémerie** dairy store, **6.1**

le **créole** Creole (language)

la **crêpe** crepe, pancake, **BV**
   **crevé(e)** exhausted

la **crevette** shrimp, **6.1**
   **croire** to believe, think, **7.2**

le **croissant** croissant, crescent roll, **5.1**

le **croque-monsieur** grilled ham and cheese sandwich, **5.1**

la **cuillère** spoon, **5.2**

la **cuisine** kitchen, **4.2**; cuisine (food)
   **faire la cuisine** to cook, **6**
   **cuit(e)** cooked
   **bien cuit(e)** well-done (meat), **5.2**
   **cultiver** to cultivate

la **culture** culture
   **culturel(le)** cultural

### D

**d'accord: être d'accord** to agree, **2.1**

**dans** in, **1.2**

la **danse** dance

la **date** date
   **d'autres** some other, **2.2**
   **de** from, **1.1**; of, belonging to, **1.2**; about

**de la, de l'** some, any, **6**
   **De quelle couleur est… ?** What color is . . . ?, **7.2**

le **début** beginning

le **décalitre** decaliter
   **décider (de)** to decide (to)

la **décision** decision
   **découvrir** to discover
   **décrire** to describe

la **déformation** alteration
   **déjà** already; ever; yet, **BV**
   **déjeuner** to eat lunch, **3.1**

le **déjeuner** lunch, **5.2**
   **le petit déjeuner** breakfast, **5.2**
   **délicieux, délicieuse** delicious
   **demain** tomorrow, **BV**
   **À demain.** See you tomorrow., **BV**
   **demander** to ask (for), **3.2**
   **demi(e)** half
   **et demie** half past (time), **BV**

le **demi-frère** half brother, **4.1**

la **demi-sœur** half sister, **4.1**

le **département d'outre-mer** French overseas department
   **désagréable** disagreeable, unpleasant
   **désespéré(e)** desperate, L4
   **désirer** to want, **5.1**

le **dessin** art, **2.2**; drawing, illustration

la **destinée** destiny
   **détester** to hate, **3.1**
   **deuxième** second, **4.2**
   **deviner** to guess

la **devinette** riddle

le **devoir** homework (assignment)
   **faire ses devoirs** to do homework
   **dévoué(e)** devoted
   **d'habitude** usually, **12.2**

le **diagnostic** diagnosis, **14.2**

le **dialecte** dialect
   **difficile** difficult, **2.1**
   **diffuser** to spread, to propagate

**dîner** to eat dinner, **5.2**
le **dîner** dinner, **5.2**
le **diplôme** diploma
la **direction** direction
**discuter** to discuss
la **disquette** diskette, floppy disk
**distinguer** to distinguish, to tell apart
**divers(e)** various
**divisé(e)** divided
**diviser** to divide
la **djellaba** djellaba (long, loose garment)
le **document** document
le **doigt** finger
le **dollar** dollar, **3.2**
le **dolmen** dolmen
le **domaine** domain, field
**donc** so, therefore
les **données** (f. pl.) data
**donner** to give, **4.1**
　**donner une fête** to throw a party, **4.1**
　**donner sur** to face, overlook, **4.2**
**dormir** to sleep
**douloureux, douloureuse** painful
le **doute** doubt
la **douzaine** dozen, **6.2**
**du coin** neighborhood (adj.)
**dynamique** dynamic, **1.2**

l' **eau** (f.) water, **6.2**
　**l'eau minérale** mineral water, **6.2**
l' **échange** (m.) exchange
**échanger** to exchange
l' **école** (f.) school, **1.2**
　**l'école primaire** elementary school
　**l'école secondaire** junior high, high school, **1.2**
l' **économie** (f.) economics, **2.2**
**écouter** to listen (to), **3.1**
**écrire** to write
l' **écrivain** (m.) writer (m. and f.), **L2**

l' **égoïste** egotistical, **1.2**
l' **élément** (m.) element
l' **élève** (m. et f.) student, **1.2**
**élevé(e)** high
　**bien élevé(e)** well-behaved
l' **e-mail** (m.) e-mail
l' **emploi** (m.) **du temps** schedule
**emprisonné(e)** imprisoned
**en** in, **3.2;** by, **5.2**
　**en général** in general
　**en l'honneur de** in honor of
　**en solde** on sale, **7.1**
　**en ville** in town, in the city
　**en voiture** by car, **5.2**
l' **énergie** (f.) energy
**énergique** energetic, **1.2**
l' **enfance** (f.) childhood
l' **enfant** (m. et f.) child, **4.1**
**enfin** finally, at last
**ensemble** together, **5.1**
l' **ensemble** (m.) outfit; whole, entirety
**enthousiaste** enthusiastic, **1.2**
**entier, entière** entire, whole
**entre** between, among, **3.2**
l' **entrée** (f.) entrance, **4.2;** admission
l' **entreprise** (f.) firm
**entrer** to enter, **7.1**
**environ** about
**envoyer** to send, **10.1**
l' **épicerie** (f.) grocery store, **6.1**
les **épinards** (m. pl.) spinach, **6.2**
l' **époque** (f.) period, times
l' **escalier** (m.) staircase, **4.2**
l' **espagnol** (m.) Spanish (language), **2.2**
l' **esprit** (m.) spirit
**essayer** to try on, **7.2;** to try
**et** and, **BV**
**établir** to establish
l' **étage** (m.) floor (of a building), **4.2**

les **États-Unis** (m. pl.) United States
**étranger, étrangère** foreign
**être** to be, **1.1**
　**être d'accord** to agree, **2.1**
l' **étude** (f.) study
l' **étudiant(e)** (university) student
**étudier** to study, **3.1**
l' **euro** (m.) euro, **6.2**
l' **Europe** (f.) Europe
**européen(ne)** European
l' **examen** (m.) test, exam, **3.1**
　**passer un examen** to take a test, **3.1**
　**réussir à un examen** to pass a test
**excellent(e)** excellent
**excepté(e)** except
l' **exception** (f.) exception
**exceptionnel(le)** exceptional
**exécuter** to carry out
l' **exemple** (m.) example
　**par exemple** for example
l' **exercice** (m.) exercise
**exister** to exist, to be
l' **explication** (f.) explanation
l' **express** (m.) espresso, black coffee, **5.1**
**expulser** to expel, banish
l' **extérieur** (m.) exterior, outside
　**à l'extérieur** outside, outside the home
**extraordinaire** extraordinary, **13.2**

la **fable** fable
**facile** easy, **2.1**
la **façon** way, manner
**faible** weak, **L1**
**faim: avoir faim** to be hungry, **5.1**
**faire** to do, make, **6.1**
　**faire du (+ nombre)** to take size (+ number), **7.2**

**faire des achats** to shop
**faire attention** to pay attention, **6**
**faire des courses** to go shopping, **7.2**
**faire les courses** to do the grocery shopping, **6.1**
**faire la cuisine** to cook, **6**
**faire ses devoirs** to do homework
**faire des études** to study
**faire du français (des maths, etc.)** to study French (math, etc.), **6**
**faire du jogging** to jog
**faire un pique-nique** to have a picnic
**Vous faites quelle pointure?** What size shoe do you take?, **7.2**
**Vous faites quelle taille?** What size do you take (wear)?, **7.2**
la **famille** family, **4.1**
    le **nom de famille** last name
**fantastique** fantastic
le **fast-food** fast-food restaurant
**fatigué(e)** tired
la **faute** fault, mistake
**faux, fausse** false
**favori(te)** favorite, **7.2**
la **femme** woman, **7.1;** wife, **4.1**
**fermé(e)** closed
la **fête** party, **4.1**
    **donner une fête** to throw a party, **4.1**
la **feuille de papier** sheet of paper, **3.2**
le **feutre** felt-tip pen, **3.2**
le **fichier** file (computer)
la **fille** girl, **1.1;** daughter, **4.1**
le **film** film, movie,
le **fils** son, **4.1**
la **fleur** flower, **4.2**
**fleuri(e)** in bloom, **L2**
**fleurir** to bloom
le **fleuve** river
la **fois** time (in a series)

à la **fois** at the same time
    **deux fois** twice
**fonder** to found
le **football américain** football
la **forme** form, shape
**former** to form
**fort(e)** strong, **2.2**
    **fort(e) en maths** good in math, **2.2**
la **fourchette** fork, **5.2**
la **fourniture** supply
    les **fournitures scolaires** school supplies, **3.2**
la **fracture** fracture (of bone)
la **fraise** strawberry, **6.2**
le **français** French (language), **2.2**
le/la **Français(e)** Frenchman (-woman)
    **français(e)** French, **1.1**
la **France** France
    **francophone** French-speaking
    **fréquenter** to frequent, patronize
le **frère** brother, **1.2**
le **frigidaire** refrigerator, **12.2**
les **frites** (f. pl.) French fries, **5.1**
le **fromage** cheese, **5.1**
la **frontière** border
    **frugal(e)** light, simple
le **fruit** fruit, **6.2**
le **futur** future, **L2**

**gagner** to earn; to win, **10.1**
le **garage** garage, **4.2**
le **garçon** boy, **1.1**
    **garder** to guard, watch; to keep
le **gâteau** cake, **4.1**
le **général** general, **7**
    **en général** in general
    **généralement** generally
les **gens** (m. pl.) people
    **gentil(le)** nice (person), **6.2**
la **géographie** geography, **2.2**
la **géométrie** geometry, **2.2**

la **glace** ice cream, **5.1;** ice
la **gomme** eraser, **3.2**
le **gourmet** gourmet
    **grâce à** thanks to
la **grammaire** grammar
le **gramme** gram, **6.2**
    **grand(e)** tall, big, **1.1;** great
    le **grand magasin** department store, **7.1**
    **de grand standing** luxury (adj.)
    la **grande surface** large department store; large supermarket
    **grandir** to grow (up) (children)
la **grand-mère** grandmother, **4.1**
le **grand-père** grandfather, **4.1**
les **grands-parents** (m. pl.) grandparents, **4.1**
la **griffe** label
    **gris(e)** gray, **7.2**
le **groupe** group
    **guillotiné(e)** guillotined
la **guitare** guitar
le/la **guitariste** guitarist
la **gymnastique** gymnastics, **2.2**

**habillé(e)** dressy, **7.1**
**habiter** to live (in a city, house, etc.), **3.1**
**haïtien(ne)** Haitian
le **hamburger** hamburger
le **hameau** hamlet
**handicapé(e)** handicapped
le **hardware** (computer) hardware
les **haricots** (m. pl.) **verts** green beans, **6.2**
la **harpe** harp
l' **hectomètre** (m.) hectometer
l' **heure** (f.) time (of day), **BV;** hour, **3.2**
    **à quelle heure?** at what time?, **2**
    **À tout à l'heure.** See you later., **BV**

**Il est quelle heure?** What time is it?, **BV**
l' **histoire** *(f.)* history, **2.2;** story
le/la **H.L.M.** low-income housing
l' **homme** *(m.)* man, **7.1**
**horrible** horrible
le **hot-dog** hot dog, **5.1**
l' **huile** *(f.)* oil, **6.1**
**humain(e)** human
**hyper: J'ai hyper faim.** I'm super hungry.
l' **hypermarché** *(m.)* large department store/supermarket

**idéal(e)** ideal
l' **idée** *(f.)* idea
**il y a** there is, there are, **4.1**
**immense** immense
l' **immeuble** *(m.)* apartment building, **4.2**
**important(e)** important
**impossible** impossible
l' **imprimante** *(f.)* printer
**indiquer** to indicate, show
**indiscret, indiscrète** indiscreet
**individuel(le)** individual
**industriel(le)** industrial
**inférieur(e)** lower
**infini(e)** infinite
l' **influence** *(f.)* influence
l' **information** *(f.)* information
**les informations** *(f. pl.)* news *(TV)*
l' **informatique** *(f.)* computer science, **2.2**
**insister** to insist
**inspirer** to inspire
les **instructions** *(f. pl.)* instructions
**intellectuel(le)** intellectual
l' **intellectuel(le)** intellectual
**intelligent(e)** intelligent, **1.1**
**intéressant(e)** interesting, **1.1**
**intéresser** to interest

l' **intérêt** *(m.)* interest
**inviter** to invite, **4.1;** to pay for someone's meal, **5.2**
l' **italien** *(m.)* Italian *(language)*, **2.2**
**italien(ne)** Italian
l' **Ivoirien(ne)** *(m. et f.)* Ivorian *(inhabitant of Côte d'Ivoire)*

**jaloux, jalouse** jealous
le **jambon** ham, **5.1**
**janvier** *(m.)* January, **BV**
le **jardin** garden, **4.2**
**jaune** yellow, **7.2**
**je** I, **1.2**
**Je t'en prie.** You're welcome. *(fam.)*, **BV**
**je voudrais** I would like, **5.1**
**Je vous en prie.** You're welcome. *(form.)*, **BV**
le **jean** jeans, **7.1**
le **jeu** game
**jeune** young
les **jeunes** *(m. pl.)* young people
le **jogging: faire du jogging** to jog
**joli(e)** pretty, **4.2**
**jouer** to play, **3.2**
le **jour** day, **BV**
**tous les jours** every day
la **journée** day, **3.1**
**Belle journée!** What a nice day!, **4.2**
**Joyeux anniversaire!** Happy birthday!
le **jumeau, la jumelle** twin, **L1**
la **jupe** skirt, **7.1**
le **jus** juice, **5.1**
**le jus d'orange** orange juice, **5.1**
**le jus de pomme** apple juice, **5.1**
**juste** just, **2.1**
**juste à sa taille** fitting (him/her) just right
**juste là** right there

le **kilo(gramme)** kilogram, **6.2**

**là** there
le **laboratoire** laboratory
**laisser** to leave *(something behind)*, **5.2;** to let, allow
**laisser un pourboire** to leave a tip, **5.2**
le **lait** milk, **6.1**
la **langue** language, **2.2**
**large** loose, wide, **7.2**
le **latin** Latin, **2.2**
**latin(e)** Latin
la **leçon** lesson
la **lecture** reading
la **légende** legend
le **légume** vegetable, **6.2**
**lever** to raise, **3.1**
**lever la main** to raise one's hand, **3.1**
la **liaison** liaison, linking
la **liberté** freedom
**libre** free, **5.1**
le **lieu** place
**avoir lieu** to take place
la **ligne** line
la **limite** limit
la **limonade** lemon-lime drink, **BV**
le **liquide** liquid
le **litre** liter, **6.2**
la **littérature** literature, **2.2**
la **livre** pound, **6.2**
le **livre** book, **3.2**
le **logement** housing
le **logiciel** computer program
**loin** far (away)
**loin de** far from, **4.2**
**long(ue)** long, **7.1**
le **look** style
le **lycée** high school, **2.1**
le/la **lycéen(ne)** high school student

**Madame (Mme)** Mrs., Ms., **BV**

**Mademoiselle (Mlle)** Miss, Ms., **BV**

le **magasin** store, **3.2**
  **le grand magasin** department store, **7.1**

le **Maghreb** Maghreb

la **main** hand, **3.1**
  **maintenant** now, **2.2**
  **mais** but, **2.1**

la **maison** house, **3.1**
  **la maison d'édition** publishing house

la **maisonnette** cottage

la **majorité** majority
  **mal** badly
  **Pas mal.** Not bad., **BV**
  **malade** ill, sick, **L1**
  **malheureusement** unfortunately
  **malheureux, malheureuse** unhappy

la **maman** mom

la **manche** sleeve, **7.1**
  **à manches longues (courtes)** long- (short-) sleeved, **7.1**
  **manger** to eat, **5.1**
  **la salle à manger** dining room, **4.2**

le **manteau** coat, **7.1**

le/la **marchand(e) (de fruits et légumes)** (produce) seller, merchant, **6.2**

la **marchandise** merchandise

le **marché** market, **6.2**
  **bon marché** inexpensive
  **le marché aux puces** flea market

le **mari** husband, **4.1**

le **mariage** marriage; wedding

le **Maroc** Morocco
  **marocain(e)** Moroccan
  **marron** (*inv.*) brown, **7.2**
  **martiniquais(e)** from or of Martinique

les **mathématiques** (*f. pl.*) mathematics, **2.2**

les **maths** (*f. pl.*) math, **2.2**

la **matière** subject (*school*), **2.2;** matter

le **matin** morning, **BV**
  **du matin** A.M. (*time*), **BV**
  **mauvais(e)** bad; wrong, **2.2**

la **médina** medina

le **melon** melon, **6.2**
  **même** (*adj.*) same, **2.1;** (*adv.*) even
  **tout de même** all the same, **5.2**

la **mer** sea
  **la mer des Antilles** Caribbean Sea
  **la mer des Caraïbes** Caribbean Sea
  **la mer Méditerranée** Mediterranean Sea
  **merci** thank you, thanks, **BV**

la **mère** mother, **4.1**

le **message** message

la **mesure** measurement
  **mesurer** to measure

le **mètre** meter

le **métro** subway, **4.2**
  **la station de métro** subway station, **4.2**
  **mettre** to put (on), to place, **7.1;** to turn on (*appliance*), **7**
  **mettre la table** to set the table, **7**

le **microbe** microbe, germ
  **microbien(ne)** microbial

le **microprocesseur** microprocessor

le **microscope** microscope
  **midi** (*m.*) noon, **BV**
  **mieux** better, **7.2**
  **aimer mieux** to prefer, **7.2**

le **milligramme** milligram
  **minuit** (*m.*) midnight, **BV**

la **mode: à la mode** in style

le **modem** modem
  **moderne** modern
  **modeste** modest; reasonably priced
  **moins** less, **7.1;** minus
  **plus ou moins** more or less

le **mois** month, **BV**

le **moment** moment, time

le **monde** world
  **tout le monde** everyone, everybody, **1.2**

le **moniteur** (*computer*) monitor
  **Monsieur** (*m.*) Mr., sir, **BV**

le **mont** mount, mountain

la **montagne** mountain, **11.2**
  **monter** to go up, **4.2**

le **mot** word

la **moule** mussel

la **moutarde** mustard, **6.2**

le **mouvement** movement
  **multiplier** to multiply

le **musée** museum

la **musique** music, **2.2**

le **mythe** myth

la **nappe** tablecloth, **5.2**
  **nationalité** (*f.*) nationality
  **nature** plain (*adj.*), **5.1**
  **naturel(le)** natural
  **naviguer sur Internet** to surf the Net
  **ne: ne... pas** not, **1.2**
  **ne... plus** no longer, no more, **6.1**
  **né(e): elle est née** she was born
  **nécessaire** necessary

la **négritude** black pride
  **n'est-ce pas?** isn't it?, doesn't it (he, she, etc.)?, **2.2**

le **neveu** nephew, **4.1**

la **nièce** niece, **4.1**
  **noir(e)** black, **7.2**

le **nom** name; noun
  **le nom de famille** last name

le **nombre** number
  **non** no

le **nord** north
  **nord-africain(e)** North African

la **note** note; grade
  **nourrir** to feed

la **nourriture** food, nutrition

nouveau (nouvel), nouvelle new, 4.2
la Nouvelle-Angleterre New England
nul(le) (slang) bad
le numéro number
le numéro de téléphone telephone number

ô oh
l' objet (m.) object
obligatoire mandatory
obliger to oblige, force
observer to observe
occidental(e) western
occupé(e) occupied, taken, 5.1; busy
l' océan (m.) ocean
l' œuf (m.) egg, 6.1
l'œuf à la coque poached egg
l'œuf brouillé scrambled egg
l'œuf sur le plat fried egg
l' œuvre (f.) work(s) (of art or literature)
officiel(le) official
l' oignon (m.) onion, 5.1
l' oiseau (m.) bird
l' omelette (f.) omelette, 5.1
l'omelette aux fines herbes omelette with herbs, 5.1
l'omelette nature plain omelette, 5.1
on we, they, people, 3.2
l' oncle (m.) uncle, 4.1
l' opéra (m.) opera
l' orange (f.) orange, 6.2
orange (inv.) orange (color), 7.2
l' oranger (m.) orange tree, L2
ordinaire ordinary
l' ordinateur (m.) computer
l' organisme (m.) organism
oriental(e) eastern
originaire de native of

l' origine (f.): d'origine américaine (française, etc.) from the U.S. (France, etc.)
orner to decorate
ôter to take off (clothing)
ou or, 1.1
où where, 1.1
d'où from where, 1.1
oublier to forget
oui yes, BV
ouvert(e) open, 13.2

le pain bread, 6.1
le pain complet whole-wheat bread
la tartine de pain beurré slice of bread and butter
la paire pair, 7.1
le palais palace
le pantalon pants, 7.1
la papeterie stationery store, 3.2
le papier paper, 3.2
la feuille de papier sheet of paper, 3.2
le paquet package, 6.2
par by, through
par exemple for example
par semaine a (per) week, 3.2
le parc park
parce que because
par-dessus over (prep.)
pardon excuse me, pardon me
les parents (m. pl.) parents, 4.1
le parfum flavor
parisien(ne) Parisian
le parking parking lot
parler to speak, talk, 3.1
parler au téléphone to talk on the phone, 3.2
les paroles (f. pl.) words, lyrics
la partie part
partout everywhere
pas not, 2.1
pas du tout not at all, 3.1

Pas mal. Not bad., BV
passer to spend (time), 3.1; to go (through)
passer un examen to take an exam, 3.1
les pâtes (f. pl.) pasta
pauvre poor, L1
le pavillon small house, bungalow
payer to pay, 3.2
le pays country
le/la paysan(ne) peasant, L1
le/la peintre painter, artist
la peinture painting
pendant during, for (time), 3.2
le père father, 4.1
la période period
la périphérie outskirts
permanent(e) permanent
la personnalité personality
la personne person
personnel(le) personal
petit(e) short, small, 1.1
le petit déjeuner breakfast, 5.2
les petits pois (m.) peas, 6.2
la petite-fille granddaughter, 4.1
le petit-fils grandson, 4.1
les petits-enfants (m. pl.) grandchildren, 4.1
peu (de) few, little
un peu a little, 2.1
en très peu de temps in a short time
très peu seldom, 5.2
peur: avoir peur to be afraid, L1
le phénomène phenomenon
la photo photograph
la phrase sentence
le/la physicien(ne) physicist
la physique physics, 2.2
la pièce room, 4.2; play
la pièce de théâtre play
le pied: à pied on foot, 4.2
pittoresque picturesque
la pizza pizza, BV
la place place; square
la plante plant
le plat dish (food)

**pleurer** to cry, **L1**
**plissé(e)** pleated, **7.1**
la **plupart (des)** most (of)
**plus** plus; more, **7.1**
   **ne… plus** no longer, no more, **6.1**
le **poème** poem
la **poésie** poetry
le **poète** poet *(m. and f.)*
le **poids** weight
**point: à point** medium-rare *(meat)*, **5.2**
la **pointure** size *(shoes)*, **7.2**
   **Vous faites quelle pointure?** What (shoe) size do you take?, **7.2**
la **poire** pear, **6.2**
le **poisson** fish, **6.1**
la **poissonnerie** fish store, **6.1**
le **poivre** pepper, **6.1**
la **politesse** courtesy, politeness, **BV**
le **polo** polo shirt, **7.1**
la **pomme** apple, **6.2**
   **la tarte aux pommes** apple tart, **6.1**
la **pomme de terre** potato, **6.2**
**populaire** popular, **1.2**
le **porc** pork, **6.1**
le **port** port, harbor
**porter** to wear, **7.1**
le/la **portraitiste** portraitist
**portugais(e)** Portuguese
**poser une question** to ask a question, **3.1**
la **position** position
**posséder** to possess, own
le **pot** jar, **6.2**
le **poulet** chicken, **6.1**
   **pour** for, **2.1**; in order to
   **pour cent** percent
le **pourboire** tip *(restaurant)*, **5.2**
   **pourquoi** why, **6.2**
   **pourquoi pas?** why not?
**pouvoir** to be able to, can, **6.1**
**préféré(e)** favorite
**préférer** to prefer, **6**
le **préfixe** prefix
**premier, première** first, **4.2**
**prendre** to have *(to eat or drink)*, **5.1**; to take, **5.2**; to buy
   **prendre le petit déjeuner** to eat breakfast, **5.2**
   **prendre le métro** to take the subway, **5.2**
**préparer** to prepare
**près de** near, **4.2**
**prie: Je vous en prie.** You're welcome., **BV**
**primaire: l'école** *(f.)* **primaire** elementary school
**principal(e)** main, principal
le **prix** price, cost, **7.1**
le **problème** problem
**prochain(e)** next
le **produit** product
le/la **prof** teacher *(inform.)*, **2.1**
le **professeur** teacher *(m. and f.)*, **2.1**
**professionnel(le)** professional
la **programmation** programming
le **programme** program
**promotion: en promotion** on special, on sale
les **provisions** *(f. pl.)* food
la **publicité** advertisement
**publier** to publish
les **puces** *(f. pl.):* **le marché aux puces** flea market
le **pull** sweater, **7.1**

la **qualité** quality
**quand** when, **4.1**
le **quart: et quart** a quarter past *(time)*, **BV**
   **moins le quart** a quarter to *(time)*, **BV**
le **quartier** neighborhood, district, **4.2**
**quatrième** fourth
**que** as; that; than *(in comparisons)*, **7.2**
**québécois(e)** from or of Quebec

**quel(le)** which, what
**quelque** some *(sing.)*
   **quelque chose** something, **11**
   **quelque chose à manger** something to eat, **5.1**
   **quelque chose de spécial** something special
**quelquefois** sometimes, **5.2**
la **question** question, **3.1**
   **poser une question** to ask a question, **3.1**
**qui** who, **1.1**; whom; which, that
**quitter** to leave *(a room, etc.)*, **3.1**

**R**

la **race** race
la **radio** radio, **3.2**
le **rap** rap *(music)*
**rapide** quick, fast
**rapidement** rapidly, quickly
le **rayon** department *(in a store)*, **7.1**
   **le rayon des manteaux** coat department, **7.1**
la **récré** recess, **3.2**
la **récréation** recess, **3.2**
**refléter** to reflect
**regarder** to look at, **3.1**
le **reggae** reggae
la **région** region
la **règle** ruler, **3.2**; rule
**regretter** to be sorry, **6.1**
la **reine** queen
**religieux, religieuse** religious
**rencontrer** to meet
**rendre** to give back
   **rendre bien service** to be a big help
**renommé(e)** renowned
**rentrer** to go home; to return, **3.2**
le **repas** meal, **5.2**
**répéter** to repeat
**respirer** to breathe
**ressembler à** to resemble
le **restaurant** restaurant, **5.2**

la **restauration** food service
  **la restauration rapide**
   fast food
**retrouver** to meet, get
  together with
la **révolution** revolution
**révolutionnaire**
  revolutionary
la **revue** magazine, **L2**
le **rez-de-chaussée** ground
  floor, **4.2**
**riche** rich
**rigoler** to joke around, **3.2**
  **Tu rigoles!** You're
   kidding!, **3.2**
**rigolo** funny, **4.2**
la **rivière** river
la **robe** dress, **7.1**
le **roman** novel
**rose** pink, **7.2**
**rouge** red, **7.2**
**royal(e)** royal
la **rue** street, **3.1**
**rural(e)** rural
le **russe** Russian *(language)*

le **sac** bag, **6.1**
  **le sac à dos** backpack, **3.2**
**saignant(e)** rare *(meat)*, **5.2**
la **salade** salad, **5.1;** lettuce,
  **6.2**
**sale** dirty
la **salle** room
  **la salle à manger** dining
   room, **4.2**
  **la salle de bains**
   bathroom, **4.2**
  **la salle de classe**
   classroom, **2.1**
  **la salle de séjour** living
   room, **4.2**
  **Salut.** Hi.; Bye., **BV**
la **salutation** greeting
les **sandales** *(f. pl.)* sandals, **7.1**
le **sandwich** sandwich, **BV**
**sans** without
la **sardine** sardine
la **sauce** sauce
la **saucisse** sausage

  **la saucisse de Francfort**
   hot dog, **BV**
le **saucisson** salami, **6.1**
**sauvegarder** to safeguard,
  to save
**sauver** to save
le **savant** scientist
les **sciences** *(f. pl.)* science, **2.1**
  **les sciences naturelles**
   natural sciences, **2.1**
  **les sciences sociales**
   social studies, **2.1**
**scientifique** scientific
**scolaire** school *(adj.)*, **3.2**
la **sculpture** sculpture
**second(e)** second
**secondaire: l'école** *(f.)*
  **secondaire** junior high,
  high school, **1.2**
**secret, secrète** secret
le **séjour** stay
  **la salle de séjour** living
   room, **4.2**
le **sel** salt, **6.1**
la **semaine** week, **3.2;**
  allowance
  **la semaine prochaine**
   next week
  **par semaine** a (per)
   week, **3.2**
**semblable** similar, **L1**
le/la **Sénégalais(e)** Senegalese
  *(person)*
**séparer** to separate
**sérieux, sérieuse** serious, **7**
**serré(e)** tight, **7.2**
le **serveur, la serveuse**
  waiter, waitress, **5.1**
le **service** service, **5.2**
  **Le service est compris.**
   The tip is included., **5.2**
la **serviette** napkin, **5.2;**
  towel, **11.1**
**seul(e)** alone, **5.2;** single;
  only *(adj.)*
  **tout(e) seul(e)** all alone,
   by himself/herself, **5.2**
**seulement** only *(adv.)*
le **shopping** shopping, **7.2**
le **short** shorts, **7.1**
**si** if; yes *(after neg.*
  *question)*, **7.2;** so *(adv.)*

le **sifsari** type of veil worn
  by North African women
la **signification** meaning,
  significance
**signifier** to mean
**simple** simple
le **site** Web site
**situé(e)** located
**sociable** sociable,
  outgoing, **1.2**
la **sœur** sister, **1.2**
le **software** software
**soi** oneself, himself, herself
**soif: avoir soif** to be
  thirsty, **5.1**
le **soir** evening , **BV**
  **ce soir** tonight
  **du soir** in the evening,
   P.M., **BV**
  **le soir** in the evening, **5.2**
les **soldes** *(m. pl.)* sale *(in a*
  *store)*, **7.1**
la **solidarité** solidarity
**solide** solid
**solitaire** lonely
la **solution** solution
**sombre** dark
la **sorte** sort, kind, type
**souffrir** to suffer
le **souk** North African market
la **soupe** soup, **5.1**
  **la soupe à l'oignon**
   onion soup, **5.1**
la **source** source
la **souris** mouse
**sous** under
**soustraire** to subtract
**souterrain(e)** underground
**souvent** often, **5.2**
**spécial(e)** special
la **spécialité** specialty
  **sport** *(inv.)* casual *(clothes)*,
   **7.1**
  **standing: de grande**
  **standing** luxury
la **station** station, **4.2;** resort
  **la station de métro**
   subway station, **4.2**
la **station-service** gas station
la **statue** statue
le **steak frites** steak and
  French fries, **5.2**

**stocker** to store
la **stratégie** strategy
**strict(e)** strict, **2.1**
le **studio** studio (apartment)
le **stylo-bille** ballpoint pen, **3.2**
le **succès** success
le **sud** south
**suivant(e)** following
le **sujet** subject
**super** terrific, super
**supérieur(e)** higher
le **supermarché** supermarket, **6.2**
**sur** on, **4.2**
**donner sur** to face, overlook, **4.2**
**sûr(e)** sure, certain
**bien sûr**, of course
**surgelé(e)** frozen, **6.2**
**surtout** especially, above all; mostly
le **survêtement** warmup suit, **7.1**
le **sweat-shirt** sweatshirt, **7.1**
**sympa** *(inv.)* nice *(abbrev. for **sympathique**)*, **1.2**
**sympathique** nice *(person)*, **1.2**
le **système** system
le **système métrique** metric system

la **table** table, **5.1**
le **tableau** painting; chart
la **taille** size *(clothes)*, **7.2**
**juste à sa taille** fitting (him/her) just right
**la taille au-dessous** next smaller size, **7.2**
**la taille au-dessus** next larger size, **7.2**
**Vous faites quelle taille?** What size do you take/wear?, **7.2**
le **tailleur** suit *(woman's)*, **7.1**
le **talent** talent
la **tante** aunt, **4.1**
la **tarte** pie, tart, **6.1**

la **tarte aux pommes** apple tart, **6.1**
la **tartine** slice of bread with butter or jam
**la tartine de pain beurré** slice of bread and butter, **5.1**
la **tasse** cup, **5.2**
la **télé** TV
**télécharger** to download
le **téléphone** telephone, **3.2**
**le numéro de téléphone** telephone number
**téléphoner** to call (on the telephone)
**téléphonique** telephone *(adj.)*
**temporaire** temporary
le **temps** time
**l'emploi** *(m.)* **du temps** schedule
**en très peu de temps** in a short time
la **terrasse** terrace, patio, **4.2**
**la terrasse d'un café** sidewalk café, **5.1**
le **texte** text
**thaïlandais(e)** Thai
le **thé** tea
le **théâtre** theater
**la pièce de théâtre** play
**timide** shy, timid, **1.2**
**tirer** to take, to draw
les **toilettes** *(f. pl.)* bathroom, toilet, **4.2**
le **toit** roof
**le toit de chaume** thatched roof
la **tomate** tomato, **6.2**
**tomber** to fall, **11.2**
**tomber malade** to get sick, **L1**
**toujours** always, **4.2**; still
la **tour** tower
**la tour Eiffel** Eiffel Tower
le **tour: À votre tour.** (It's) your turn.
**tous, toutes** *(adj.)* all, every, **2.1**
**tous (toutes) les deux** both
**tout** *(pron.)* all, everything

**C'est tout.** That's all., **6.1**
**pas du tout** not at all, **3.1**
**tout(e)** *(adj.)* the whole, the entire; all, any
**tout le monde** everyone, everybody, **1.2**
**tout** *(adv.)* very, completely, all, **4.2**
**À tout à l'heure.** See you later., **BV**
**tout de même** all the same, **5.2**
**tout près de** very near, **4.2**
**tout(e) seul(e)** all alone, all by himself/herself, **5.2**
la **tradition** tradition
**traditionnel(le)** traditional
**traiter** to treat
la **tranche** slice, **6.2**
**transporter** to transport
le **travail** work
**travailler** to work, **3.1**; to practice
**très** very, **BV**
la **trigonométrie** trigonometry, **2.2**
**triste** sad, **L1**
**troisième** third, **4.2**
**trop** too *(excessive)*, **2.1**
**tropical(e)** tropical
**trouver** to find, **5.1**; to think *(opinion)*, **7.2**
le **t-shirt** T-shirt, **7.1**
la **tunique** tunic
la **Tunisie** Tunisia
**tunisien(ne)** Tunisian
le **type** type; guy *(inform.)*
**typique** typical

l' **un(e)... l'autre** one . . . the other
**unique** single, only one
**l'enfant unique** only child
l' **unité** *(f.)* unit
l' **université** *(f.)* university
**utiliser** to use

les **vacances** *(f. pl.)* vacation
le **val** valley
la **valeur** value
la **vanille: à la vanille**
　vanilla *(adj.)*, **5.1**
　**varié(e)** varied
le **vendeur, la vendeuse**
　salesperson, **7.1**
le **verre** glass, **5.2**
　**vert(e)** green, **5.1**
la **veste** (sport) jacket, **7.1**
les **vêtements** *(m. pl.)* clothes,
　**7.1**
la **viande** meat, **6.1**
la **vidéo** video, **3.1**
la **vie** life
　**vieille** old *(f.)*, **4.2**
　**vietnamien(ne)**
　　Vietnamese, **6**
　**vieux (vieil)** old *(m.)*, **4.2**
la **villa** house
le **village** village, small town
la **ville** city, town
　**en ville** in the
　　city
le **vinaigre** vinegar, **6.1**
　**violent(e)** violent; rough
le **violon** violin
le **virus** virus
　**visionner** to view
　**visiter** to visit *(a place)*
　**vite** fast *(adv.)*
la **vitrine** (store) window, **7.1**

**vivant(e)** living
**voici** here is, here are, **4.1**
**voilà** there is, there are;
　here is, here are
　*(emphatic)*, **1.2**
le **voile** veil
**voir** to see, **7.1**
le/la **voisin(e)** neighbor, **4.2**
la **voiture** car, **4.2**
　**en voiture** by car, **5.2;**
　　"All aboard!"
la **voix** voice
**voudrais: je voudrais** I
　would like, **5.1**
**vouloir** to want, **6.1**
**vrai(e)** true, real, **2.2**
**vraiment** really, **1.1**
la **vue** view, **4.2**

le **week-end** weekend

le **yaourt** yogurt, **6.1**
les **yeux** *(m. pl; sing. œil)* eyes,
　**L1**

la **zoologie** zoology
**Zut!** Darn!, **BV**

This English-French Dictionary *contains all productive vocabulary from the text. The numbers following each entry indicate the chapter and vocabulary section in which the word is introduced. For example,* **2.2** *means that the word first appeared in* **Chapitre 2, Mots 2.** **BV** *refers to the introductory* **Bienvenue** *lessons.* **L** *refers to the optional literary readings. If there is no number or letter following an entry, this means that the word or expression is there for receptive purposes only.*

**a** un, une, **1.1**
  **a week** par semaine, **3.2**
  **a lot** beaucoup, **3.1**
**able** capable
  **to be able to** pouvoir, **6.1**
**about** *(on the subject of)* de; *(approximately)* à peu près
**above all** surtout
**accessible** accessible
**accessory** l'accessoire *(m.)*
to **accompany** accompagner
to **add** additionner
**address** l'adresse *(f.)*
**adolescent** l'adolescent(e)
**adorable** adorable, **4.1**
**adult** l'adulte *(m. et f.)*
**advertisement** la publicité
**afraid: to be afraid** avoir peur, **L1**
**Africa** l'Afrique *(f.)*
**African** africain(e)
**after** après, **3.2**
**afternoon** l'après-midi *(m.)*, **3.2**
  **five o'clock in the afternoon** cinq heures de l'après-midi, **BV**
**age** l'âge *(m.)*, **4.1**
to **agree** être d'accord, **2.1**
**aid** l'aide *(f.)*
**album** l'album *(m.)*
**algebra** l'algèbre *(f.)*, **2.2**
**Algeria** l'Algérie *(f.)*
**algerian** algérien(ne)
**all** tout(e), tous, toutes, **2.1**
  **all alone** tout(e) seul(e), **5.2**

**all the same** tout de même, **5.2**
  **not at all** pas du tout
  **That's all.** C'est tout., **6.1**
**alone** seul(e), **5.2**
  **all alone** tout(e) seul(e), **5.2**
**along** le long de
**already** déjà, **BV**
**also** aussi, **1.1**
**always** toujours, **4.2**
**a.m.** du matin, **BV**
**American** *(adj.)* américain(e), **1.1**
**among** entre, **3.2**
to **analyse** analyser
**analysis** l'analyse *(f.)*
**analytical** analytique
**and** et, **BV**
**animal** l'animal *(m.)*
to **announce** annoncer
  **Anything else?** Avec ça?, **6.1**; Autre chose?, **6.2**
**apartment** l'appartement *(m.)*, **4.2**
  **apartment building** l'immeuble *(m.)*, **4.2**
**apple** la pomme, **6.2**
  **apple tart** la tarte aux pommes, **6.1**
to **appreciate** apprécier
**April** avril *(m.)*, **BV**
**Arab** arabe
**Arabic** *(language)* l'arabe *(m.)*
**arithmetic** le calcul
**around** autour de, **4.2**
to **arrive** arriver, **3.1**
**art** le dessin *(m.)*, **2.2**

**article** l'article *(m.)*
**artist** l'artiste *(m. et f.)*; le/la peintre *(painter)*
**artistic** artistique
**as** aussi *(comparisons)*, **7**; comme
  **as . . . as** aussi... que, **7**
  **the same . . . as** le (la, les) même(s)... que
**Asian** asiatique
to **ask (for)** demander, **3.2**
  **to ask a question** poser une question, **3.1**
**at** à, **3.1**; chez, **3.2**
  **at the home (business) of** chez, **3.2**
  **at what time?** à quelle heure?, **2**
**attention** l'attention *(f.)*
**August** août, *(m.)*, **BV**
**aunt** la tante, **4.1**
**author** l'auteur *(m.)*
**avenue** l'avenue *(f.)*

**baby** le bébé
**backpack** le sac à dos, **3.2**
**bad** mauvais(e), **2.2**; nul(le) *(slang)*
  **Not bad.** Pas mal., **BV**
**badly** mal, **14.1**
**bag** le sac, **6.1**
**bagpipes** la cornemuse
**bakery** la boulangerie-pâtisserie, **6.1**
**balcony** le balcon, **4.2**

**ballpoint pen** le stylo-bille, **3.2**
**banana** la banane, **6.2**
**base** la base
**baseball cap** la casquette, **7.1**
**based** basé(e)
**based on** à base de
**basis** la base
**bathroom** la salle de bains, les toilettes *(f. pl.)*, **4.2**
to **be** être, **1.1**
**to be able to** pouvoir, **6.1**
**to be afraid** avoir peur, **L1**
**to be hungry** avoir faim, **5.1**
**to be in luck** avoir de la chance
**to be lucky** avoir de la chance
**to be on time** être à l'heure, **8.1**
**to be part of** faire partie de
**to be sorry** regretter, **6.1**
**to be thirsty** avoir soif, **5.1**
**to be . . . years old** avoir... ans, **4.1**
**bean: green beans** les haricots verts *(m. pl.)*, **6.2**
**beautiful** beau (bel), belle, **4.2**
**because** parce que
**bedroom** la chambre à coucher, **4.2**
**beef** le bœuf, **6.1**
**before** avant; avant de
**beginning** le début
**beige** beige *(inv.)*, **7.2**
**Belgian** belge
**Belgium** la Belgique
to **believe** croire, **7.2**
**better** *(adv.)* mieux, **7.2**
**between** entre, **3.2**
**beverage** la boisson; la consommation, **5.1**
**bicycle** la bicyclette
**big** grand(e), **1.1**
**biological** biologique

**biologist** le/la biologiste
**biology** la biologie, **2.2**
**bird** l'oiseau *(m.)*
**birthday** l'anniversaire *(m.)*, **4.1**
　**Happy birthday!** Bon (Joyeux) anniversaire!
**black** noir(e), **7.2**
　**black pride** la négritude
**blond** blond(e), **1.1**
**bloom: in bloom** fleuri(e), **L2**
to **bloom** fleurir
**blouse** le chemisier, **7.1**
**blue** bleu(e), **7.2**
　**navy blue** bleu marine *(inv.)*, **7.2**
**body** le corps
**bohemian** bohème
**book** le livre, **3.2**
**border** la frontière
**botany** la botanique
**both** tous (toutes) les deux
**bottle** la bouteille, **6.2**
**boutique** la boutique, **7.1**
**bowl** le bol
**boy** le garçon, **1.1**
**brave** courageux, courageuse; brave
**bread** le pain, **6.1**
　**loaf of French bread** la baguette, **6.1**
　**slice of bread and butter** la tartine de pain beurré
　**whole-wheat bread** le pain complet
**breakfast** le petit déjeuner, **5.2**
　**to eat breakfast** prendre le petit déjeuner, **5.2**
to **breathe** respirer
**Breton** breton(ne)
**Brittany** la Bretagne
**brother** le frère, **1.2**
**brown** brun(e), marron *(inv.)*, **7.2**
**brunette** brun(e), **1.1**
**bungalow** le bungalow
**bus** le bus; l'autocar *(m.)*
　**by bus** en bus
**bush** *(wilderness)* la brousse
**busy** occupé(e)

**but** mais, **2.1**
**butcher** le boucher, la bouchère
**butcher shop** la boucherie, **6.1**
**butter** le beurre, **6.1**
to **buy** acheter, **3.2**
**by** par
**Bye.** Salut., **BV**

**cabaret** le cabaret
**café** le café, **BV**
**cafeteria** la cafétéria
**cake** le gâteau, **4.1**
**calculator** la calculatrice, **3.2**
**calculus: differential calculus** le calcul différentiel
　**integral calculus** le calcul intégral
to **call** appeler; *(on the telephone)* téléphoner
**calm** calme
**Camembert cheese** le camembert
**can** pouvoir, **6.1**
**can of food** la boîte de conserve, **6.2**
**Canadian** *(adj.)* canadien(ne), **6**
**candle** la bougie, **4.1**
**cap** la casquette, **7.1**
**capital** la capitale
**car** la voiture, **4.2**
　**by car** en voiture, **5.2**
**Careful!** Attention!, **4.2**
**Caribbean Sea** la mer des Caraïbes, la mer des Antilles
**carnival** *(season)* le carnaval
**carpenter** le charpentier
**carrot** la carotte, **6.2**
to **carry out** exécuter
**cash register** la caisse, **3.2**
**cassette** la cassette, **3.1**
**castle** le château
**casual** *(clothes)* sport *(adj. inv.)*, **7.1**

cat le chat, **4.1**
catalog le catalogue
category la catégorie
CD le CD, **3.1**
**CD-ROM** le CD-ROM
**Celtic** celte, celtique
**centiliter** le centilitre
**cereal** les céréales *(f. pl.)*
**chain** la chaîne
to **change** changer (de)
**characteristic** la
   caractéristique
**charm** le charme
**chart** le tableau
to **chat** bavarder
**check** *(in restaurant)*
   l'addition *(f.)*, **5.2**
**checkout counter** la
   caisse, **3.2**
**cheese** le fromage, **5.1**
**chemist** le/la chimiste
**chemistry** la chimie, **2.2**
**chic** chic *(inv.)*
**chicken** le poulet, **6.1**
**child** l'enfant *(m. et f.)*, **4.1**
**childhood** l'enfance *(f.)*
**Chinese** chinois(e)
**chocolate** le chocolat; *(adj.)*
   au chocolat, **5.1**
**circle** le cercle
**circus** le cirque
to **cite** citer
**city** la ville
   **in the city** en ville
**civilized** civilisé(e)
**class** *(people)* la classe, **2.1;**
   *(course)* le cours, **2.1**
   **in (French, etc.) class** en
      cours de (français, etc.)
**classmate** le/la camarade
   de classe
**classroom** la salle de
   classe, **2.1**
**closed** fermé(e)
**clothes** les vêtements
   *(m. pl.)*, **7.1**
**clown** le clown
**coat** le manteau, **7.1**
**code** le code, **4.2**
**coffee** le café, **5.1**
   **black coffee** l'express
      *(m.)*, **5.1**

**coffee with cream** le
   crème, **5.1**
**cola** le coca, **5.1**
**collection** la collection
**color** la couleur, **7.2**
   **What color is . . . ?** De
      quelle couleur est... ?,
      **7.2**
**comfortable** confortable
to **compare** comparer
**compatriot** le/la
   compatriote
**complete** complet,
   complète
to **complete** compléter
**completely** complètement
**composer** le compositeur,
   la compositrice
**computer** l'ordinateur *(m.)*
   **computer science**
      l'informatique *(f.)*, **2.2**
**concept** le concept
**concert** le concert
to **connect** connecter; relier
**contest** la compétition, le
   concours
**continent** le continent
to **continue** continuer
**conversation** la
   conversation
to **converse** converser
to **cook** faire la cuisine, **6**
   **cooked** cuit(e)
   **correct** bon(ne), **6.2**
**correspondence** la
   correspondance
**cost** le prix, **7.1**
to **cost** coûter, **3.2**
**cottage** la maisonnette
to **count** compter
**country** le pays
**courageous** courageux,
   courageuse
**course** le cours, **2.1**
   **of course** bien sûr; mais
      oui
**court** la cour
**courtesy** la politesse, **BV**
**courtyard** la cour, **3.2**
**cousin** le/la cousin(e), **4.1**
**crab** le crabe, **6.1**
**cream: coffee with cream**
   le crème, **5.1**

to **create** créer
**Creole** *(language)* le créole
**crepe** la crêpe, **BV**
**croissant** le croissant, **5.1**
to **cry** pleurer, **L1**
to **cultivate** cultiver
**cultural** culturel(le)
**culture** la culture
**cup** la tasse, **5.2**
**customer** le/la client(e)

**dairy store** la crémerie, **6.1**
to **dance** danser
**dark** sombre
**dark haired** brun(e), **1.1**
**Darn!** Zut!, **BV**
**data** les données *(f. pl.)*
**date** la date
   **What is today's date?**
      Quelle est la date
      aujourd'hui?, **BV**
**daughter** la fille, **4.1**
**day** le jour, **BV;** la journée,
   **3.1**
   **every day** tous les jours
   **What a nice day!** Belle
      journée!, **4.2**
   **What day is it today?**
      C'est quel jour
      aujourd'hui?, **BV**
**dear** cher, chère
**decaliter** le décalitre
**December** décembre *(m.)*,
   **BV**
to **decide (to)** décider de
**decimal** *(adj.)* décimal(e)
to **decorate** orner
**delicatessen** la
   charcuterie, **6.1**
**delicious** délicieux,
   délicieuse
**department (in a store)**
   le rayon, **7.1**
   **coat department** le rayon
      des manteaux, **7.1**
**department store** le grand
   magasin, **7.1**
   **large department store**
      la grande surface
**descendant** le/la
   descendant(e)

to **describe** décrire
**designer** (clothes) le couturier
**desperate** désespéré(e)
**dessert** le dessert
**destiny** la destinée
**devoted** dévoué(e)
**dialect** le dialecte
**different** différent(e), **8.1**
**difficult** difficile, **2.1**
**dining hall** (school) la cantine, **3.1**
**dining room** la salle à manger, **4.2**
**dinner** le dîner, **5.2**
   **to eat dinner** dîner, **5.2**
**diploma** le diplome
**direction** la direction; le sens
**dirty** sale
**disagreeable** désagréable
to **discover** découvrir
to **discuss** discuter
**dish** (food) le plat
**diskette** la disquette
to **distinguish** distinguer
**district** le quartier, **4.2**; (Paris) l'arrondissement (m.)
to **divide** diviser
to **do** faire, **6.1**
   **to do the grocery shopping** faire les courses, **6.1**
**document** le document
**dog** le chien, **4.1**
**dollar** le dollar, **3.2**
**domain** le domaine
**doubt** le doute
to **download** télécharger
**downtown** le centre-ville
**dozen** la douzaine, **6.2**
**dress** la robe, **7.1**
**dressy** habillé(e), **7.1**
**drink** la boisson; la consommation, **5.1**
to **drink** boire
   **something to drink** quelque chose à boire
**druid** le druide
**during** pendant, **3.2**
**dynamic** dynamique, **1.2**

# E

**each** (adj.) chaque
**each (one)** chacun(e), **5.2**
to **earn** gagner
**eastern** oriental(e)
**easy** facile, **2.1**
to **eat** manger, **5.1**
   **to eat breakfast** prendre le petit déjeuner, **5.2**
   **to eat lunch** déjeuner, **3.1**
**economics** l'économie (f.), **2.2**
**egg** l'œuf (m.), **6.1**
**egotistical** égoïste, **1.2**
**electric** électrique
**electronic** électronique
**element** l'élément (m.)
**elevator** l'ascenseur (m.), **4.2**
**else: something else** autre chose
   **Anything else?** Avec ça?, **6.1**; Autre chose?, **6.2**
**e-mail** l'e-mail (m.)
**energetic** énergique, **1.2**
**energy** l'énergie (f.)
**English** anglais(e)
**English** (language) l'anglais (m.), **2.2**
**enough** assez, **1.1**
to **enter** entrer, **7.1**
**enthusiastic** enthousiaste, **1.2**
**entire** entier, entière
**entrance** l'entrée (f.), **4.2**
**equation** l'équation (f.)
**equivalent** l'équivalent (m.)
**eraser** la gomme, **3.2**
**especially** surtout
**espresso** l'express (m.), **5.1**
to **establish** établir
**euro** l'euro (m.)
**Europe** l'Europe (f.)
**European** (adj.) européen(ne)
**evening** le soir, **BV**
   **in the evening** le soir, **5.2**

   **in the evening** (P.M.) du soir, **BV**
**every** tous, toutes, **2.1, 8**; chaque
**everybody** tout le monde, **1.2**
**everyone** tout le monde, **1.2**
**everything** tout
**everywhere** partout
**exam** l'examen (m.), **3.1**
   **to take an exam** passer un examen, **3.1**
**example: for example** par exemple
**excellent** excellent(e)
**except** excepté(e); sauf
**exception** l'exception (f.)
**exceptional** exceptionnel(le)
**exchange** l'échange (m.)
to **exchange** échanger
**excuse me** pardon
to **execute** exécuter
**exercise** l'exercice (m.)
**exhausted** crevé(e); épuisé(e)
to **exist** exister
to **expel** expulser
**expensive** cher, chère, **7.1**
**exterior** l'extérieur (m.)
**extraordinary** extraordinaire
**eyes** les yeux (m. pl.), **L1**

# F

**fable** la fable
to **face** donner sur, **4.2**
**fairly** assez, **1.1**
**false** faux, fausse
**family** la famille, **4.1**
**famous** célèbre; connu(e)
**fantastic** fantastique
**far (away)** loin
   **far from** loin de, **4.2**
**fast** (adj.) rapide; (adv.) vite
**fast-food** (adj.) de restauration rapide
   **fast-food restaurant** le fast-food
**father** le père, **4.1**

**fault** la faute
**favorite** favori(te); préféré(e)
**February** février *(m.)*, **BV**
to **feed** nourrir
**felt-tip pen** le feutre, **3.2**
**field** le champ, **L1;** le domaine
**file** *(computer)* le fichier
**finally** enfin, finalement
to **find** trouver, **5.1**
**fine** ça va, bien, **BV**
**finger** le doigt
**firm** l'entreprise *(f.)*
**first** premier, première *(adj.)*, **4.2**
**fish** le poisson, **6.1**
　**fish store** la poissonnerie, **6.1**
**fitting room** la cabine d'essayage
**flavor** le parfum
**flea market** le marché aux puces
**floor** *(of a building)* l'étage *(m.)*, **4.2**
　**ground floor** le rez-de-chaussée, **4.2**
**flower** la fleur, **4.2**
**following** suivant(e)
**food** la nourriture; l'aliment *(m.)*; les provisions *(f. pl.)*
　**food service** la restauration
**foot** le pied
　**on foot** à pied, **4.2**
**football** le football américain
**for** pour; *(time)* pendant, **3.2**
　**for example** par exemple
**foreign** étranger, étrangère
to **forget** oublier
**fork** la fourchette, **5.2**
**form** la forme
to **form** former
to **found** fonder
**fourth** quatrième
**fracture** la fracture
**free** libre, **5.1;** gratuit(e)

**French** français(e) *(adj.)*, **1.1;** *(language)* le français, **2.2**
　**French fries** les frites *(f. pl.)*, **5.1**
**French-speaking** francophone
to **frequent** fréquenter
**Friday** vendredi *(m.)*, **BV**
**friend** l'ami(e), **1.2;** *(pal)* le copain, la copine, **2.1;** le/la camarade
**from** de, **1.1**
**frozen** surgelé(e), **6.2**
**fruit** le fruit, **6.2**
**fun** amusant(e), **1.1**
**funny** amusant(e), **1.1;** rigolo, **4.2;** comique
**future** l'avenir *(m.)*, le futur, **L2**

**game** le jeu
**garage** le garage, **4.2**
**garden** le jardin, **4.2**
　**gas station** la station-service
**generally** généralement
**geography** la géographie, **2.2**
**geometry** la géometrie, **2.2**
**germ** le microbe
**German** *(language)* l'allemand *(m.)*, **2.2**
**Germany** l'Allemagne *(f.)*
to **get: to get sick** tomber malade, **L1**
**gift** le cadeau, **4.1**
**girl** la fille, **1.1**
to **give** donner, **4.1**
　**to give back** rendre
**glad** content(e)
**glass** le verre, **5.2**
to **go** aller, **5.1**
　**to go (and) get** aller chercher, **6.1**
　**to go home** rentrer, **3.2**
　**to go up** monter, **4.2**
　**to go with** accompagner
**good** bon(ne), **6.2**

**good in math** fort(e) en maths, **2.2**
**good-bye** au revoir; ciao *(inform.)*, **BV**
**gourmet** le gourmet
**grade** la note
**grains** les céréales *(f. pl.)*
**gram** le gramme, **6.2**
**grammar** la grammaire
**granddaughter** la petite-fille, **4.1**
**grandfather** le grand-père, **4.1**
**grandmother** la grand-mère, **4.1**
**grandparents** les grands-parents *(m. pl.)*, **4.1**
**grandson** le petit-fils, **4.1**
**gray** gris(e), **7.2**
**great** grand(e)
**green** vert(e), **5.1**
　**green beans** les haricots *(m. pl.)* verts, **6.2**
**greeting** la salutation
**grilled ham and cheese sandwich** le croque-monsieur, **5.1**
**grocery store** l'épicerie *(f.)*, **6.1**
**ground floor** le rez-de-chaussée, **4.2**
　**on the ground** à terre
**group** le groupe
to **grow (up)** grandir
to **guard** garder
to **guess** deviner
**guillotined** guillotiné(e)
**guitarist** le/la guitariste
**gymnastics** la gymnastique, **2.2**

**Haitian** haïtien(ne)
**half** demi(e)
　**half brother** le demi-frère, **4.1**
　**half hour** la demi-heure
　**half past** *(time)* et demie, **BV**
　**half sister** la demi-sœur, **4.1**

**ham** le jambon, **5.1**
**hamburger** le hamburger
**hamlet** le hameau
**hand** la main, **3.1**
**handicapped** handicapé(e)
**handsome** beau (bel), **4.2**
**happy** content(e); heureux, heureuse
  **Happy birthday!** Bon (Joyeux) anniversaire!
**harbor** le port
**hardware** *(computer)* le hardware
**harp** la harpe
to **hate** détester, **3.1**
to **have** avoir, **4.1**; *(to eat or drink)* prendre, **5.1**
  **Have a nice day!** Belle journée!, **4.2**
**he** il, **1.1**
**hello** bonjour, **BV**
**help** l'aide *(f.)*
  **to be a big help** rendre bien service
  **with the help of** à l'aide de
to **help** aider
  **here is, here are** voici, **4.1**; *(emphatic)* voilà, **1.2**
**hi** salut, **BV**
**high school** le lycée, **2.1**
**higher** supérieur
**his** sa, son, ses
**history** l'histoire *(f.)*, **2.2**
**home: at (to) the home of** chez, **3.2**
  **to go home** rentrer, **3.2**
**homework** *(assignment)* le devoir
**horrible** horrible
**hot** chaud(e)
  **hot chocolate** le chocolat
  **hot dog** la saucisse de Francfort, **BV**
**house** la maison, **3.1**; la villa
  **publishing house** la maison d'édition
  **small house** le pavillon
**housing** le logement
**how** comment, **1.1**

**How are you?** Ça va? Comment vas-tu? Comment allez-vous?, **BV**
**How's it going?** Ça va?, **BV**
**how much, how many** combien (de), **3.2**
**How much is it?** C'est combien?, **3.2**
**human** humain(e)
  **human being** l'être humain *(m.)*
**hundred** cent, **2.2**
  **hundreds** les centaines *(f. pl.)*
**hungry: to be hungry** avoir faim, **5.1**
  **I'm super hungry.** J'ai hyper faim.
**husband** le mari, **4.1**

**I** je, **1.2**
**ice cream** la glace, **5.1**
**idea** l'idée *(f.)*
**ideal** idéal(e)
**if** si
**ill** malade, **L1**
**immense** immense
**important** important(e)
**impossible** impossible
**imprisoned** emprisonné(e)
**in** dans, **1.2**; à, **3.1**; en, **3.2**
**In what month?** En quel mois?, **BV**
**included** compris(e), **5.2**
  **The tip is included.** Le service est compris., **5.2**
to **indicate** indiquer
**indiscreet** indiscret, indiscrète
**industrial** industriel(le)
**inexpensive** bon marché *(inv.)*
**infinite** infini(e)
**influence** l'influence *(f.)*
**information** l'information *(f.)*

to **insist** insister
to **inspire** inspirer
**instructions** les instructions *(f. pl.)*
**intellectual** intellectuel(le)
**intelligent** intelligent(e), **1.1**
**interest** l'intérêt *(m.)*
**interesting** intéressant(e), **1.1**
to **invite** inviter, **4.1**
**island** l'île *(f.)*
**Italian** *(adj.)* italien(ne)
**Italian** *(language)* l'italien *(m.)*, **2.2**
**Ivory Coast** la Côte d'Ivoire

**jacket** le blouson, **7.1**
  **(sport) jacket** la veste, **7.1**
  **ski jacket** l'anorak *(m.)*, **7.1**
**jam** la confiture, **6.2**
**January** janvier *(m.)*, **BV**
**jar** le pot, **6.2**
**jealous** jaloux, jalouse
**jeans** le jean, **7.1**; le blue-jean
to **jog** faire du jogging
to **joke around** rigoler, **3.2**
**juice** le jus, **5.1**
  **apple juice** le jus de pomme, **5.1**
  **orange juice** le jus d'orange, **5.1**
**July** juillet *(m.)*, **BV**
**June** juin *(m.)*, **BV**
**junior high student** le/la collégien(ne)
**just** juste, **2.1**
  **fitting (him/her) just right** juste à sa taille

**keyboard** le clavier
to **kid: You're kidding!** Tu rigoles!, **3.2**

**kilogram** le kilo(gramme), **6.2**
**kind** la sorte; le genre
**kitchen** la cuisine, **4.2**
**knife** le couteau, **5.2**

**label** la griffe
**laboratory** le laboratoire
**lamb** l'agneau *(m.)*, **6.1**
**lame** boiteux, boiteuse
**large** grand(e); ample
**last** dernier, dernière, **10.2**
  **last name** le nom de famille
**later** plus tard
  **See you later.** À tout à l'heure., **BV**
**Latin** le latin, **2.2**
to **learn (to)** apprendre (à), **5**
to **leave (a room, etc.)** quitter, **3.1**
  **to leave (something behind)** laisser, **5.2**
  **to leave a tip** laisser un pourboire, **5.2**
**legend** la légende
**lemonade** le citron pressé, **5.1**
**lemon-lime drink** la limonade, **BV**
**less** moins, **7.1**
  **less than** moins de
  **less . . . than** moins... que, **7**
**lesson** la leçon, **11.1**
**lettuce** la salade, **6.2**
**liaison** la liaison
**life** la vie
**light** *(color)* clair(e)
**like** comme
to **like** aimer, **3.1**
  **I would like** je voudrais, **5.1**
  **What would you like?** *(café, restaurant)* Vous désirez?, **5.1**
**limit** la limite
**line** la ligne
**linked** en liaison
**linking** la liaison
**liquid** le liquide

to **listen (to)** écouter, **3.1**
**liter** le litre, **6.2**
**literature** la littérature, **2.2**
**little: a little** un peu, **2.1;** un peu de
to **live** *(in a city, house, etc.)* habiter, **3.1**
**living** vivant(e)
  **living room** la salle de séjour, **4.2**
**located** situé(e)
**lonely** solitaire
**long** long(ue), **7.1**
**longer: no longer** ne... plus, **6.1**
to **look** *(seem)* avoir l'air
to **look at** regarder, **3.1**
to **look for** chercher
  **loose** *(clothing)* large, **7.2**
  **loose-leaf binder** le classeur, **3.2**
  **lot: a lot** beaucoup, **3.1**
  **a lot of** beaucoup de, **3.2**
to **love** aimer, **3.1;** adorer
**lower** inférieur(e)
**low-income housing** le/la H.L.M.
**luck** la chance
  **to be in luck** avoir de la chance
**lucky: to be lucky** avoir de la chance
**lunch** le déjeuner, **5.2**
  **to eat lunch** déjeuner, **3.1**
**luxury** *(adj.)* de grand standing
**lyrics** les paroles *(f. pl.)*

**ma'am** madame, **BV**
**magazine** le magazine; la revue, **L2**
**Maghreb** le Maghreb
**main** principal(e)
**majority** la majorité
to **make** faire, **6.1;** fabriquer
  **mall** le centre commercial, **7.1**
  **man** l'homme *(m.)*, **7.1**
**mandatory** obligatoire
**manner** la façon

**many** beaucoup de, **3.2**
**map** la carte
**March** mars *(m.)*, **BV**
**market** le marché, **6.2**
  **flea market** le marché aux puces
**marriage** le mariage
**masculine** masculin(e)
**math** les maths *(f. pl.)*, **2.2**
**mathematics** les mathématiques *(f. pl.)*, **2.2**
**May** mai *(m.)*, **BV**
**meal** le repas, **5.2**
to **mean** signifier
  **meaning** la signification; le sens
to **measure** mesurer
  **measurement** la mesure
**meat** la viande, **6.1**
**medina** la médina
**Mediterranean Sea** la mer Méditerranée
**medium-rare** *(meat)* à point, **5.2**
to **meet** rencontrer; retrouver *(get together with)*; faire la connaissance de
**melon** le melon, **6.2**
to **mention** citer
**menu** la carte, **5.1**
**merchandise** la marchandise
**merchant** le/la marchand(e), **6.2**
  **produce merchant** le/la marchand(e) de fruits et légumes, **6.2**
**message** le message
**meter** le mètre
**metric system** le système métrique
**microbe** le microbe
**microbial** microbien(ne)
**microprocessor** le microprocesseur
**microscope** le microscope
**middle school student** le/la collégien(ne)
**midnight** minuit *(m.)*, **BV**
**milk** le lait, **6.1**
**milligram** le milligramme
**mineral water** l'eau *(f.)* minérale, **6.2**

**minus** moins
**minute** la minute, **9.2**
**Miss (Ms.)** Mademoiselle (Mlle), **BV**
**mistake** la faute
**modem** le modem
**modern** moderne
**modest** modeste
**mom** la maman
**moment** le moment
**Monday** lundi *(m.)*, **BV**
**money** l'argent *(m.)*, **5.2**
**monitor** *(computer)* le moniteur
**month** le mois, **BV**
**more** *(comparative)* plus, **7.1**
  **more . . . than** plus... que, **7**
  **no more** ne... plus, **6.1**
**morning** le matin, **BV**; le mat *(fam.)*
  **in the morning** le matin
  **in the morning (A.M.)** du matin, **BV**
**Moroccan** marocain(e)
**Morocco** le Maroc
**most (of)** la plupart (des)
**mother** la mère, **4.1**
**mount** le mont
**mountain** le mont; la montagne
**mouse** la souris
**movement** le mouvement
**Mr.** Monsieur (M.), **BV**
**Mrs. (Ms.)** Madame (Mme), **BV**
**multicolored** multicolore
to **multiply** multiplier
**museum** le musée
**music** la musique, **2.2**
**musician** le/la musicien(ne)
**mussel** la moule
**mustard** la moutarde, **6.2**
**my** ma, mon, mes, **4**
**myth** le mythe

**name** le nom
  **first name** le prénom

**last name** le nom de famille
**My name is . . .** Je m'appelle... , **BV**
**What's your name?** Tu t'appelles comment?, **BV**
**napkin** la serviette, **5.2**
**nationality** la nationalité
**natural** naturel(le)
  **natural sciences** les sciences naturelles *(f. pl.)*, **2.1**
**nature** la nature
**navy blue** bleu marine *(inv.)*, **7.2**
**near** près de, **4.2**
  **very near** tout près, **4.2**
**necessary** nécessaire
**neighbor** le/la voisin(e), **4.2**
**neighborhood** le quartier, **4.2**; *(adj.)* du coin
**nephew** le neveu, **4.1**
**new** nouveau (nouvel), nouvelle, **4.2**
**New England** la Nouvelle-Angleterre
**news** *(TV)* les informations *(f. pl.)*
**next** prochain(e), **9.2**
**nice** *(person)* sympa, **1.2**; aimable; sympathique; gentil(le), **6.2**
**niece** la nièce, **4.1**
**no** non
  **no longer** ne... plus, **6.1**
  **no more** ne... plus, **6.1**
**noble** noble
**noon** midi *(m.)*, **BV**
**north** le nord
**North African** nord-africain(e)
**not** ne... pas, **1.2**; pas, **2.1**
  **isn't it?, doesn't it (he, she, etc.)?,** n'est-ce pas?, **2.2**
  **not at all** pas du tout, **3.1**
  **not bad** pas mal, **BV**
**note** la note
**notebook** le cahier, **3.2**
**notepad** le bloc-notes, **3.2**
**novel** le roman
**November** novembre *(m.)*, **BV**

**now** maintenant, **2.2**
**number** le nombre; le numéro
  **telephone number** le numéro de téléphone

**object** l'objet *(m.)*
to **oblige** obliger
**oboe** le hautbois
**occupied** occupé(e)
**ocean** l'océan *(m.)*
**o'clock: It's . . . o'clock.** Il est... heure(s)., **BV**
**October** octobre *(m.)*, **BV**
**of** *(belonging to)* de, **1.2**
  **of course** bien sûr
**official** officiel(le)
**often** souvent, **5.2**
**oil** l'huile *(f.)*, **6.1**; le pétrole
**okay** *(health)* Ça va.; *(agreement)* d'accord, **BV**
  **Okay!** Bon!, **6.1**
**old** vieux (vieil), vieille, **4.2**; âgé(e); ancien(ne)
  **How old are you?** Tu as quel âge? *(fam.)*, **4.1**
**older** l'aîné(e), **L1**
**omelette (with herbs/plain)** l'omelette *(f.)* (aux fines herbes/nature), **5.1**
**on** sur, **4.2**
  **on foot** à, **4.2**
  **on sale** en solde, **7.1**
**onion** l'oignon *(m.)*, **5.1**
**only** seulement; *(adj.)* seul(e)
**open** ouvert(e), **13.2**
**opera** l'opéra *(m.)*
**opinion** l'avis *(m.)*, **7.2**
  **in my opinion** à mon avis, **7.2**
**or** ou, **1.1**
  **or else** sinon, **9.2**
**orange** *(fruit)* l'orange *(f.)*, **6.2**; *(color)* orange *(inv.)*, **7.2**
  **orange tree** l'oranger *(m.)*, **L2**
**order: in order to** pour

to **order** commander, **5.1**
**ordinary** ordinaire
**organism** l'organisme (m.)
**other** autre
  **some other** d'autres, **2.2**
**our** notre, nos, **4**
**outfit** l'ensemble (m.)
**outgoing** sociable, **1.2**
**outside** (n.) l'extérieur
  (m.); (adv.) à l'extérieur;
  (prep.) au dehors de
**outskirts** la périphérie
**over** (prep.) par-dessus,
  **10.2**
to **overlook** donner sur, **4.2**
**overseas** (adj.) d'outre-mer
to **own** posséder

**package** le paquet, **6.2**
**pain in the neck** (slang)
  casse-pieds
**painful** douloureux,
  douloureuse
**pair** la paire, **7.1**
**pal** le copain, la copine,
  **2.1**
**palace** le palais
**pancake** la crêpe, **BV**
**pants** le pantalon, **7.1**
**paper** le papier, **3.2**
  **sheet of paper** la feuille
  de papier, **3.2**
**pardon me** pardon
**parents** les parents (m. pl.),
  **4.1**
**Parisian** (adj.) parisien(ne)
**park** le parc
**parking lot** le parking
**part** la partie
**party** la fête, **4.1**
  **to throw a party** donner
  une fête, **4.1**
**patient** patient(e), **1.1**
**patio** la terrasse, **4.2**
to **pay** payer, **3.2**
  **pear** la poire, **6.2**
  **peas** les petits pois (m. pl.),
  **6.2**
  **peasant** le/la paysan(ne),
  **L1**

**pen: ballpoint pen** le
  stylo-bille, **3.2**
  **felt-tip pen** le feutre, **3.2**
**pencil** le crayon, **3.2**
**people** les gens (m. pl.)
**pepper** le poivre, **6.1**
**percent** pour cent
**period** l'époque (f.); la
  période
**permanent** permanent(e)
**person** la personne
**personal** personnel(le)
**personality** la
  personnalité
**phenomenon** le
  phénomène
**photograph** la photo
**physical** physique
**physicist** le/la
  physicien(ne)
**physics** la physique, **2.2**
**picnic** le pique-nique
**picturesque** pittoresque
**pie** la tarte, **6.1**
**pink** rose, **7.1**
**pizza** la pizza, **BV**
**plant** la plante
**plate** l'assiette (f.), **5.2**
to **play** jouer, **3.2**
  **please** s'il vous plaît
  (form.), s'il te plaît (fam.),
  **BV**
  **pleated** plissé(e), **7.1**
  **plus** plus
  **p.m.** de l'après-midi; du
  soir, **BV**
  **poem** le poème
  **poet** (m. and f.) le poète
  **politeness** la politesse,
  **BV**
  **polo shirt** le polo, **7.1**
  **poor** pauvre, **L1**
  **popular** populaire, **1.2**
  **pork** le porc, **6.1**
  **port** le port
  **Portuguese** portugais(e)
  **position** la position
to **possess** posséder
  **poster** l'affiche (f.)
  **potato** la pomme de terre,
  **6.2**
  **pound** la livre, **6.2**

to **prefer** préférer, **6**
**prefix** le préfixe
to **prepare** préparer
**present** le cadeau, **4.1**
**pretty** joli(e), **4.2**
**price** le prix, **7.1**
**principal** principal(e)
**printer** l'imprimante (f.)
**private** individuel(le);
  privé(e)
**problem** le problème; la
  difficulté
**product** le produit
**professional**
  professionel(le)
**program** le programme;
  (computer) le logiciel
**programming** la
  programmation
to **publish** publier
**purchase** l'achat (m.)
to **put (on)** mettre, **7.1**

**quality** la qualité
**quarter: quarter after**
  (time) et quart, **BV**
  **quarter to** (time) moins le
  quart, **BV**
**Quebec: from or of**
  **Quebec** québécois
**queen** la reine
**question** la question, **3.1**
  **to ask a question** poser
  une question, **3.1**
**quick** rapide
**quickly** rapidement
**quite** assez, **1.1**

**race** (human population) la
  race
**radio** la radio, **3.2**
**rain** la pluie
to **raise** lever
  **to raise one's hand** lever
  la main, **3.1**
**rap** (music) le rap

**rapidly** rapidement
**rare** *(meat)* saignant(e), **5.2**
**reading** la lecture
**real** vrai(e), **2.2**
**really** vraiment, **1.1**
**recess** la récré(ation), **3.2**
**red** rouge, **7.1**
to **reflect** refléter
**refrigerator** le frigidaire
**region** la région
**religious** religieux, religieuse
**renowned** renommé(e)
to **resemble** ressembler à
**restaurant** le restaurant, **5.2**
to **return** rentrer
**revolution** la révolution
**revolutionary** révolutionnaire
**rich** riche
**riddle** la devinette
**river** le fleuve; la rivière
**Riviera** *(French)* la Côte d'Azur
**roof** le toit
　**thatched roof** le toit de chaume
**room** *(in house)* la pièce, **4.2;** la salle
　**dining room** la salle à manger, **4.2**
　**living room** la salle de séjour, **4.2**
**royal** royal(e)
**rule** la règle
**ruler** la règle, **3.2**
**running shoe** la basket, **7.1**
**rural** rural(e)
**Russian** *(language)* le russe

**sad** triste, **L1**
to **safeguard** sauvegarder
**salad** la salade, **5.1**
**salami** le saucisson, **6.1**
**sale: on sale** en solde, **7.1;** en promotion
**sales** les soldes *(m. pl.)*, **7.1**
**salesperson** le vendeur, la vendeuse, **7.1**

**salt** le sel, **6.1**
**same** même, **2.1**
　**all the same** tout de même, **5.2**
**sandals** *(f. pl.)* les sandals, **7.1**
**sandwich** le sandwich, **BV**
　**grilled ham and cheese sandwich** le croque-monsieur, **5.1**
**sardine** la sardine
**Saturday** samedi *(m.)*, **BV**
**sauce** la sauce
to **save** sauver; sauvegarder
**schedule** l'emploi *(m.)* du temps
**school** l'école *(f.)*, **1.2;** *(adj.)* scolaire, **3.2**
　**elementary school** l'école primaire
　**junior high/high school** l'école secondaire, **1.2**
　**high school** le lycée, **2.1**
　**school supplies** la fourniture scolaire, **3.2**
**science** les sciences *(f. pl.)*, **2.1**
　**natural sciences** les sciences naturelles, **2.1**
　**social sciences** les sciences sociales, **2.1**
**scientific** scientifique
**scientist** le savant
**screen** l'écran *(m.)*, **8.1**
**second** *(adj.)* deuxième, **4.2;** second(e)
**secret** *(adj.)* secret, secrète
to **see** voir, **7.1**
　**See you later.** À tout à l'heure., **BV**
　**See you soon!** À bientôt!, **BV**
　**See you tomorrow.** À demain., **BV**
**seldom** très peu
**seller** le/la marchand(e), **6.2**
　**produce seller** le/la marchand(e) de fruits et légumes, **6.2**
**separate** séparer
**September** septembre *(m.)*, **BV**

**serious** sérieux, sérieuse, **7;** grave
**service** le service, **5.2**
to **set the table** mettre la table, **7**
**shape** la forme
**she** elle, **1.1**
**sheet of paper** la feuille de papier, **3.2**
**shirt** la chemise, **7.1**
**shoe** la chaussure, **7.1**
**shop** la boutique, **7.1**
to **shop** faire des achats
**shopkeeper** le/la commerçant(e)
**shopping** le shopping, **7.2**
　**to do the grocery shopping** faire les courses, **6.1**
　**to go shopping** faire des courses, **7.2**
　**shopping cart** le chariot, **6.2**
　**shopping center** le centre commercial, **7.1**
**short** petit(e), **1.1;** court(e), **7.1**
　**in a short time** en très peu de temps
**shorts** le short, **7.1**
to **show** montrer; *(movie)* jouer
**shrimp** la crevette, **6.1**
**shy** timide, **1.2**
**sick** malade, **L1**
　**to get sick** tomber malade, **L1**
**side** le côté
**sidewalk café** la terrasse (d'un café), **5.1**
**significance** la signification
**similar** semblable, **L1**
**simple** simple
**single** unique; seul(e)
**sir** monsieur, **BV**
**sister** la sœur, **1.2**
**size** *(clothes)* la taille; *(shoes)* la pointure, **7.2**
　**the next larger size** la taille au-dessus, **7.2**
　**the next smaller size** la taille au-dessous, **7.2**

**to wear size (number)** faire du (nombre), **7.2**
**What size do you wear?** Vous faites quelle taille (pointure)?, **7.2**
**ski jacket** l'anorak *(m.)*, **7.1**
**skirt** la jupe, **7.1**
to **sleep** dormir
**sleeve** la manche, **7.1**
**long-(short-)sleeved** à manches longues (courtes), **7.1**
**slice** la tranche, **6.2**
**slice of bread with butter or jam** la tartine
**slice of bread and butter** la tartine de pain beurré
**small** petit(e), **1.1**
**sneaker** la basket, **7.1**
**so** alors, **BV;** donc; si *(adv.)*
**sociable** sociable, **1.2**
**social sciences** les sciences sociales *(f. pl.)*, **2.1**
**sock** la chaussette, **7.1**
**software** le software
**solid** solide
**solidarity** la solidarité
**solution** la solution
**some** du, de la, de l', des, **6;** *(adj.)* quelques *(pl.)*, **9.2;** *(pron.)* certains
**some other** d'autres, **2.2**
**someone** quelqu'un, **10.1**
**something** quelque chose, **11**
**something else** autre chose
**something special** quelque chose de spécial
**something to drink** quelque chose à boire
**sometimes** quelquefois, **5.2**
**son** le fils, **4.1**
**song** la chanson
**soon** bientôt
**See you soon.** À bientôt., **BV**
**sorry: to be sorry** regretter, **6.1**
**so-so** comme ci, comme ça

**soup** la soupe, **5.1**
**source** la source
**south** le sud
**Spanish** espagnol(e)
**Spanish** *(language)* l'espagnol *(m.)*, **2.2**
to **speak** parler, **3.1**
**special** spécial(e)
**specialty** la spécialité
to **spend** *(time)* passer, **3.1**
**spinach** les épinards *(m. pl.)*, **6.2**
**spirit** l'esprit *(m.)*
**spoon** la cuillère, **5.2**
**square** la place
**staircase** l'escalier *(m.)*, **4.2**
**station** la station, **4.2**
**gas station** la station-service
**subway station** la station de métro, **4.2**
**stationery store** la papeterie, **3.2**
**statue** la statue, **13.2**
**stay** le séjour
**steak and French fries** le steak frites, **5.2**
**stepfather** le beau-père, **4.1**
**stepmother** la belle-mère, **4.1**
**still** toujours; encore, **11**
**store** le magasin, **3.2**
**department store** le grand magasin, **7.1**
to **store** stocker
**strategy** la stratégie
**strawberry** la fraise, **6.2**
**street** la rue, **3.1**
**strict** strict(e), **2.1**
**strong** fort(e), **2.2**
**student** l'élève *(m. et f.)*, **1.2;** *(university)* l'étudiant(e)
**studio** *(artist's)* l'atelier *(m.)*
**studio** *(apartment)* le studio
**study** l'étude *(f.)*
to **study** étudier, **3.1;** faire des études
**to study French** *(math, etc.)* faire du français (des maths, etc.), **6**

**style** le look
**in style** à la mode
**subject** le sujet; *(in school)* la matière, **2.2**
to **subtract** soustraire
**subway** le métro, **4.2**
**subway station** la station de métro, **4.2**
**success** le succès
to **suffer** souffrir
**suit** *(men's)* le complet; *(women's)* le tailleur, **7.1**
**Sunday** dimanche *(m.)*, **BV**
**super** super
**supermarket** le supermarché, **6.2**
**supply** la fourniture
**school supplies** les fournitures scolaires, **3.2**
**sure** sûr(e)
to **surf the Net** naviguer sur Internet
**sweater** le pull, **7.1**
**sweatshirt** le sweat-shirt, **7.1**
**system** le système
**metric system** le système métrique

**table** la table, **5.1**
**table setting** le couvert, **5.2**
**tablecloth** la nappe, **5.2**
to **take** prendre, **5.2**
**What size do you take?** Vous faites quelle taille (pointure)?, **7.2**
**to take an exam** passer un examen, **3.1**
**to take place** avoir lieu
**to take size** *(number)* faire du (nombre), **7.2**
**to take the subway** prendre le métro, **5.2**
**taken** occupé(e)
to **talk** parler, **3.1**
**to talk on the phone** parler au téléphone, **3.2**
**tall** grand(e), **1.1**

**tape** la cassette, **7.1**
**tart** la tarte, **6.1**
  **apple tart** la tarte aux pommes, **6.1**
**tea** le thé
**teacher** le/la prof *(inform.)*, **2.1**; le professeur, **2.1**
**teenager** l'adolescent(e)
**telephone** le téléphone, **3.2**; *(adj.)* téléphonique
  **telephone number** le numéro de téléphone
**temporary** temporaire
**ten** dix, **BV**
**terrace** la terrasse, **4.2**
**terrific** super; terrible
**test** l'examen *(m.)*, **3.1**
  **to take a test** passer un examen, **3.1**
**Thai** thaïlandais(e)
**than** *(in comparisons)* que, **7.2**
**thank you** merci, **BV**
**thanks** merci, **BV**
  **thanks to** grâce à
**that** ça; ce (cet), cette, **9**
  **that is** c'est-à-dire
  **That's all.** C'est tout., **6.1**
**thatched roof** le toit de chaume
**the** le, la, les, **1.1**
**theater** le théâtre, **13.1**
**their** leur(s), **4**
**then** alors, **BV**
**there** là; y, **5.2**
  **there are** il y a, **4.1**
  **there is** il y a, **4.1**
**therefore** donc
**they** ils, elles, **2**; on, **3.2**
**thing** la chose
to **think** croire, **7.2**; *(opinion)* trouver, **7.2**
**third** troisième, **4.2**
**thirsty: to be thirsty** avoir soif, **5.1**
**thousand** mille, **3.2**
**through** par
to **throw a party** donner une fête, **4.1**
**Thursday** jeudi *(m.)*, **BV**
**tie** la cravate, **7.1**

**tight** serré(e), **7.2**
**time** *(of day)* l'heure *(f.)*, **BV**; *(in a series)* la fois; le temps
  **at the same time** à la fois
  **at what time?** à quelle heure?, **2**
  **in a short time** en très peu de temps
  **times** l'époque *(f.)*
  **What time is it?** Il est quelle heure?, **BV**
**tip** *(restaurant)* le pourboire, **5.2**
  **to leave a tip** laisser un pourboire, **5.2**
  **The tip is included.** Le service est compris., **5.2**
**tired** fatigué(e)
**to** à, **3.1**
**today** aujourd'hui, **BV**; de nos jours
**together** ensemble, **5.1**
**tomato** la tomate, **6.2**
**tomorrow** demain, **BV**
  **See you tomorrow.** À demain., **BV**
**tonight** ce soir
**too** *(also)* aussi, **1.1**; *(excessive)* trop, **2.1**
**totally** complètement; totalement
**tower** la tour
  **Eiffel Tower** la tour Eiffel
**town** la ville, le village
  **in town** en ville
  **small town** le village
**tradition** la tradition
**traditional** traditionel(le)
to **transport** transporter
to **treat** traiter
  **tree** l'arbre *(m.)*, **L3**
**trigonometry** la trigonométrie, **2.2**
**tropical** tropical(e)
**true** vrai(e), **2.2**
to **try on** essayer, **7.2**
  **T-shirt** le t-shirt, **7.1**
**Tuesday** mardi *(m.)*, **BV**
**tunic** la tunique
**Tunisian** tunisien(ne)

to **turn on** *(appliance)* mettre, **7**
**TV** la télé
**twin** le jumeau, la jumelle, **L1**
**type** le type, la sorte, le genre, **13.1**
**typical** typique

**uncle** l'oncle *(m.)*, **4.1**
**under** sous, **8.2**
**underground** souterrain(e)
to **understand** comprendre, **5**
**unhappy** malheureux, malheureuse
**unit** l'unité *(f.)*
**United States** les États-Unis *(m. pl.)*
**university** l'université *(f.)*
to **use** utiliser
**usually** d'habitude, **12.2**

**vacation** les vacances *(f. pl.)*
**valley** la vallée; le val
**value** la valeur
**vanilla** *(adj.)* à la vanille, **5.1**
**varied** varié(e)
**various** divers(e)
**vegetable** le légume, **6.2**
**veil** le voile
**very** très, **BV**; tout
  **very near** tout près, **4.2**
  **very well** très bien, **BV**
**video** la vidéo, **3.1**
**Vietnamese** vietnamien(ne), **6**
**view** la vue
**village** le village
**vinegar** le vinaigre, **6.1**
**violent** violent(e)
**violin** le violon
**viral** viral(e)
**virus** le virus

to **visit** *(a place)* visiter
**voice** la voix

**waiter** le serveur, **5.1**
**waitress** la serveuse, **5.1**
to **want** désirer, vouloir,
avoir envie de
**warmup suit** le
survêtement, **7.1**
**Watch out!** Attention!, **4.2**
**water** l'eau *(f.)*, **6.2**
**way** la façon
**we** nous, **2**; on, **3.2**
**weak** faible, **L1**
to **wear** porter, **7.1**
**What size do you wear?**
Vous faites quelle
taille?, **7.2**
**Web site** le site
**wedding** le mariage
**Wednesday** mercredi *(m.)*,
**BV**
**week** la semaine, **3.2**
**a week** huit jours
**a (per) week** par
semaine, **3.2**
**last week** la semaine
dernière, **10.2**
**next week** la semaine
prochaine
**weekend** le week-end
**weight** le poids
**welcome** le/la
bienvenu(e)
**Welcome!** Bienvenue!
**You're welcome.** Je t'en
prie. *(fam.)*, **BV**; Je vous
en prie. *(form.)*, **BV**
**well** bien, **BV**; eh bien;
ben *(slang)*
**well then** alors, **BV**
**well-behaved** bien
élevé(e)
**well-done** *(meat)* bien
cuit(e), **5.2**
**well-known** connu(e),
**13.1**
**well-to-do** aisé(e)

**western** occidental(e)
**what** qu'est-ce que, **3.2;**
quel(le), **6;** quoi *(after
prep.)*
**What color is . . . ?** De
quelle couleur est... ?,
**7.2**
**What is . . . like?**
Comment est... ?, **1.1**
**What is it?** Qu'est-ce que
c'est?, **3.2**
**What is today's date?**
Quelle est la date
aujourd'hui?, **BV**
**What's your name?** Tu
t'appelles comment?,
**BV**
**when** quand, **4.1**
**where** où, **1.1**
**from where** d'où, **1.1**
**which** quel(le), **6**
**white** blanc, blanche, **7.2**
**who** qui, **1.1**
**whole** *(adj.)* entier, entière;
*(n.)* l'ensemble *(m.)*
**whole-wheat bread** le
pain complet
**whom** qui
**why** pourquoi, **6.2**
**why not?** pourquoi pas?
**wide** large, **7.2**
**wife** la femme, **4.1**
**wind** le vent, **11.1**
**window** *(seat)* (une place)
côté fenêtre, **8.1**
**window** *(store)* la vitrine,
**7.1**
**windsurfing** la planche à
voile, **11.1**
**to go windsurfing** faire
de la planche à voile,
**11.1**
**windy: It's windy.** Il y a
du vent., **11.1**
**winner** le/la gagnant(e),
**10.2**
**winner's cup** la coupe,
**10.2**
**winter** l'hiver *(m.)*
**with** avec, **3.2;** auprès de;
muni(e) de

**without** sans
**woman** la femme, **7.1**
**wood** le bois
**word** le mot
**words** *(of song, etc.)* les
paroles *(f. pl.)*
**work** le travail; *(of art or
literature)* l'œuvre *(f.)*, **13.1**
**worker** l'ouvrier,
l'ouvrière
**world** le monde
**wounded** blessé(e)
to **write** écrire, **9.2**
**to write a prescription**
faire une ordonnance,
**14.2**
**writer** l'écrivain *(m.)*, **L2**
**wrong** mauvais(e), **2.2**
**What's wrong?** Qu'est-ce
qui ne va pas?
**What's wrong with him?**
Qu'est-ce qu'il a?, **14.1**

**yeah** ben oui
**year** l'an *(m.)*, **4.1;** l'année
*(f.)*
**to be . . . years old**
avoir... ans, **4.1**
**yellow** jaune, **7.2**
**yes** oui, **BV;** si *(after neg.
question)*, **7.2**
**yogurt** la yaourt, **6.1**
**you** tu, **1**; vous, **2**
**young** jeune
**young people** les jeunes
*(m. pl.)*
**younger** le cadet, la
cadette, **L1**
**your** ton, ta, tes; votre,
vos, **4**

**zoology** la zoologie

# Index

à contractions with definite articles, **166 (5)**

**adjectives** agreement with singular nouns, **28 (1)**; agreement with plural nouns, **58 (2)**; comparative of, **230 (7)**; irregular, **126 (4)**; possessive, **123 (4)**; position of, **126 (4)**; **100 (4)**; **138 (5)**

**agreement** adjectives with singular nouns, **28 (1)**, adjectives with plural nouns, **58 (2)**; definite and indefinite articles with singular nouns, **26 (1)**; definite and indefinite articles with plural nouns; **58 (2)**; subject and verb, **30 (1)**; **60 (2)**

**aller** present tense, **162 (5)**; with expressions of health, **162 (5)**; with infinitive to express near future, **165 (5)**; with **y**, **162 (5)**

**apprendre** present tense, **168 (5)**

**articles** (*see definite articles, indefinite articles, and partitive*)

**au, aux** contractions of à + definite articles, **166 (5)**

**aussi… que 230 (7)**

**avoir** present tense, **120 (4)**; to express age, **120 (4)**

**beau 126 (4)**

**colors 225 (7)**

**comparative of adjectives 230 (7)**

**contractions** au, aux, **166 (5)**; du, des, **166 (5)**

**croire** present tense, **232 (7)**

**dates** days of the week, **(BV)**; months of the year, **(BV)**

**de** after **pas** to replace indefinite article, **120 (4)**; after **pas** to replace the partitive, **198 (6)**; contractions with definite articles, **166 (5)**; to indicate possession, **166 (5)**; with plural adjectives, **126 (4)**

**definite articles** gender and agreement with noun, **26 (1)**; plural, **58 (2)**; singular, **26 (1)**; vs. the partitive, **196 (6)**

**des** contraction of **de** + **les**, **166 (5)**; partitive **196 (6)**; plural indefinite article, **94 (3)**

**du** contraction of **de** + **le**, **166 (5)**; partitive **196 (6)**

**elision 26 (1)**; **90 (3)**; **94 (3)**

**-er verbs** (*see present tense*)

**être** present tense: plural forms, **60 (2)**; present tense: singular forms **30 (1)**

**faire** expressions with, **194 (6)**; present tense **194 (6)**

**future** expressed with **aller** + infinitive, **165 (5)**

**gender** of adjectives, **28 (1)**; of definite articles, **26 (1)**; of indefinite articles, **26 (1)**; of nouns, **26 (1)**

**il y a 120 (4)**

**indefinite articles** gender and agreement with noun, **26 (1)**; in negative sentences, **94 (3)**; plural, **76 (3)**; singular, **26 (1)**

**indefinite pronoun on, 90 (3)**

**infinitives** with **aller** to express near future, **165 (5)**; with other verbs, **95 (3)**

**irregular verbs** (*see individual verb entries*)

**liaison 26 (1)**; **90 (3)**; **123 (4)**; **126 (4)**; **230 (7)**

**mettre** present tense **228 (7)**

**moins… que, 230 (7)**

**negation** ne… pas, **33 (1)**; **165 (5)**; of indefinite articles, **94 (3)**; of the partitive, **196 (6)**

**nouveau 126 (4)**

**numbers** cardinal, 1–30, **10 (BV)**; 30–60, **23 (1)**; 70–100, **55 (2)**; 100–1000, **87 (3)**

**on 90 (3)**

**partitive 196 (6)**

**plural** of adjectives, **58 (2)**; of adjectives like **beau, nouveau, vieux, 126 (4)**; of definite articles, **58 (2)**; of indefinite articles, **58 (2)**; of nouns, **45 (2)**; of subject pronouns, **60 (2)**

**plus… que 230 (7)**

**possession** with **de, 166 (5)**; (*see also possessive adjectives*)

# Credits

Glencoe would like to acknowledge the artists and agencies who participated in illustrating this program: Meg Aubrey represented by Cornell & McCarthy; Domenick D'Andrea; Len Ebert; Judy Love; Glencoe; Fanny Mellet Berry represented by Anita Grien Representing Artists; Joseph Hammond; Studio InkLink; Carlos Lacamara; Ortelius Design Inc.; Shannon Stirnweis; Carol Strebel; Joe Veno represented by Gwen Walters; Susan Jaekel, Jane McCreary and DJ Simison represented by Remen-Willis Design Group. **COVER** (t to b)Koji Yamashita/Panoramic Images, Michelle Busselle/Stone, Shankar/Panoramic Images, Koji Yamashita/Panoramic Images, (students)Philippe Gontier; **i** (t)Rlexion Phototec/International Stock, (tc c)Oleg Cajko/ Panoramic Images, (bc)David L. Brown/Panoramic Images, (b)Philippe Gontier; **iv** (l)Photowood Inc/U-AT/The Stock Market, (r)Mark Burnett; **v** (l)Larry Hamill, (r)Travelpix/FPG; **vi** (tl)Timothy Fuller, (tr)Jenny Andre/Photo 20-20, (b)Zephyr Images/Sunset; **vii** (l)John Evans, (r)Mark Antman/Scribner; **viii** Timothy Fuller; **ix** (tl)Explorer/Photo Researchers, (tr b)Larry Hamill; **x** (tl)Moulo/Sunset, (tr)Musee d'Orsay, Paris/Lauros-Giraudon, Paris/SuperStock, (b)PhotoDisc; **xi** Owen Franken/Stock Boston; **xii** (t)Massimo Listri/CORBIS; **xiii** (tl tr)Philippe Gontier; (t)Chris Sorenson/The Stock Market, (cl)Mark Antman/The Image Works, (b)Mark Burnett; **xxix** (t c)Larry Hamill, (bl)Walter Bibikow/FPG, (bc)Michele Burgess/The Stock Market, (br)Alain Even/DIAF; **0** (t)Michael Krasowitz/FPG, (tc)Photobank USA/Sunset, (bc)Curt Fischer, (b)David Florenz/Option Photo; **0–1** Curt Fischer; **1** (5)Curt Fischer, (6)Robert Fried Photography, (7)Timothy Fuller, (8)Gio Barto/The Image Bank, (9)Larry Hamill; **2** Larry Hamill; **3** (tl tc bc)Larry Hamill, (tr bl)Catherine et Bernard Desjeux, (br)Timothy Fuller; **4** (l)Timothy Fuller, (r)Catherine et Bernard Desjeux; **5** Timothy Fuller; **6** Larry Hamill; **7** Mark Burnett; **8** Larry Hamill; **9** (tl)Ilico/Wallis Phototheque, (c cr)LCI/Wallis Phototheque, (others)John Evans; **11** (tl tr)Ken Karp, (bl)Jean-Daniel Sudres/DIAF, (br)Photowood Inc/U-AT/The Stock Market; **13** Mark Burnett; **14** Larry Hamill; **15** Mark Burnett; **16** Bridgeman Art Library; **16–17** Catherine et Bernard Desjeux; **18** Larry Hamill; **19** Timothy Fuller; **20** (t c br)Larry Hamill, (bl)Jill Connelly/The Image Works; **21** (tl)Pacha/CORBIS, (tr)Bettmann/CORBIS, (bl)Mitchell Gerber/CORBIS, (br)Christie's Images/CORBIS; **22** (tl tr bc)Larry Hamill, (bl)John Evans, (br)Dale Durfee/Getty Images; **23** (l)John Evans, (r)file photo; **24** (tl)Curt Fischer, (tr)Robert Fried Photography, (bl)Garufi/Wallis Phototheque, (br)Telegraph Colour Library/ FPG; **25** (t)Jose Fusta Raga/The Stock Market, (c)Dannic/DIAF, (b)Goumare/Wallis Phototheque; **26** Pascal Crapet/Getty Images; **27** P. Wysocki/S. Frances/Hémisphères Images; **28** Getty Images; **30** Ken Karp; **31** (t)Peter McCabe/The Image Works, (b)Monika Graff/The Image Works; **32** (t)Larry Hamill, (b)Claudie/Sunset, (inset)Wayne Rowe; **33** Owen Franken/ CORBIS; **34** (t)Travelpix/FPG, (b)Larry Hamill; **35** Bruno DeHogues/Getty Images; **36** (l)Fernand/Sunset, (r)Robert Holmes/CORBIS; **37** (t)Chris Sorenson/The Stock Market, (b)David Simson/Stock Boston; **38** (t)Brian A. Vikander, (cl)Mark Antman/The Image Works, (cr)C. Capel/Sunset, (b)Yvan Travert/DIAF; **39** (t)Private Collection/The Bridgeman Art Library International, Ltd, (b)Jean-Daniel Sudres/DIAF; **40** (t)Camille Moirenc/DIAF, (b)Sitki Tarlan/Panoramic Images; **40–41** Fototeca Storica Nazionale/PhotoDisc; **41** (t)Doug Armand/Getty Images, (b)Ric Ergenbright/CORBIS; **42** (t)Larry Hamill, (c)Peter McCabe/The Image Works, (b)Chris Duranti/ Wallis Phototheque; **44** Ozu Kiki/La Phototheque/SDP-DIAF; **45** J. Brun/Explorer; **47** (t)Robert Holmes/CORBIS, (b)Larry Hamill; **48** Barnes Foundation, Merion, Pennsylvania/ SuperStock; **48–49** Larry Hamill; **50** Catherine et Bernard Desjeux; **51** (t)Larry Hamill, (b)Timothy Fuller; **52** (t)Marge/ Sunset, (b)Timothy Fuller; **53** John Evans; **54** Curt Fischer; **55** John Evans; **56–57** Larry Hamill; **59** Larry Hamill; **60** (tr)Gabe Palmer/CORBIS, (c)Ken Karp, (l)Monika Graff/The Image Works; **63** (t)Robert Fried Photogaphy, (b)Photobank/Sunset;

**65** (tl)Zephyr Images/Sunset, (tc)Sierpinski/DIAF, (tr)Robert Fried Photography, (bl)Sylva Villerot/DIAF, (bc)Stuart Cohen/ The Image Works, (br)Robert Fried Photography; **66** Larry Hamill; **68** (tl)Michele Burgess/The Stock Market, (tr)Larry Hamill, (b)Beryl Goldberg; **69** (t)David Grunfeld/The Image Works, (b)SuperStock; **70** (t)Larry Hamill, (b)Curt Fischer; **71** (tl)Larry Hamill, (tr)Stephane Cande/Mission/Wallis Phototheque, (b)Robert Holmes/CORBIS; **72** (t)Jean-Paul Garcin/DIAF, (b)Art Wolfe/Getty; **72–73** The Studio Dog/ PhotoDisc; **73** (t)Beryl Goldberg, (b)Mark Burnett; **74–75** Larry Hamill; **77** Jenny Andre/Photo 20-20; **79** (t)Larry Hamill, (b)Curt Fischer; **80** Musee Du Louvre, Paris/SuperStock; **80–81** Bob Handelman/Getty Images; **82** Larry Hamill; **83** (t)Aaron Haupt, (b)Alain Le Bot/DIAF; **84** (t)R. Lucas/The Image Works, (b)Larry Hamill; **85** Ken Karp; **86** (tl)Aaron Haupt, (tr bcl bc br)Curt Fischer, (others)Amanita Pictures; **87** Larry Hamill; **88** (t c)Amanita Pictures, (b)Valerie Simmons; **89** Amanita Pictures; **91** (t)John Evans, (bl br)Ken Karp; **92** Ken Karp; **92–93** Matthieu Colin/Hémisphères Images; **94** Beryl Goldberg; **95** file photo; **96** (t)Larry Hamill, (b)John Evans; **98** (l)John Evans, (c)Hartmut Krinitz/Hémisphères Images, (r)Robert Fried Photography; **99** Larry Hamill; **100** (t)Guido Cozzi/Agence ANA, (c)Beryl Goldberg; **101** (t)Larry Hamill, (b)Christian Roger/Wallis Phototheque; **102** (t)Getty Images, (c b)Cheryl Fenton; **103** Ed Taylor Studio/FPG; **104–105** Larry Hamill; **107** Mark Antman/Scribner; **109** Curt Fischer; **110** Metropolitan Museum of Art, New York City/SuperStock; **110–111** file photo; **112** (b)PhotoDisc, (others)Larry Hamill; **113** Timothy Fuller; **114** (t)Mark Burnett, (b)Peter Marlow/ Magnum Photos; **115** Giraudon/Art Resource, NY; **117** Larry Hamill; **118** Karin Ansara/Wallis Phototheque; **119** (l)Grant V. Faint/The Image Bank, (c)Stéphane Frances/Hémisphères Images, (r)Claude/Sunset; **121** (t)Michelle Chaplow, (b)Zephyr Images/Sunset; **122** file photo; **123** Michelle Chaplow; **124** Pawel Wysocki/Hémisphères Images; **125** Daniel Thierry/DIAF; **126** Walter Bibikow/FPG; **128** Larry Hamill; **129** (l)file photo, (r)Ken Karp; **130** (l)Pratt-Pries/DIAF, (r)Andrew Payti; **131** (t)Weststock/Sunset, (b)Sandra Baker/ Liaison Agency; **132** (tl)SuperStock, (tr)Jean-Daniel Sudres/ DIAF, (b)LCI/Wallis Phototheque; **134** (t)Lauros-Giraudon/Art Resource, NY, (b)Renunion des Musees Nationaux/Art Resource, NY; **134–135** CORBIS; **135** (t)David Noble/FPG, (c)Desvignes/ Sunset, (b)Gianni Dagli Orti/CORBIS; **137** Travelpix/FPG; **139** Curt Fischer; **141** (t)Timothy Fuller, (b)Travelpix/FPG; **142** (t)Larry Hamill, (b)Mark Burnett; **143** Wayne Rowe; **144** (t)Timothy Fuller, (b)Larry Hamill; **145** R. Rozencwajg/ DIAF; **147** Larry Hamill; **148** (2)Laurent Rebours, AP/Wide World Photos, (3)Bernard Boutrit/Photo Researchers, (4)Marie-José Jarry & Jean-François Tripelon/Agence Top/National Geographic Image Collection, (5)Steve McCurry/National Geographic Image Collection; **148–149** Michael Busselle/Stone; **149** (6)P. Bennett/AA Photo Library, (7)Martha Bates/Stock Boston; **150** (9)Steve Vidler/Leo de Wys Stock Photo Agency, (10)Patrick Ingrand/Stone, (11)Patrick Zachmann/Magnum, (12)Christophe Ena, AP/Wide World Photos; **150–151** Chad Ehlers/Stone; **151** (13)Craig Aurness/CORBIS, (14)Suzanne & Nick Geary/Stone; **152** Erich Lessing/Art Resource; **152–153** John Lawrence/Getty Images; **155** (orange juice, apple juice) Timothy Fuller, (fries)Aaron Haupt, (others)John Evans; **156** Timothy Fuller; **157** Gérard Gsell/DIAF; **158** Larry Hamill; **159** (l)John Evans, (c r)Aaron Haupt; **160** (t)Timothy Fuller, (b)Curt Fischer; **162** H. Gyssels/DIAF; **164** (l)Eve Morcrette/ Wallis Phototheque, (r)file photo; **166** Gerard Lacz/Sunset; **167** Bill Deering/FPG; **168** James Davis/International Stock; **169–170** Larry Hamill; **172** (t)Catherine et Bernard Desjeux, (b)Timothy Fuller; **173** Wayne Rowe; **174** (t)Larry Hamill, (c)Bob Krist/The Stock Market, (b)Explorer/Photo Researchers; **175** (t)Robert Fried Photography, (c)Quinard/Wallis Phototheque; **176–177** Sami Sarkis/PhotoDisc; **178** Larry Hamill; **179** David Simson/Stock Boston; **180** Wayne Rowe; **183** (t)Gerard Lacz/